YALE COLLEGE
LEARNING RESOURCE CENTRE

D0806426

access to religion and philosophy

r
p

Christian Theology

Michael Wilcockson

HODDER
EDUCATION
AN HACHETTE UK COMPANY

Author's acknowledgements

I am very grateful to The Master and Fellows of Pembroke College, Cambridge for electing me to the position of Visiting Scholar, Michaelmas term 2010 and so by their generous support enabling me to write this book. In addition I thank the following for their much valued comments and advice: Trevor Allan, Andrew Barrott, Julian Dobson, James Gardom, Nicholas Heap and Douglas Hedley.

I am especially indebted to Michael Wilkinson and Alison Wilcockson for their detailed criticisms and advice.

Bible quotations are taken from the Revised Standard Version translation.

The Publishers would like to thank the following for permission to reproduce copyright material:

Photo credits

Cover © Danny Lehman/CORBIS; **p.4** *L* © Rex Features, *R* © Rex Features; **p.6** © Classic Image/Alamy; **p.22** © INTERFOTO/Alamy; **p.23** © INTERFOTO/Alamy; **p.43** © CSU Archives/Everett Collection/Rex Features; **p.58** *L* © Carson Ganci/Design Pics Inc./Rex Features, *C* © Ivan Vdovin/Alamy, *R* © Matteo Rossetti/Rex Features; **p.80** © INTERFOTO/Alamy; **p.92** © Marco Simoni/Robert Harding/Rex Features; **p.115** © AFP/Getty Images; **p.134** © Photo Art Resource/Bob Schalkwijk/Scala, Florence; **p.145** © Mike Goldwater/Alamy; **p.152** Frederic Sierakowski/Rex Features; **p.160** © Peter Horvath/Rex Features

Revised Standard Version of the Bible, copyright 1952 [2nd edition, 1971] by the Division of Christian Education of the National Council of the Churches of Christ in the United States of America. Used by permission. All rights reserved. Every effort has been made to trace all copyright holders, but if any have been inadvertently overlooked the Publishers will be pleased to make the necessary arrangements at the first opportunity.

Although every effort has been made to ensure that website addresses are correct at time of going to press, Hodder Education cannot be held responsible for the content of any website mentioned in this book. It is sometimes possible to find a relocated web page by typing in the address of the home page for a website in the URL window of your browser.

Hachette's policy is to use papers that are natural, renewable and recyclable products and made from wood grown in sustainable forests. The logging and manufacturing processes are expected to conform to the environmental regulations of the country of origin.

Orders: please contact Bookpoint Ltd, 130 Milton Park, Abingdon, Oxon OX14 4SB. Telephone: +44 (0)1235 827720. Fax: +44 (0)1235 400454. Lines are open 9.00a.m.–5.00p.m., Monday to Saturday, with a 24–hour message answering service. Visit our website at www.hoddereducation.co.uk

© Michael Wilcockson 2011

First published in 2011

by Hodder Education,
an Hachette UK company
338 Euston Road
London NW1 3BH

Impression number 5 4 3 2 1

Year   2015 2014 2013 2012 2011

All rights reserved. Apart from any use permitted under UK copyright law, no part of this publication may be reproduced or transmitted in any form or by any means, electronic or mechanical, including photocopying and recording, or held within any information storage and retrieval system, without permission in writing from the publisher or under licence from the Copyright Licensing Agency Limited. Further details of such licences (for reprographic reproduction) may be obtained from the Copyright Licensing Agency Limited, Saffron House, 6–10 Kirby Street, London EC1N 8TS.

Typeset in Bembo by Greengate Publishing Services, Tonbridge, Kent

Printed by MPG Books, Bodmin

A catalogue record for this title is available from the British Library

ISBN 978 0340 95773 8

CONTENTS

PREFACE

About the series

Access books are written mainly for students studying for examinations at higher levels, particularly GCE AS level and A level. A number of features have been included to assist students, such as the study guides at the end of chapters.

To use these books most effectively, you should be aware of the following features:

- At the beginning of each chapter there is a checklist, which is a brief introduction about the key elements that the chapter covers.
- Key questions, words, people, thoughts and quotes in the margin highlight specific points from the main text.
- Profiles of key individuals give information on a philosopher's background and work.
- There are summary diagrams throughout the chapters to aid revision.
- The revision checklist at the end of each chapter summarises the main points.

General advice on answering essay questions

Structured questions will tell you what to include. The following advice is for those questions which leave it to you to work out.

- The most important thing is to read the question carefully and work out what it really means. Make sure you understand all the words in the question (you may need to check some of them in the dictionary or look up technical terms in the glossary at the back of this book).
- Gather the relevant information for answering the question. You will probably not need everything you know on the topic. Keep to what the question is asking.
- Organise your material by drawing up a plan of paragraphs. Make sure that each paragraph is relevant to the question. Include different views within your answer (most questions require arguments for and against).
- Start with an introduction that explains in your own words what the question is asking and defines any technical words. Work through your answer in carefully planned paragraphs. Write a brief conclusion in which you sum up your answer to the question (without repeating everything in the essay).

About this book

Christian theology covers a very wide area and has developed from the very first moment the early Christians reflected on the significance of Jesus' teaching and the new circumstances in which they found themselves. Theology cannot be static and in trying to articulate often difficult beliefs which each new era raises, new problems have to be answered. To do this, Christian theology has to cover a wide range of disciplines including philosophy, literature, history, psychology, science, sociology and linguistics.

This book does two things: first it outlines some of the major building blocks of Christian theology; second it looks at the way theology can work in practice.

Part 1 Foundations of Christian theology

Part 1 aims to do the following:

- to set out a general problem focusing on a particular theological issue
- to look at one influential theologian's response to this issue
- to consider how this theologian's teaching is still part of a live discussion today.

The theologians selected therefore cover an important historical moment in the development of Christian theology:

- Augustine: late antiquity and early medieval (Chapter 1)
- Aquinas: medieval (Chapter 2)
- Calvin: Reformation (Chapter 3)
- Schleiermacher: eighteenth to nineteenth century (Chapter 5)
- Cone: twentieth century (Chapter 4).

The 'contemporary discussion' section of each chapter provides ways of analysing the ideas of each of these significant theologians.

Part 2 Liberation theology

Part 2 aims to do the following:

- to look at the birth of one of the most significant movements in modern Christian theology
- to consider whether theology can actually *do* anything other than think theoretically
- to consider how far the theological foundations set out in Part 1 have been modified.

However, theology is not just something to be learnt: it is an imaginative and intellectual exercise. The hope is that this book will give readers just enough to get started and to develop their own reasoned responses to the central ideas raised by Christian theology.

1 HUMAN NATURE

Chapter checklist

This chapter considers the paradoxes which describe the human condition when humans equally appear to do great acts of good and evil. The ancient problem of weakness of will is first considered and then contrasted with Augustine's account of the Fall, original sin and the divided will. The chapter concludes by considering some contemporary theological and non-theological discussions of the issues raised by Augustine.

1 The human condition

Key word

Doctrine means teaching and has come to mean the official teaching of the Church on key areas of Christian theology such as the Incarnation, the Trinity, Grace, God and so on. Doctrines are frequently discussed and refined by theologians.

Key question

Are human beings naturally good or bad?

The Christian theological narrative begins and ends with humans: their creation, relationship with God, corruption and restoration. All the central Christian teachings, or **doctrines**, are ways of explaining these ideas according to the time and culture in which they were developed. As society in every age changes according to its moral, scientific and philosophical views, so Christian doctrine adapts and rethinks its central claims. The doctrine of human nature is one such area.

a) The paradox of human nature

Human nature is paradoxical or apparently contradictory. There are countless numbers of people who, throughout the ages, have acted with considerable generosity to others: ruled wisely, beautified the environment through art and music and exemplified an aspect of being human which is probably not matched by any other living creature. On the other hand, the Holocaust where six million Jews were exterminated, and the brutal, sadistic and cold-hearted murders of children by people such as the **Moors Murderers**, Ian Brady and Myra Hindley, illustrate the darker, evil aspect of human nature.

Not everyone thinks there is a paradox. Those who hold an optimistic view of human nature consider that humans only behave badly through poor education or psychological deprivation. Conversely, others argue that humans are naturally egocentric and violent because these are the qualities required simply to survive.

Key thought

The Moors Murders took place around Manchester between 1963 and 1965. Ian Brady and Myra Hindley abducted, tortured, sexually abused and murdered five children. They buried their victims on Saddleworth Moor. What shocked the world was the cold-blooded way Brady and Hindley had recorded the final moments of some of their victims as they pleaded for mercy and cried out for their parents.

Myra Hindley

Ian Brady

Key people

Thomas Hobbes (1588–1679) was educated at Oxford and later began writing political pieces, of which *Leviathan* (1651) is his most developed work.

In the seventeenth century the political philosopher **Thomas Hobbes** wrote that the natural state of humans is 'solitary, poor, nasty, brutish and short'. It is only through the power of reason that we can agree, through making contracts with each other, not to kill or steal, but to create civilised communities. But what happens when reason does not prevail? In William Golding's novel *Lord of the Flies* a group of school children are shipwrecked on a desert island and without the imposition of adult reason they quickly become murderous savages, living only under the law of the survival of the strongest.

Even though Hobbes and Golding represent the pessimistic view of human nature, they still suppose that humans can be better than their base instincts. This suggests that although humans are driven by a range of animal desires, they are also able to make rational decisions and have the ability to sympathise and cooperate with each other. It is the tension between these characteristics that determines what is meant by human nature. How these characteristics are ordered and weighted determines the kind of answers given to these standard questions about human nature:

- Can there be true friendships?
- Can we achieve happiness through reason alone?
- Do we always act in our own best interests?
- How free are we to make our own decisions?
- Do people ever act in a totally unselfish way?
- Do men and women have the same human nature?
- Are we uniquely different from non-human animals?

These questions form the basis of the doctrine of human nature. But it is not just theologians who have attempted to give an account of the odd way in which we behave, it is also a basic question for philosophers. The oddity of human behaviour is the apparent way in which we don't always do what we intend to do, what philosophers have termed the weakness of will paradox.

b) Weakness of will

Key question

Do we always act in our own best interests?

In your New Year's resolution you promise that you will not answer your parents back even when you know that they are in the wrong. You know that when you do, it only causes a row and then everyone is angry and no one is happy. Then, on New Year's Day your mother asks you to do the washing up even though it is your brother's turn, and before you know what has happened, you answer back.

Key word

Akrasia is the paradox that when a person S chooses voluntarily to do action B, they do so even though they appear to think that alternative A is better.

This illustrates a moral problem which the ancient Greek philosophers called **akrasia**. We all know this phenomenon well. The paradox is that I think I know what is in my best interests, but I find myself doing something quite different which turns out not to be for the best. This demonstrates something very basic about human nature. The question is whether we have a will which we are not able to control through reason, or whether in fact what we will is always for the best but we are not always clear or conscious that this is so.

In **Plato**'s *Protagoras*, Socrates argues that there is no such thing as akrasia; when we act we do what really, deep down, gives us pleasure. This is sometimes referred to as evaluative hedonism and can be summarised as follows:

Key people

Plato (477–347BC) was from a noble Athenian family and around 407BC became a pupil of the great philosopher Socrates. After his master's death he established his own school, the Academy. His central idea was that there is a division between reality (the world of forms which can be known only through reason) and the imperfect material world.

- People choose hedonism or pleasures over other alternatives.
- If I choose to accompany a friend in his car even though I know he is a bad driver, then the reason is that I value his friendship more than I fear his driving.
- Reason is used to calculate short- and long-term happiness.
- A painful short-term option might be preferred because it is believed to have a long-term pleasurable result.

Evaluative hedonism also supports psychological hedonism, which is the view that people always act in a way they believe will be for the best (most happiness) as opposed to any other kind of action. A variation of this view is proposed by **Aristotle**. Aristotle suggests that often we don't know all the facts and so we might act for what we think is for the best, but owing to ignorance it turns out not to be in our best interest.

Key people

Aristotle (384–322BC) was a pupil of Plato in ancient Athens. Unexpectedly, he did not take over the running of Plato's Academy and instead established his own school, the Lyceum in 335BC. Unlike Plato, Aristotle did not think there is an abstract world of forms or ideas, but that all things are governed by different types of cause. Aristotle's teachings had great influence on the medieval Christian thinkers such as Thomas Aquinas and Albertus Magnus.

However, if I am really motivated by deeper desires, does this mean that I am not fully in control? If reason indicates that what I choose is contrary to my own best interests, then it appears that I am not making a genuine free choice. In other words, our wills are weak and we are not always able to control them. In the Christian tradition, weakness of will is a universal condition of being human; neither Plato or Aristotle had a word for the 'will' and so were unable to give it an explanation.

Having been brought up in the ancient Greek philosophical tradition, Augustine concluded through his own life experiences and reflection on the letters of St Paul, that weakness of will is the defining characteristic of human nature. He went further. The paradox for him was not just that we are weak willed, but that weakness of will is the reason for God's greatest gift to the world in the person of Jesus Christ. Augustine's deep theological, psychological and philosophical insights into human nature have affected Western thought for over one and a half thousand years, and so it is to him that we now turn.

2 Augustine on human nature

Augustine's influence on Western Christianity is fundamental both for Catholics and Protestants. Even today, when, in the light of modern science, history and psychology, his judgements appear obscure and often harsh, so many of his insights continue to be the source of fruitful reflection. It is largely because he is so honest about his own inner experiences that his theology of human nature rings true to us today. Augustine's ideas change. As a young academic his view of human nature was optimistic and he shared with the **Neo-Platonists** the view that the happy life can be achieved through living virtuously. But over time his viewed hardened, and he became increasingly pessimistic, doubting that humans can ever live the happy life through their own efforts. Central to his analysis is his view that the **will** has become irreparably damaged.

Key quote

'The philosopher's assumption about everyone being basically persuadable in terms of rational freedom just doesn't hold.'

GEORGE PATTISON, *A SHORT COURSE IN CHRISTIAN DOCTRINE*, 20

Key words

Neo-Platonism is the term scholars use to refer to the followers of Plato in the third century AD, notably Plotinus (c. 205–270). They were dualists believing there are sharp differences between thought and reality, matter and the One (or God), body and soul. The One can only be achieved once the soul has separated itself from all thought and material influences.

The **will** in Augustine's thought is the aspect of the image of God which distinguishes humans from all other animals.

Manichees believed that suffering and evil in the world are not caused by God but by a lower power. Humans have two souls: one which desires God and the other desires evil.

Augustine of Hippo (354–430)

PROFILE

Augustine was born in Thagaste, North Africa. His mother Monica was a devout, though uneducated, Christian. His father was a merchant and although they were not well off, he realised his son's genius and gave him the best education he could. Augustine studied rhetoric (philosophy) at Carthage (370) where he also became a Manichaean and lived a rowdy student life. The **Manichees** offered him a rational view of the world which could be reconciled with faith. In essence they believed that suffering and evil in the world are not caused by God but by a lower power. Humans have two souls – one which desires God, the other evil. He taught rhetoric at Carthage (374) and Rome (383) and was appointed official orator to the imperial court at Milan (384). Here he met the Christian bishop Ambrose and was impressed by his sincere faith and allegorical interpretation of the Bible. After a disappointing discussion with the Manichaean bishop Faustus in 383, he abandoned Manichaeism and embraced Platonism – especially the works of Plotinus. Although he never rejected Platonism, his conversion to Christianity in 386 (when he was 32) was partly due to his dissatisfaction with the Platonic view that all that is needed to live a happy life is the pursuit of virtue, and partly due to St Paul's vivid description of human nature and God's grace.

Augustine was baptised by Ambrose on Easter Eve 387 and in 389 he returned to North Africa where he was ordained priest in 391. In 395 he was consecrated bishop of Hippo where he remained until his death. He was a prolific writer of books, sermons and letters; amongst his most influential books are: *On Free Will* (388) *Confessions* (started 397), *The City of God* (written between 413 and 426) and *On the Trinity* (written between 399 and 420). His life was marked by conflict: first with the Manichaeans and the Donatists (the Christian Church in North Africa who considered that the sacraments of the Catholic Church were not valid); then, from 411 onwards, with the **Pelagians** – Christians who did not believe that original sin caused universal guilt which only God could remove. The Pelagians argued that humans have sufficient free will to overcome personal sin. The Pelagian controversy caused him to take an increasingly hard-line view of sin and **predestination**.

Although Augustine's theology is based on his philosophical reflections, it is equally informed by his own experiences. He frequently refers back to his early life where, until his conversion to Christianity, he had, like many young men of his class, kept a concubine (or mistress) and fathered a child. This relationship was in every respect a marriage, and when Augustine eventually had to give her up for a socially acceptable marriage, both he and his concubine suffered considerable anguish. Augustine could therefore talk knowledgably about the pleasures of sex, the joys of love and the power of lust. His relationship with his concubine and with Monica is a possible reason why Augustine's view of women was far more sympathetic than some of his more austere contemporaries.

Key people

Pelagius (c. 354–c. 440) was born either in Britain or France and became a monk and taught in Rome. After the sack of Rome in 410 he fled to Carthage where he briefly met Augustine before settling in Palestine. His unorthodox teaching on free will had branded him a heretic.

Cross-reference

See page 32 for an explanation of predestination.

a) The human will before the Fall

So, when the woman saw that the tree was good for food, and that it was a delight to her eyes, and that the tree was to be desired to make one wise, she took of its fruit and ate; and she also gave some to her husband, and he ate. Then the eyes of both were opened, and they knew that they were naked.

(Genesis 3:6–7)

Augustine's starting point is Genesis 1–3. Here we are given accounts of the creation of man and woman, their time in the Garden of Eden (paradise), their relationship with each other, the

Key word

The Fall is the moment described in Genesis 3 when Adam and Eve rebelled against God and were punished by being expelled from Eden (paradise).

Key word

Cupiditas and *caritas* are two Latin key words used by Augustine meaning love. *Cupiditas* is selfish love. *Caritas* is generous love.

Key quote

'Then (had there been no sin) the man would have sowed the seed and woman would have conceived the child when their sexual organs had been aroused by the will, at the appropriate time and in the necessary degree, and had not been excited by lust.'

AUGUSTINE, *CITY OF GOD*,
BOOK 14, CHAPTER 24

natural world and God. Until **the Fall** humans enjoyed a time of harmony. Harmony is expressed in the complete obedience of Adam and Eve to God and in their duties to other living creatures. It is also, according to Augustine, a time when the human will, the body and reason are in complete cooperation with each other.

i) The will as love

The will is God-given, created along with humans *ex nihilo* (from nothing) and can choose to do good or evil, to believe in God or to reject him. The will determines the kind of people we are. Above all, the will is synonymous with love – a kind of force or weight pulling us in various directions. Therefore, if the will is driven by selfish love (*cupiditas*) it diminishes us as human beings, but used generously (*caritas*) in willing our neighbour's good it completes us as humans, as it expresses the divine love of God for his creation.

ii) Sex and friendship

Augustine wrote extensively on friendship. In his ground-breaking commentary on Genesis, Augustine argued that in paradise, Adam and Eve were not only married (other theologians of the time argued that marriage only occurred after the Fall to control lust) but married as friends, where they equally and mutually participated in the friendliness of God. Augustine argued that as God had commanded Adam and Eve to be 'fruitful and occupy the earth' (Genesis 1:28), then friendship between men and women also included reproduction as well as the pleasure of sex. Nevertheless, sex is always secondary to friendship, friendship being the highest expression of human existence. Therefore, sex, when required, would occur without lust and Adam could summon an erection at will, so perfectly tuned was the will to the body.

Even after the Fall, friendship continues to express *caritas* as *amor Dei* (love of God). But in a fallen world friendship is far more complicated and fraught with anguish. Even so, as he wrote in one of his letters, 'There is nothing truly enjoyable without a friend'. The solution is that true friendship (as experienced before the Fall) is only possible for those who love Christ first. Love for neighbour is then generous, forgiving and non-judgemental if it is removed from *cupiditas*. Christ, Augustine famously said, did not choose his friends because they were senators but because they were fishermen.

b) The human will after the Fall

Augustine discusses the Fall (from Genesis 3) at length in his *City of God*. Adam, led on by his friendship with Eve and tempted by the snake, caused himself and Eve to discover their nakedness; their disobedience was at once forever linked with their own realisation of their sexual bodies. The reason for Adam's disobedience,

Augustine suggests, is unclear, but it originates in human perversity and pride and was an entirely voluntary act:

> *For they would not have arrived at the evil act if an evil will had not preceded it. Now, could anything but pride have been the start of the evil will? For 'pride is the start of every kind of sin'. And what is pride except a longing for a perverse kind of exaltation?*

> (Augustine, *City of God*, Book 4, Chapter 13)

i) The divided will

Augustine argued that the distorted soul or will had now become divided. Although it was still rational enough to know what is good, the damage done to it in the Fall meant that what it willed was often motivated by desire rather than good. This paradoxical state of the will is the one Augustine found described by St Paul in his *Letter to the Romans*. Paul says:

> *I do not understand my own actions. For I do not do what I want, but I do the very thing I hate. Now if I do what I do not want, I agree that the law is good. So then it is no longer I that do it, but sin which dwells within me … For I do not do the good I want, but the evil I do not want is what I do. Now if I do what I do not want, it is no longer I that do it, but sin which dwells within me … but I see in my members another law at war with the law of my mind and making me captive to the law of sin which dwells in my members. Wretched man that I am! Who will deliver me from this body of death?*

> (Romans 7:15–24)

In his *Confessions* Book 8, Augustine offers his own commentary on Romans 7. Here he describes the will as half wounded (*Confessions* 8.8) and divided, ingrained out of habit (*Confessions* 8.5), like trying to leave a comfortable bed, realising that God would heal him of lust which he would rather not give up. The will is at war with itself and unable to obey its own orders (*Confessions* 8.8–10). Augustine realises that he cannot put behind him his past relationships with women and embrace celibacy. As Plato argued, the memory is a powerful aspect of the soul and Augustine agrees it is not possible to shake it off (*Confessions* 8.11). Even the vision of Lady **Continence** is not enough:

> *But by now the voice of habit was very faint. I had turned my eyes elsewhere, and while I stood trembling at the barrier, in the barrier, on the other side I could see the chaste beauty of Continence in all her serene, unsullied joy, as she modestly beckoned me to cross and hesitate no more … I was overcome with shame, because I was still listening to the futile mutterings of my lower self.*

> (Augustine, *Confessions* 8:11)

Key quote

'Human nature then is, without any doubt, ashamed about lust, and rightly ashamed.'

AUGUSTINE, *CITY OF GOD*, BOOK 4, CHAPTER 20

Key word

Continence means self-restraint especially to abstain from sexual pleasures. Augustine describes continence using the metaphor of a beautiful woman.

Key word

Concupiscence is sexual lust but can also refer to uncontrolled desires of all kinds.

Cross-reference

See pages 6–7 on Manichaeism.

Key quote

'The snare of concupiscence awaits me in the very process of passing from the discomfort of hunger to the contentment which comes when it is satisfied.'

AUGUSTINE, *CONFESSIONS* 10:31

Key quote

'Augustine's legacy with regard to friendship was at once powerful and ambivalent.'

LIZ CARMICHAEL, *FRIENDSHIP*, 66

Key words

Original sin is the Christian notion that, despite being created in the image of God, all humans fail to fulfil this potential. This is the human condition. Original sin is different from actual sins which are committed by individuals.

Post-Lapsarian means the world after the Fall of Adam and Eve, or simply the fallen world.

Ontological refers to being or the nature of existence.

Key quote

'If Christian doctrine were to say of human beings only that they are created in the image of God, it would become sheer idealism.'

DANIEL L. MIGLIORE, *FAITH SEEKING UNDERSTANDING*, 149

ii) Concupiscence

In his fallen state, man is no longer able to control his libido and the appetitive or desiring aspect of his soul is completely dominated by **concupiscence**. Augustine was careful not to accept either the **Manichaean** argument that the body is evil and sinful or the neo-Platonic notion that because it belongs to the realm of flesh the body is necessarily imperfect. The body cannot be sinful because it was created to be good by God. But now that the will is weak and divided, concupiscence dominates human existence. Unmoderated, the body craves power, food, money and, above all, sexual intercourse.

Concupiscence is most clearly and painfully experienced in friendships. Augustine shared with his philosophical friends the idea that nothing could be better than a community of friends as equals. But in reality, even with the closest friends, jealousy, betrayal and even death all conspire to cause pain and undermine true friendship. We also invest so heavily in friendships that we are distracted from loving God. Friendship, as Liz Carmichael comments, illustrates Augustine's deep ambivalence about human nature. For example, he had many women amongst his friends and yet, as Peter Brown notes:

> *He would never visit a woman unchaperoned, and he did not allow even his own female relatives to enter the bishop's palace. He expelled a young clergyman who had been found speaking with a nun 'at an inappropriate hour of the day'.*

(Peter Brown, *The Body and Society*, 396)

iii) Original sin

In the **post-Lapsarian** world the effects of Adam's sin can be seen in the continued rebellious state of the will. Everywhere one looks the effects of the Fall on human nature can be seen. Men have spontaneous erections, wet dreams and loss of rational control during sexual orgasm. The presence of concupiscence illustrates the lack of control that the rational soul has over sin. Even impotence or lack of libido is a sign that the uncontrolled body mocks the weak and divided will.

Augustine had now forged a very distinctive view of original sin. Whereas other theologians took the phrase from St Paul, 'through Adam all have fallen' to describe the inadequacies that all humans are prone to, Augustine made this sin an **ontological** condition of human existence, not just a description of our behaviour on occasions. No one is good however virtuous they might appear to be. The sin of Adam is passed on through every sexual act, because every act of sexual intercourse is tainted by concupiscence. Therefore, with the exception of Mary, Jesus' mother, who conceived without lust, all other humans are tainted with the original sin of Adam.

iv) Free will

Cross-reference

Read Augustine, *City of God*, Book 14, Chapters 16–25.

Augustine's view of free will changed over time. In Book 1 of *On Free Will* Augustine argues the platonic view that using reason and aspiring to the Good by living the virtuous life was possible through free will. Sin and evil were merely the absence or failure to do good. But in Books 2 and 3 (written sometime later) Augustine concluded that the sex drive, ignorance and death were punishments for human rebellion which no amount of human reasoning could ever overcome. Sin is no longer voluntary but involuntary: we can't but fall into error. We prefer falsehoods to truth because (and he uses platonic type language) our souls are 'fettered' and chained down by sin.

Even living the ascetic life (as a monk or nun) or by dedicating oneself to a chaste life (Augustine encouraged married couples to abstain from sex after having children) – both ways of getting closer to the virtuous life – would never enable the will to be free or strong enough to resist various forms of concupiscence.

v) Men and women's natures

> *So God created man in his own image, in the image of God he created him; male and female he created them.*

> (Genesis 1:27)

Key people

Philo of Alexander (c. 20BC– c. 50 AD) Philo was an influential philosopher who combined Greek and Jewish thinking and was famous for his allegorical interpretation of the Jewish Scriptures and the development of God's creative word as Logos.

Augustine also disagreed with other contemporaries in their explanation of the woman's subordinate relationship with man. He rejected the interpretation of Genesis by the Jewish philosopher **Philo of Alexander** who blamed Adam's sin on Eve's evil nature, preferring the interpretation that men and women were created equal though different.

Key word

Image of God (or in Latin *imago Dei*) as used in Genesis 1:27 has been the subject of considerable interpretation: a) the human rational self; b) the power for humans to act as God's stewards on earth; c) human free will; d) human ability to be in relationship with God as mirror of the divine.

Before the Fall men and women are created in the **image of God** and so both share equally in God's *rational* nature. The difference in roles is determined by their bodies and role in society. As the active partner in sex the man also has the role of being active in the public sphere and he has to exercise the **deliberative** rational aspect of his soul to rule over the irrational animal world, but at the same time to be obedient to God. A woman's body is not inferior to a man's, but her genitals suggest that she is passive in sex and is therefore the homemaker and must be obedient to her husband as his 'helpmate' and child bearer. She is to use her deliberative reason in the private realm of the household as mother and housewife and to be obedient to her husband as St Paul teaches.

Key thought

Deliberative soul. Although the soul is a single entity, according to Plato it has various functions which include reason and desire, or as Augustine terms it, the deliberative and obedient.

> *And just as in man's soul there are two forces, one which is dominant because it deliberates and one which obeys because it is subject to such guidance, in the same way, in the physical sense, woman has been made for man. In her mind and her rational intelligence she has a nature the equal of man's, but in sex she is physically subject to him in the same way as our natural impulses need to be subjected to the reasoning power*

Key quote

'Wives, be subject to your husbands, as is fitting in the Lord.'
ST PAUL, *LETTER TO THE COLOSSIANS*, 3:18

of the mind, in order that the actions to which they lead may be inspired by the principles of good conduct.

(Augustine, *Confessions* 13:32)

The taking of the rib from Adam's side (Genesis 2:22–24) illustrates that both men and women share the same spiritual nature – Augustine rejected the view of others that women were in that sense inferior.

However, the Fall affects men and women differently because their bodies are different. According to Genesis men are punished with the pain of work and women the painfulness of childbirth. Unlike his contemporaries, Augustine did not consider that Eve was punished more because she was the evil temptress – after all, he met and corresponded with any number of virtuous and spiritual women (his mother Monica being one of them) – but that her body made her less spiritually pure than those of men. The justification is based on a rather odd idea from St Paul that women have to wear a veil because of their subordination to men.

> *For a man ought not to cover his head, since he is the image and glory of God; but woman is the glory of man … That is why a woman ought to have a veil on her head, because of the angels.*

(1 Corinthians 11:7, 10)

Paul has in mind a passage in the Old Testament where Moses had to wear a veil as a sign that he had come into the presence of God. Paul suggests that by the same token a woman must wear a veil as an indication of her obedience to her husband and a sign that his image is less corrupt than her image. Augustine's view is often ambiguous. As the following passage suggests, women may be subordinate rationally but not spiritually. If this were not the case, then they would be unable to know God and be offered the possibility of redemption.

> *But because she differs from man by her bodily sex, that part of the reason which is turned aside to regulate temporal things, could be properly symbolised by her corporeal veil; so that the image of God does not remain except in that part of the mind in which it clings to the contemplation and consideration of the eternal reasons, which, as is evident, not only men but also women possess.*

(Augustine, *On the Trinity XII*, Chapter 8)

c) Grace

Key quote

'His ideal was a human soul, a human body and a human society unfissured by the dark twist of the fallen will.'

PETER BROWN, *BODY AND SOCIETY*, 407

Human nature offers a tantalising possibility that with just a bit more effort we could achieve the harmonious relationship with God which would lead to the *summum bonum* – the greatest good. Augustine's experience of life, his memories of past pleasures

Key words

Grace is God's generous, undeserved and free act of love for the world, expressed supremely in the giving of his son Jesus Christ in order that humans might overcome their sinful natures.

Election is the Christian doctrine that salvation is possible because God chooses to redeem humans first.

Key question

Why is grace an essential part of Augustine's theology?

which continued to haunt his dreams, led him frequently to ask the question posed by St Paul, 'who will deliver me from this body of death?' (Romans 7:24). There is only one answer and that is God. It is through God's generous love that the damaged will can be healed and the human relationship with God restored. The wound is healed through God's **grace**, an act of love in the gift of his son Jesus Christ in which the guilt of the original sin committed by Adam and Eve is removed. If this were not so, then there would be no possibility of redemption for any of humankind. Of course, people will continue to sin but God has chosen or **elected** those he knows will respond to his love and be restored to paradise. For the individual, the experience of election is the process by which the Holy Spirit assists those who believe in moving beyond the merely moral life to the life of spiritual freedom.

Augustine concludes that, although he admires the philosophy of the Platonists and Stoics, their ambition to live the good life will always fall short. Unless, he argued, one has sufficient humility to acknowledge the failings of human nature and faith in the love of God, no amount of reason will bring ultimate happiness, or *eudaimonia*. He quotes from Isaiah, 'Unless you believe, you will not understand' (Isaiah 7:9).

3 Contemporary discussion

Key thought

The **Enlightenment** refers primarily to the eighteenth-century thinkers such as Hume and Kant who argued that knowledge could only be obtained through human reason and observation and not through divine revelation or other authorities.

Key people

Richard Dawkins (1941–) is an evolutionary biologist and outspoken atheist critic of religion. He was professor of the public understanding of science at Oxford University and has published widely. His many books include *The Selfish Gene* (1976), *The Blind Watchmaker* (1986) and *The God Delusion* (2006).

Augustine's influence on Western theology has been profound. However, since the **Enlightenment** two factors have challenged or modified his views. The first is the place of modern evolutionary biology and psychology, and the second is the emphasis philosophy has given to the independence of human reason.

a) Biology and sex
i) Evolutionary biology

Richard Dawkins finds the whole Christian notion of original sin not only entirely contrary to evolutionary biology but also absurd and dangerous. He blames a great deal on the 'original sin' tradition which he considers Augustine created. He argues that:

- It is absurd to imagine the corruption of all humans rests on two individuals. As evolutionary biology considers that humans (as *homo sapiens*) emerged from less sophisticated animal forms who did not have the kind of consciousness which enabled them to make an active decision to rebel, then a literal belief in Adam and Eve makes no sense.
- Even a symbolic account of the Fall of humans does not rid Christianity of its unhealthy obsession with sin associated with sex.

Key quote

'What kind of ethical philosophy is it that condemns every child, even before it is born, to inherit the sin of a remote ancestor? … But now, the sado-masochism. God incarnated himself as a man, Jesus, in order that he should be tortured and executed in *atonement* for the hereditary sin of Adam.'

RICHARD DAWKINS, *THE GOD DELUSION*, 251–2

Key people

Ian Barbour (1923–) is Bean Professor Emeritus of Science, Technology and Society at Carleton College Minnesota, USA. He is one of the most influential theologians today in the area of science and religion.

Key question

Has Christianity focused too much on sex and sin?

Key people

Sigmund Freud (1856–1939) lived and worked for most of his life in Vienna and was one of the founders of psychoanalysis. In helping his patients overcome their psychological disorders he developed an idea that the ego (the conscious self) represses traumatic experiences into the id (the unconscious self). Once the ego can confront these repressed experiences often the disorders can be resolved. Freud argued that many traumas are caused by sexual problems relating back to childhood.

- The idea that God should wish to restore human nature by killing Jesus on the cross is sado-masochistic.

However, many theologians argue that Dawkins dismisses the idea of original sin too quickly. **Ian Barbour**, for example, agrees that evolutionary biology means that the idea of an original event makes little sense, but suggests that 'suffering, conflict, and death long preceded the advent of humanity' (*Nature, Human Nature and God* page 52). Furthermore, many Christians have long ago rejected the idea of the creation, Fall and redemption as separate historical events, but consider they should be seen as continuing processes in each person's individual life. In other words, Genesis 3 is an imaginative story about humans' use of their potential and relationship with the world. Augustine's great insights into friendship and love can still be used but not his view of the Fall as an actual moment in history.

ii) Psychology of sex

Others following **Sigmund Freud**'s understanding of sexuality, reject Augustine's unfortunate connection between the original sin of Adam and Eve and its transmission to future generations through sexual intercourse. The connection has regrettably reduced sexual human relations to be necessary only for reproduction, whereas sex, as Freud argued, is an important and natural aspect of human development. While it is true that many human disorders can be traced back to sexual problems, sin is not an original moment passed on through sexual intercourse but the result of environment (such as family, education, religion). Augustine's repressive teaching on sex fails to acknowledge that pleasure in sex is part of the natural relationship men and women enjoy in marriage.

Interestingly, Freud offers his own re-interpretation of Augustine's original sin in terms of his explanation of the origins of religion. For Freud the origins of monotheistic religion are due to repressed sexual guilt caused by an act of gross indecency in the human tribal past, which is atoned for by making offerings to God who is the projection of the tribal father figure who was abused and killed. This is why religion is bad because, for Freud, it perpetuates guilt and keeps alive the sense of sexual repression.

There are few people today who would agree with Freud that Judaism and Christianity were founded because of some traumatic sexual offence. But the lessons offered by both the Augustinian and Freudian accounts of human nature indicate that the misuse of sex and relationships are frequently a reason for individual and social disorder.

b) Reason and will

For many post-Enlightenment thinkers the paradox of free will and original sin is rejected in favour of more naturalistic and rational

Cross-reference

On his account of original sin read, for example, Sigmund Freud, *Totem and Taboo*, IV.6.

Key question

Have modern views of morality made the idea of sin irrelevant?

Key people

Immanuel Kant (1724–1804) was a German philosopher who lived all his life in Königsberg and taught at the university, becoming professor of logic in 1770. He developed his own distinctive rational theory of knowledge based on the mind's innate capacity and experience. From this basis he developed his moral philosophy in a number of books and lectures.

explanations. So, for example, whereas for Augustine the perfect state, the City of God, cannot be established in a fallen world, the post-Enlightenment philosophers considered that, as human nature is not in that sense flawed, the world can become a better place by letting reason rule over the emotions.

i) Immanuel Kant: the good will

The moral philosophy of **Immanuel Kant** marks a clear break from the Augustinian tradition. Whereas for Augustine only God's grace can save humans from themselves, for Kant 'salvation' is through human reason alone. However, even Kant recognises that there are powerful human emotions, appetites and desires which drive humans to act for their own selfish ends. The moral life, on the other hand, seeks to rise above this animal level of existence and create authentic, happy and free lives. As there is no original sin there are no essential defects in human nature which make this impossible, and 'sin' (not a term used by Kant) is merely the lack of reason and the inability to live according to our innate good will. The 'good will' is what makes humans uniquely human. Being good means being able to distinguish between what may appear to be moral duties but which on closer inspection turn out to be no more than our own selfish desires (what he calls hypothetical imperatives) and genuine duties which treat all people with equal dignity (what he calls categorical imperatives).

Kant's view of human nature is therefore essentially optimistic. It suggests the enticing notion that if we could all treat each other as we would like to be treated ourselves, then conflict, war, hatred and suffering, while not being completely overcome, would be very uncommon. In his essay *Toward Perpetual Peace* (1795) Kant sets out how this might occur. He begins by agreeing with Thomas Hobbes that the natural state of humans is war and, left to our own devices, humans would treat territory, property and other people as fair game for anyone who had sufficient power to take it for themselves; this is the state of barbaric peoples. But human reason, rightly educated, can overcome these base instincts and establish a higher level of civilised existence in which war would be no more. This is why peace has to be *established*, it does not occur naturally by itself.

Importantly, Kant argues that individual morality is no different from the way the state should behave; what is possible at the private level is also possible at the public level. It is a matter of dispute whether Kant's moral philosophy is compatible with Christian theology, as Kant makes humans the sole judge of what is right and wrong. This makes God's role in moral decision-making redundant.

Key people

Jean-Paul Sartre (1905–1980) was a French philosopher, novelist, playwright and political activist. He developed the ideas of Heidegger into what was popularly called existentialism. His major philosophical work is *Being and Nothingness* (1943).

Key word

Bad faith or *mauvaise foi* is the inauthentic life which is not lived freely but according to a stereotype or preconceived image or idea.

Key quote

'Man is nothing else but that which he makes of himself. That is the first principle of existentialism … Before the projection of the self nothing exists; not even in the heaven of intelligence: man will only attain existence when he is what he purposes to be.'

JEAN-PAUL SARTRE, *EXISTENTIALISM AND HUMANISM,* 28

Key people

Reinhold Niebuhr (1892–1971) was an American theologian and influential writer on ethics and politics. As a young man he embraced liberal Christianity but in the 1930s he transferred to neo-orthodoxy because of its realistic understanding of sin and the human condition. For most of his career he was professor of Christian ethics at the Union Theological Seminary, New York. His books include *Moral Man and Immoral Society* (1932) and *The Nature and Destiny of Man* (1941).

ii) Jean-Paul Sartre: bad faith

An even more radical account of the human will is developed by the atheist existentialist philosopher **Jean-Paul Sartre**. Sartre's non-theological and post-Enlightenment view of human nature shares something of Augustine's paradoxical presentation of the human psyche. However, the battle is not between the sinful body and the spirit or will, but the body as a fixed existence and the will which has the power to overcome it. Sartre rejects the Christian notion of an essential human nature because to have a human nature characterised by original sin means that we can never truly and freely develop our own personalities. If that were the case then free will would mean nothing.

Sin, therefore in Sartre's atheistic philosophy, is the failure to live the authentic life by becoming a stereotyped person (as a mother, as a lover, as a student) because it is easy to do so. He calls this state **bad faith**. As there is no God who can overcome our deficiencies, no original sin or unconscious self tainted by concupiscence, we have no excuse not to act and engage fully with life. That does not mean life is easy. The existential life requires great effort and is one which is accompanied by a sense of dread or *Angst*, as nothing can guarantee that what we do is right.

Even though as an atheist Sartre rejected the traditional Christian idea of human nature, many contemporary Christian theologians have used existentialism as a means of reworking the tradition in ways which they think are more in tune with the way we think about our existence today and our relationship with God. Like Sartre, they agree that the Augustinian ideas of sin and original sin do not mean much today, but rather should be radically reinterpreted as expressions of alienation, lack of authentic existence and *Angst* in our relationship with ourselves, others and God.

iii) Reinhold Niebuhr: immoral society

Niebuhr argued that, although the post-Enlightenment thinkers have made it unfashionable to talk about sin, failure to understand original sin leads to colossal mistakes being made by society and especially by those in power. Niebuhr's argument is quite simply that the rationalism of Western philosophy and politics has failed. The optimistic vision of Kant and others has not only failed (war, poverty and cruelty abound) but more worryingly has also corrupted the human sense of responsibility. By rationalising and rejecting the traditional notion of sin, humans at every level fail to realise that no action can ever be entirely good and this causes greater injustices and more suffering. This may not be so apparent at the individual level, but collectively when people act in groups then their faults become greatly exaggerated.

In Augustine's terms the inner spiritual will is defeated by egoism and self-interest. In particular, Niebuhr accuses both religious and non-religious leaders of bad faith if they think that the power of reason and belief in moral goodness is enough to bring about just and fair societies. This ill-founded idea must be rejected. But Niebuhr is no fatalist; he does not think, as some Augustinians have, that there is nothing we can do to remedy the human condition as this would remove all responsibility; the solution is for the human ego to understand its own nature fully by coming into a proper relationship with God. Once the ego comes into contact with the Absolute it is able to realise both its limitations and possibilities.

Niebuhr has had enormous influence on a wide range of theologians. Although he did not offer a rational account of original sin, his explanation of its paradoxical nature has reminded theologians that reason alone is inadequate when describing human nature. Three such paradoxes are that:

- original sin is both 'inevitable but not necessary'
- sin is apparent in evil as well as good acts because even the good person's ego desires self-affirmation
- at an individual level good people may do good things but collectively they do not.

Niebuhr's teaching on sin shares similarities with Augustine's sense of its power and pervasiveness while avoiding linking it to sex and the body. But it is in his challenge to moral and political philosophy and theology where his impact has been most felt. At a popular level, **Martin Luther King** claimed that it was Niebuhr who made him reconsider the over-optimistic liberal Protestantism which he had studied at university and understand that even his own motives for a fairer society were motivated by egoism and the desire to be famous and admired. In one sermon he likened his ego to a drum major who likes to be at the front of the band enjoying the power and adulation of the crowds. In reply to his critics who accused him of using the civil rights movement for his own gain, King argued that even if this was the case, when subject to God's love, the ego can be directed to achieve great things for the greater good.

c) Religious dimension of the human person

Whilst science and philosophy have challenged many aspects of the Augustinian tradition, **Colin Gunton** observes that modern debates have failed to mention Augustine's important insight that science and philosophy do not consider the *religious* dimension of being human.

Like Augustine, Gunton argues that the religious view of human nature is not something which can be proved scientifically or philosophically, but without it the paradoxes of our existence cannot

---

Key question

Would public leaders achieve more if they were more aware of the nature of sin?

Key quote

'The perennial tragedy of human history is that those who cultivate the spiritual elements usually do so by divorcing themselves from or misunderstanding the problems of collective man, where the brutal elements are most obvious … To the end of history the peace of the world, as Augustine observed, must be gained by strife. It will not be perfect peace.'

REINHOLD NIEBUHR, *MORAL MAN AND IMMORAL SOCIETY*, 256

Key people

Martin Luther King (1929–68) was a Baptist minister who became the leader of the civil rights movement to abolish racial segregation in the United States. He led the march on Washington in 1968 where he gave his famous 'I have a dream …' speech. He was assassinated shortly afterwards.

Key quote

'Yes, if you want to say that I was a drum major, say that I was a drum major for justice. Say that I was a drum major for peace. I was a drum major for righteousness. And all the other shallow things will not matter.'

MARTIN LUTHER KING, 'THE DRUM MAJOR INSTINCT', IN *THE GREAT SERMONS OF MARTIN LUTHER KING, JR*, 185

Key question

Does a belief in God offer a more complete view of human nature than a philosophical one?

Key people

Colin Gunton (1941–2003) was professor of Christian doctrine at King's College London, a United Reformed minister and author of many books including *The One, The Three and The Many* (1993) and *The Christian Faith* (2002). He is often considered to be one of the most influential theologians of his time.

Cross-reference

Colin Gunton, *The Christian Faith*, Chapter 3.

Key words

Redemption is when humans are freed from sin, suffering and death. In Christian thought redemption of the world is through Jesus Christ.

Eschatology means literally 'discussion of the last things' and is the time when the present age comes to completion and creation achieves perfection. Some consider that it refers not to the future of the world but to our own journey towards moral and spiritual completion.

Cross-reference

Colin Gunton, *The Christian Faith*, 39.

be resolved. The Bible story of the Fall and redemption, he suggests, is not to be read in a literal historical way but as a narrative which reveals God's purpose for each of us. The narrative begins (at the creation and Fall) with our potential as human beings and concludes when these potentialities are fulfilled (God's judgement).

However, Augustine's interpretation of the biblical account of the Fall is flawed. By using the Platonic distinction between body and soul Augustine misinterprets what Paul means by 'the body of sin'. What Paul meant by 'body', Gunton argues, is not a separation between the corrupted body on the one hand and soul or spirit on the other, but that the whole human personality has fallen short of perfection. The spirit is not a separate power but the aspect of our personality which is open to God and desires **redemption**.

If the Fall marks the start of the Christian narrative of ourselves, the end of the narrative is the **eschatological** moment when God completes his creation. This is crucial. But whereas Augustine considered that this was the final historical moment, it is really the time when we each achieve a state of wholeness; where body *and* spirit, through God's grace, achieve perfect union with him. Being human, therefore, is a process of growing from an infantile state to maturity. Importantly this is a religious journey because without the idea that this journey which is completed begun and ended in God's redemptive love, human existence would otherwise be defined only by death.

Finally, in correcting Augustine's understanding of the image of God, Gunton argues that Genesis does not suggest that women are more defective than men. 'Adam is created from the dust, and Eve from his side, signifying, as is sometimes commented, complementarity, rather than inferiority or superiority, because not from his head or feet.' Furthermore the image does not mean that humans are unique because of their powers to reason, but because of their relationship to God. The word *image* considers the same relationship of a statue to the person it represents. Humans therefore represent God as his agents in the world; having the freedom to act means that we can do good as well as evil, but it is not a precondition of being human to be evil. As Gunton comments:

That the possibilities for its corruption and pollution are equally great follows from this, for it remains an indisputable principle of life that the very worst derives from the corruption of the very best.

(Colin Gunton, *The Christian Faith*, 41)

Summary diagram

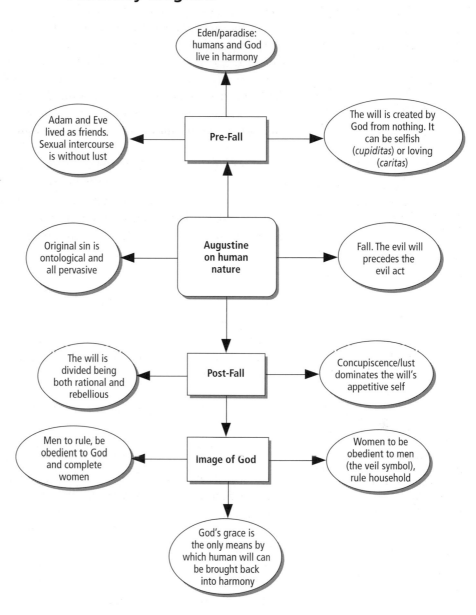

Eden/paradise: humans and God live in harmony

Adam and Eve lived as friends. Sexual intercourse is without lust

Pre-Fall

The will is created by God from nothing. It can be selfish (*cupiditas*) or loving (*caritas*)

Original sin is ontological and all pervasive

Augustine on human nature

Fall. The evil will precedes the evil act

The will is divided being both rational and rebellious

Post-Fall

Concupiscence/lust dominates the will's appetitive self

Men to rule, be obedient to God and complete women

Image of God

Women to be obedient to men (the veil symbol), rule household

God's grace is the only means by which human will can be brought back into harmony

Study guide

By the end of this chapter you should be able to explain the central aspects of Augustine's theology on human nature, including the state of the will before and after the Fall, the relationship of men and women, the significance of original sin and God's grace. You should be able to discuss and analyse these ideas using contemporary philosophical, theological and scientific views.

Essay questions

1a Explain the relationship of men and women before and after the Fall according to Augustine.

Before the Fall man and woman lived in harmony as friends. As friends neither felt lust for each other and when sex was necessary Adam could exercise his will perfectly over his body to summon an erection. Both men and women's wills were obedient to God and they carried out their duties freely. As both were created in the image of God, *ex nihilo*, their wills were, at this stage, governed by *caritas*, love for neighbour and God. However, after the Fall, the will became confused and divided. It is driven also by *cupiditas*, desire, and is unable to control the body's natural drives. Women's bodies have to be controlled more so they must be obedient to their husbands and exercise their deliberative wills only in the context of the household.

1b 'Men and women are essentially evil.' Discuss.

Arguments may wish to question the assumption that humans are evil. Evil acts occur when people lack sufficient reason or have been badly educated. The natural state of humans is neither good nor evil, although left to their own devices humans will behave according to their animal nature. On the other hand, there are sufficient evil events in the world to indicate that human nature needs more than education or right reasoning to be good. A conclusion might be that God did not create humans to be evil but with personalities which, though imperfect, can be redeemed through love.

Further essay questions

2 a   Explain Augustine's teaching on original sin and concupiscence.
2 b   'Original sin is incompatible with evolutionary biology.' Discuss.

3 To what extent was Kant right that there is no such thing as sin, merely lack of reason?

4 Assess the view that Augustine's theology is the source of an unhealthy obsession with sin and sex.

Revision checklist

Can you give brief definitions of:

- akrasia
- concupiscence
- original sin
- election
- the deliberative and obedient soul.

Can you explain:

- Augustine's idea of the will
- Augustine's teaching on the necessity of grace
- why Reinhold Niebuhr considered Augustine essential for modern politics
- how Colin Gunton adapted Augustine's theology.

Can you give arguments for and against:

- whether modern science and psychology support an idea of original sin
- whether sin is merely bad faith
- whether Augustine's understanding of human nature has continued significance today.

2

GOD AND CREATION

Chapter checklist ✓

The chapter begins by considering how creation is depicted in Genesis and then moves on to look at Aquinas' philosophical presentation of God as creator and primary cause of all matter. His teaching on God as primary and secondary cause is considered along with his explanation of angels and the role of humans. The chapter concludes by looking at contemporary discussion of these issues by theologians, scientists and philosophers.

1 Genesis

Key question

What do Genesis 1 and 2 teach about God's relationship to the creation?

In the beginning God created the heavens and the earth. The earth was without form and void, and darkness was upon the face of the deep; and the Spirit of God was moving over the face of the waters. And God said, 'Let there be light'; and there was light. And God saw that the light was good.

(Genesis 1:1–4)

In that day the Lord God made the earth and the heavens, when no plant of the field was yet in the earth and no herb of the field had yet sprung up … then the Lord God formed man of dust from the ground, and breathed into his nostrils the breath of life; and man became a living being.

(Genesis 2:4b–7)

The opening of the Bible begins with two creation accounts of the origins and purpose of the creation. According to many scholars, Genesis 1:1–2:4a was probably compiled around 586BC when the Jews were exiled in Babylon. One of the purposes of the account is to give hope in a time of despair: God is the sovereign and only creator of the universe; everything has its place and purpose; human beings are the focus of God's creation. In the second older account (Genesis 2:4b–25), possibly compiled around 960BC, God is depicted as the potter who creates man out of the dust of the earth, who, through love, gives him a companion and places them in a garden where they and the rest of the animal world live in harmony.

There are many who consider that these stories should be read as scientific accounts of the creation. But for others Genesis 1–2 are not formally scientific but poetic insights into God's relationship to the world.

However one regards Genesis, the fact is that it doesn't offer a comprehensive philosophical or scientific account of the world. For many theologians the role of science and philosophy is to provide the fuller picture using reason to reflect on and answer those questions which the biblical texts are not equipped to answer.

Although Aquinas may not have the insights of modern science, his discussion of God's relationship to matter poses the questions which continue to occupy theologians today. It is to him that we now turn.

2 Aquinas on God's relationship to matter

Key quote

Describing how Aquinas is depicted in art:

'The Buddha-like serenity attributed to him in much of the iconography is belied by the furious display of intellectual energy and passion in surviving manuscripts in his own hand.'

FERGUS KERR, IN ERNEST BAKER,
THE MEDIEVAL THEOLOGIANS, 207

PROFILE

Thomas Aquinas was, by general consent, the greatest of the medieval theologians. He was born in Roccasecca, near Naples in 1224/25 into a minor Italian aristocratic family. After school he attended the university of Naples between 1239 and 1241. There he first came into contact with the writings and philosophy of Aristotle. Aristotle was to play a very important part in the formation of his theology throughout his life and was the reason why his teaching was

Key people

The **Dominicans** were founded in 1216 by Dominic de Guzman who as friars (meaning 'brother') dedicated their lives to Christian education as travelling teachers and preachers.

Key quote

'I cannot do any more. Everything I have written seems to me as straw in comparison with what I have seen.'

THOMAS AQUINAS

often regarded with suspicion. The next important influence on his life and thought occurred in 1242 when he joined the newly founded **Dominicans**, became a friar and later around 1250 was ordained as a priest. The Dominicans sent him to Paris and then to Cologne where he became the assistant to the Aristotelian scholar, Albertus Magnus. In 1252 he returned as a lecturer in the university of Paris where he found the theology faculty deeply divided over whether to allow Dominican friars to teach. However, Aquinas' intellectual significance was becoming more influential, primarily through his commentaries on Peter Lombard's *Sentences*, where, for the first time, Aquinas deliberately integrated Aristotle's ideas with Christian doctrine. In 1256 he was made professor of divinity in Paris and began his commentary on Boethius; this was followed by his first major work the *Summa Contra Gentiles* (1256–59). The *Summa* was to help Christian missionaries in Muslim Spain and North Africa at a time when Islamic scholars were far more advanced in their use of Aristotelian philosophy than Christian theologians. Shortly afterwards in 1259 he returned home to Naples and began his most important and influential work the *Summa Theologiae*. The *Summa Theologiae* systematically sets out Christian theology in three 'parts' and develops the arguments through a system of questions and answers beginning with arguments for God's existence and the creation to ethics and the sacraments of the Church. Returning again to Paris in 1268 he continued to lecture on Aristotle and also on St John's Gospel and the Muslim scholar, Averroes.

In 1272 on his return to Naples having started the third part of the *Summa Theologiae*, on 6 December 1273 he had a mystical experience after which he said he could do no more theology. He is famously recorded as having said, 'I cannot do any more. Everything I have written seems to me as straw in comparison with what I have seen.' In February 1274 he set out to attend the council of Lyons but fell seriously ill. He ordered that he should be taken back to Fossanova (very near to where he had been born) where, soon after, he died.

a) Aristotle: Aquinas' scientist and philosopher

As we have seen, Aquinas' use of Aristotle was fundamental to the way in which he developed a rational approach to Christian theology. For him, Aristotle was simply 'The Philosopher' and he employed his technical language and ideas about matter in the same way as a theologian today uses Einstein or quantum physics.

i) The four causes

Fundamentally important for Aquinas was Aristotle's teaching on causation. Causation for Aristotle and Aquinas was a far wider idea than simply cause and effect as we tend to think today, but a description of the way something exists and how we can recognise

Key word

Aitia is the Greek used by Aristotle meaning cause, law or characteristic.

it. The term in Greek used by Aristotle for causes is **aitia** but it can also mean 'laws' or 'characteristics'. Aristotle suggested that there are four causes which determine the nature of things:

1 **Material cause** is the substance from which a thing is made. All matter has the potential for change.
2 **Formal cause** is the design of a thing and its 'organising principle'. A 'substantial form' distinguishes one thing from another.
3 **Efficient cause** is the maker, originator or designer of a thing which brings about a change in material substance. It can also be thought of as the energising (*energia*) cause.
4 **Final cause** is the material substance's purpose (*telos*) or function.

One of the most important aspects of Aristotle's philosophy which is fundamentally important for Aquinas is that matter cannot exist without form and equally form cannot exist without matter. Unlike Plato, who considered that forms or ideas *could* exist independently from matter, Aristotle argued that a form is meaningless unless it is expressed in terms of material existence.

ii) Potential, actuality and change

Aristotle argued that, at any particular moment, matter can be described in terms of what it is *potentially* and what it can become when fully actualised in its final state (*entelechia*). When matter achieves its final state it is said to be flourishing (*eudaimonia*) and complete.

Change can take place in various ways. **Substantial change** is when something goes through a process which cannot be reversed, such as an acorn growing up to become an oak tree. **Accidental change** is when matter can change according to place, decay, quality and quantity as the matters stays essentially the same, and all these accidental changes can be reversed.

Key words

Substantial and **accidental change**. A substantial change is one where matter undergoes a change which cannot be reversed; an accidental change is where matter remains the same but other factors (such as place and quantity) can be reversed.

iii) God as prime mover

God is the prime mover of all matter. As a fully actualised being he has no potential, no parts and as pure intellect he contemplates only himself as the only perfect being. Material substances are all drawn to God as their end (*telos*) because he represents the goal of all their potentials. All matter is therefore in a state of *change*, unlike God who, as a fully actualised being, undergoes no change. However, because matter is attracted to him, he can be described as the prime (or first) mover. In conclusion, and by contrast to Aquinas, as matter has always existed he is not the creator of the universe but has eternally co-existed alongside it and been its source of design and purpose.

b) Aquinas: God and creation

Aquinas' discussion on the creation and God occupies the majority of the first section of the *Summa Theologiae*. 'The Treatise on Creation' owes a great deal to Aristotle's notion of causation but Aquinas' argument is to show that, without the Christian insights as revealed in the Bible and elsewhere, the picture is incomplete. Reason therefore provides the basis on which faith takes its stand.

The Bible, and in particular the creation stories in Genesis 1 and 2, describe two characteristics of God which are fundamentally at variance with Aristotle's prime mover:

- God is the sole creator who creates all matter from nothing (*ex nihilo*)
- God is **immanent** being continually involved with the creation/matter and acts in the world generally and specifically.

i) Existence: ens and esse

A fundamentally important and technical distinction Aquinas makes is between a thing's being or *ens* and its 'act of being' or *esse*. For all material existences just being or existing is not enough unless it can do it actively. This is clearly the case for living matter: trees grow and develop just as much as animals. But it is also true for non-living matter. A rock exists (its *ens*) but it occupies space and time and affects other things (its *esse*). Furthermore, the *esse* of an entity, Aquinas argues, is always proportionate to its *ens*. This is important because it explains why even the same things can behave in slightly different ways, just as two identical cars will handle differently because each will have very slightly different *ens*.

ii) God's simplicity

From the perspective of faith God is not just the prime mover as described by Aristotle. Aristotle's idea has to be modified in several ways. First, there is no distinction between God's *esse* and his *ens* because as God is pure actuality, he has no potentiality as he is perfect. This is known as **divine simplicity**. Second, God's simplicity means he is unique, mysterious and beyond human comprehension. All that can be known of God is his effects on the world (such as its design or miracles) and from these we can *infer* his qualities often by saying what he is not. For example, we infer that: God exists as form but not matter; he is undivided; he has no dimensions; he causes but is not caused; he is changeless.

Whilst Aquinas agrees with Aristotle that God is pure actuality, he is not a passive first principle of matter or merely a final cause (*telos*) to which all matter is attracted, but the first efficient cause of everything. Finally, God is love, again not in the Aristotelian sense of a God who can only love himself, but who loves his creation and who wills every aspect of it to flourish.

Key words

Immanence describes God's omnipresence and involvement in the particular processes and events of the universe.

Ens and *esse* are two Latin terms Aquinas used to explain existence. *Ens* is a thing's being and *esse* is the way it exists.

Key word

Divine simplicity is the principle that God exists as one single entity. He cannot be divided (into matter and form), he has no parts and has no dimensions.

ii) Creation ex nihilo

The significance of Aquinas' view of Aristotle's four causes is that only the material cause is not part of God's creative command. That is because there is no pre-existing matter which God orders or designs or creates from his own substance. The answer is that God creates *ex nihilo* – from nothing. The significance of the *ex nihilo* doctrine is that it affirms that:

- God acts freely.
- God is sovereign of all matter (visible and invisible) – there are no other creators.
- God exists apart from matter and so cannot change.
- God can do anything (providing it does not create a contradiction such as squaring a triangle).
- All matter shares in God's likeness because it is created by him alone. It is therefore good. But likeness reminds us that matter is never equal to God. The doctrine of God's simplicity and creation *ex nihilo* indicate that God is uniquely different from the world.
- Creation does not involve any change in matter itself because there is no pre-existent matter from which it can be derived. Matter appears absolutely from nothing. Aquinas summarises this in the phrase, 'creation is not a change' or *creatio non est mutatio*.

Unlike **Gnostic Christians** who considered the world of matter to be evil and where hope lay in escaping this world, the *ex nihilo* doctrine is a world-affirming view that as matter is good it is there for us to enjoy. However, paradoxically, the Fall has corrupted the initial state and for Aquinas (just as much for Augustine and later Calvin) redemption in Christ provides the means to overcome this corrupted state.

iii) Actus purus

Aquinas argues that God does not just create matter and then stand back. In order for anything to exist God is everywhere and at all times the sustaining presence giving purpose and order. However, it would be quite wrong to think of these as separate actions. As God is a single being, his actions also cannot be divided. The *actus purus* or 'pure act' describes God's constant creative activity. The *actus purus* can be demonstrated equally from faith, as revealed in the Bible, as well as rational reflection. Based on Aristotle's four causes, Aquinas argues that every act of God is a triple moment when he produces, orders and preserves.

Key question

Why does it matter that God should create the world from nothing?

Key words

Gnostic Christians considered the world to be evil and corrupt and created by a lower being. Salvation lay in acquiring special knowledge or gnosis which would enable them to escape the world and be united with God.

Actus purus is Latin meaning 'pure act' and describes God's constant creative activity.

		Reason	Faith
P	Producing	God is the efficient cause of creation, producing it out of nothing	What God produces is aesthetically good, beautiful and purposeful (Genesis 1:11)
O	Ordering	God as formal cause orders matter out of chaos	God's act is a free act out of love; there is no necessity for him to create
P	Preserving	As final cause God sustains and preserves the creation so that it can fulfil its potentials	As there are no gods, the universe is solely contingent on God (Exodus 20:3)
POP is not a sequence of events but one act; every act of God is an actus purus, a single pure cause			

There is no material cause of the universe because God is not a thing. Matter does not derive from God, rather it exists as something wholly different from him. Nevertheless, all matter owes its existence to the active, ever-present will of God. This means that God is not just a rather detached abstract 'primary principle', as implied in Aristotle's thought, but pure love who acts for no other reason than that of generosity.

iv) God and time

God is not the cause *before* the universe (an idea which many modern Christian theologians have wrongly assumed) because this would imply that God undergoes a change when he causes the universe as a first cause. God is the unchanging and timeless *condition* or principle which enables everything in the universe to come into being.

v) God's actions in the world

Philosophically, these insights from faith pose difficult intellectual problems for Aquinas. First and foremost: how can God who is wholly different from matter know the material world and be involved with it? Put another way: if I have an idea about how to write an essay, the idea alone does not write the essay, it has somehow to be translated into action. This is not a problem if I think that thoughts and action are an aspect of each other (i.e. thoughts are no more than the workings of the brain) because like things can affect like things. But if I consider that minds and matter are two very different kinds of existences then I am presented with a problem that utterly different existences (mind and matter in this case) cannot affect each other.

Key question

If God is utterly different from matter, how can he interact with it?

So it is with God and the world. Aquinas does not think that God is like Aristotle's ultimate unmoved mover because Aquinas has already established the Christian view that God's simplicity means that he is utterly different from the world of matter. But if God is utterly different from the material world we appear to face the problem posed in the essay-writing example above. How can God in any sense know the world and act in it?

Aquinas' answer is given in two ways.

Cross-reference

See Alister McGrath, *Christian Theology*, page 220.

- **God is the primary cause of everything**. As all things are made in God's likeness, then there is a correspondence between them and God. God is intelligence and matter is intelligible so God knows all matter and affects it as first and final cause of everything at all times. Nothing happens by chance and even if things appear to us to be unexpected or random, their source may be traced back to God. Even bad things can be explained by the fact that God may act in favour of something rather than something else. Aquinas argues that human free will is possible because God is the designer of free will, so that like a child left on its own to do as he wishes, he is still under the control of his parents.
- **Secondary or intermediate causes**. However, Aquinas is also aware that things happen because of their effects on each other. Now, if God were to be *directly* causing these things to happen all the time then there would be no point to their existence and God would have wasted his time making anything. So, God has created everything with its own causal powers through which he affects the world *indirectly*. Some things have greater causal powers than others; human free will is one such example.

Alister McGrath explains the relationship of primary and secondary causes with an example of a pianist:

- The pianist, as the artist, is the primary cause.
- The piano as the means by which the performance occurs is the secondary or intermediate cause. The strings and hammers produce their own sound, but if they are poorly constructed then the performance will be less good.

Therefore, God as the unmoved mover usually acts through the secondary causes as the initiator of change. God initiates through the 'chain of being' (from angels, to humans, to animals, etc.). As each has its own characteristic, God's will is enacted differently. Evil, therefore, is not directly caused by God but rather is a characteristic of creatures who fail to comply with God as primary cause. However, there are times when God does act directly in the world in what we call miracles.

3 Aquinas on God's relationship to angels and humans

a) Angels

Key question

What purpose do angels serve in the creation?

It might seem strange to us for Aquinas to dedicate a long discussion on 'The Treatise on Angels' in the *Summa Theologiae* before the 'Treatise on the Six Days of Creation', but as Genesis 1 suggests, the creation is an orderly affair, designed as a hierarchy of forms from God to inert matter.

As angels are often referred to in the Bible and in the teaching of the Church, Aquinas presupposes their existence, but his treatise is to offer rational justification for this belief and to expand on his teaching on the creation.

Aquinas' philosophical reflections begin with the doctrine of **plenitude**.

Key word

Plenitude means fullness and describes the state of the greatest possible perfection.

For a universe to be truly good then it must contain the greatest possible states of goodness. So, as there is a visible and invisible realm then it is greater if it is populated with invisible incorporeal beings (beings which have no material body). Angels are incorporeal beings, therefore they must exist and belief in them cannot be irrational.

But there are other reasons why discussion of angels is important. In discussing angels Aquinas is also able to offer the following reflections:

- How humans share some characteristics with angels but in what significant ways they are different.
- How human immortality is established by the existence of angels.
- How although angels exist without bodies and are immortal they are distinguished from God.
- How God acts in the material visible world.

i) Material cause of angels

Angels have no material cause and are sometimes called 'separated substances' because they do not have a corporeal bodily existence. As pure spirits they are 'self-subsistent forms' and so, once created *ex nihilo* by God, they cannot be destroyed.

On special occasions God gives angels 'assumed (i.e. borrowed) corporeal bodies' which humans experience as visions. Therefore when people 'see' an angel it is not an actual angel but rather a projection of its essential self (it does not actually speak, eat or have sex).

ii) Efficient cause of angels

God is the efficient cause of angels as he is the cause of all creation. However, whereas other beings may be affected by intermediary or secondary causes, angels are directly affected by God. Once created they cannot undergo substantial change (they are immortal), only accidental change (they can move).

iii) Formal cause of angels

Unlike many of his contemporaries, Aquinas argued that angels do not have bodies of any kind and considered that the idea angels could have 'spiritual bodies (matter)' would confuse what is meant by the invisible world of spirit by suggesting that it could also be material like a ghost.

But this presented him with a problem because in Aristotelian terms there can be 'no form without matter'. Aquinas' conclusion was that a body is only necessary to provide sensory experience in order to gain knowledge, but for angels knowledge is their form. In other words, the form of an angel is just to know; unlike human knowledge which is acquired over time, angelic knowledge is innate – they just have it and a material body is therefore unnecessary.

A formal cause distinguishes one entity from another. Angels therefore are distinguished from each other and have their own hierarchy from archangels to lower angels. As every angel has its own form, then no angel is exactly the same as any other. Each has its own soul and potentials which can be actualised.

But as incorporeal substances angels have no ability to configure or order matter themselves. This is not so for humans. As corporeal substances the formal cause of humans also allows them to organise and order the world for God.

Finally, the formal cause of angels illustrates that an incorporeal intellectual existence means that after death the human rational soul can also come into full knowledge of God.

iv) Final cause of angels

When angels take on corporeal form their function is to convey God's will to humans. Mary, for example, is told by Gabriel that she is to bear a son conceived by the Holy Spirit. Angel means 'messenger' and in Biblical terms this is their primary function. But in their essential incorporeal form angels have other purposes. These include:

Key question

What does the existence of angels teach us about the nature of God and humans?

- **Intellect and love**. As God is pure intelligence angels are the closest beings to share in this intelligence. Angels therefore set an example to humans of what it means to love, know and serve God.
- **Evil is not a condition of existence**. Before the Fall of humans, the fall of the invisible non-corporeal world occurred when the angel Satan, through his own free will, rebelled against God's will. This fall therefore indicates that neither the material world nor the non-material world is intrinsically evil but is corrupted through the misuse of free will. So, the existence of angels serves to remind humans that the invisible world is not intrinsically superior to the visible material world. Angels and humans are designed to serve God in each sphere of existence.

- **Essence and existence**. Even though angels have no material form, they are necessarily different from God because there is a distinction between their *ens* and *esse*, their being and action. God's **simplicity** means that his existence and action are one and the same, but the purpose and function of angels are limited in proportion to their being. By contrast there is no limit to God.

b) God and humans

According to Genesis 1:26 humans are created *imago Dei*, in the image of God. All of God's creations are created in his *likeness*, but only humans are endowed with this particular quality, God's *image*.

i) Material cause of humans

Like all substances of the visible world humans are corporeal. However, in Genesis God makes man in his own image by breathing his spirit into him (Genesis 2:7). Aquinas uses Aristotle's notion that all living matter has soul (*psyche*) as soul is what enables matter to be alive. Soul animates in three ways: at the vegetative level; the appetitive level; and the intellectual or rational level. Lower life forms only possess the first or second of these characteristics of soul but humans alone possess all three. By using Aristotle, Aquinas is therefore able to give a philosophical account of humans as *imago Dei*. It is the rational soul which God breathes into humans; it is also the rational soul which enables humans to know God and act freely.

ii) Efficient cause of humans

God is first (and final) cause of humans. But as rational creatures they also have free will and are, in that sense, their own efficient causes making genuine choices and affecting the material world around them.

iii) Formal cause of humans

The intellectual soul as organising principle is, as we have observed, the first principle of the body and enables humans to know God in a limited way. The human intellectual formal cause also distinguishes humans from angels because, unlike angels, humans are able to organise matter. In biblical terms, as God's stewards (Genesis 1:28), humans are there to maintain creation and order it according to God's will.

iv) Final cause of humans

But the final state of humans is after death when the soul is reunited with its body (now transformed by God) and is able to know God and see him face to face. In Aquinas' version of **predestination**, it is God's will that all rational creatures should find salvation in eternal

Cross-reference

See page 26 on God's simplicity.

Key quote

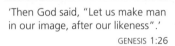

'Then God said, "Let us make man in our image, after our likeness".'

GENESIS 1:26

Key question

How are humans unique in God's creation?

Key word

Predestination is God's eternal plan or decree that humans will be saved because of God's grace in Jesus Christ. Some theologians argue that salvation is only for the few chosen elect.

life, made available through God's grace in Jesus Christ. This is not, however, theirs by right and there will be some who fall short and so do not enter into God's eternal bliss.

4 Contemporary discussion

Aquinas' presentation of God and his relationship to the material world raises many questions, especially in the light of contemporary science and philosophy. The following represent just a few of the current debates.

a) Science and creation

i) Evolution and the telos

Key question

Has evolution destroyed the need for a creator God?

Aquinas' use of Aristotle meant that his view of matter was strongly teleological. God is the first and final cause of everything. However, since Darwin, it is widely held that evolution and natural selection do not require a final cause. Nature develops 'blindly' and is not drawn to some grand *telos* but evolves as circumstances force some things to adapt and others to die out. Once the idea of *telos* is abandoned then God as the 'producing–ordering–preserving' principle of matter loses all meaning. For even if God were to produce and order matter without preserving it for some purpose, his role would be an empty one. It is a point which Richard Dawkins and many others have frequently made.

Key people

Keith Ward (1938–) was Regius Professor of Divinity at Oxford University. His areas of interest include the relationship of science and religion, the relationship of religions with one another and ethics. He has been one of the most eloquent opponents of the 'new atheism' developed by Richard Dawkins and AC Grayling. His many books include: *God, Chance and Necessity* (1996) and *Why there Almost Certainly is a God* (2008).

On the other hand, **Keith Ward** considers that a value-giving *telos* is exactly what evolutionary biology supports. He rejects Dawkins' claim that human existence is only to reproduce. Even by Dawkins' and other modern Darwinist standards this is not the way we understand ourselves. Ward concludes:

> *Bodies are not primarily machines for carrying genes. They are not machines at all. They are the generators and carriers of central nervous systems, networks of conscious interaction with the environment, making possible understanding, contemplation, happiness and rational agency … the purpose of brains is to generate consciousness and purpose, and with them, for the first time in the history of the cosmos, the existence of intrinsic values.*

(Keith Ward, *God, Chance and Necessity*, 145)

ii) Origins and ex nihilo

Key question

Should the idea of creation from nothing be removed from Christian teaching?

Key word

Quantum physics suggests that the behaviour of sub-atomic particles are predictions based on probabilities and not certainties as in Newtonian physics.

Stephen Hawking famously concluded his influential *A Brief History of Time* by saying that once we can get back to the very moment of creation we will then know the 'mind of God'. He has subsequently argued that, as modern **quantum physics** offers the paradoxical idea that we could give a description of the universe

Key people

Stephen Hawking (1942–) was until his retirement in 2009 Lucasian Professor of Mathematics at Cambridge University. He has pioneered research into theoretical cosmology and quantum gravity and through his *A Brief History of Time* (1988) popularised the complex debates about the origins of the universe.

Key word

Big Bang is the cataclysmic event scientists estimate to have taken place 14 billion years ago which brought the universe and time into being.

Key quotes

'However, if we do discover a complete theory, it should in time be understandable in broad principle by everyone, not just a few scientists. Then we shall all, philosophers, scientists, and just ordinary people, be able to take part in the discussion of the question why it is that we and the universe exist. If we find the answer to that, it would be the ultimate triumph of human reason – for then we would know the mind of God.'

STEPHEN HAWKING, *A BRIEF HISTORY OF TIME*, 175

'To say that a very complex and well-ordered universe comes into being without any cause or reason is equivalent to throwing one's hands up in the air and just saying that anything might happen, that it is hardly worth bothering to look for reasons at all. And that is the death of science.'

KEITH WARD GOD, *CHANCE AND NECESSITY*, 19

Key word

Neo-Thomism refers to the modern revival and adaptation of Aquinas' teaching.

prior to the **Big Bang**, then there is no necessity even to consider a 'mind of God' other than the conditions which made this universe possible.

Those who have argued along the lines suggested by Aquinas that God is the first cause and initiator of the Big Bang, now find themselves rescuing God to 'fill the gap' left by physicists and then find that the 'gap' has been filled by more recent scientific explanation.

Some theologians have argued that maybe Aquinas' insistence on creation *ex nihilo* needs to be revised. Their argument is that Genesis doesn't really support an *ex nihilo* explanation – at the time it would have been presumed that matter of some kind had always existed, but what God did was to give it form and purpose. A modified *ex nihilo* allows us to abandon the problem of needing a beginning without harming God's unique sovereignty. As Keith Ward argues, God provides an explanation why there is a universe. The popular scientific alternatives are:

- **Chance** – there is no reason for the universe. There is no explanation for it and we accept its existence as 'brute fact'.
- **Necessity** – all the reasons which explain the nature of universe are contained in the universe itself. In time we will be able to describe and explain them all.

Ward finds both explanations far from satisfactory. Chance is misleading because quantum science suggests that the universe is not a *random* event, rather that it is a *probable* event. That means that laws of probability exist which suggest that there is a purpose (a *telos*). Necessity suffers from the 'fallacy of misplaced concreteness'. This fallacy is the idea that we are so impressed by the power of mathematics that we assume it can explain everything in concrete or certain terms. This forgets that mathematics is itself a human and abstract process and cannot offer concrete certainty. Furthermore, as Ward concludes, those who argue for necessity would logically have to reckon that only a mind as powerful as God's could comprehend it.

Neo-Thomists and others consider that far from undermining Aquinas' idea of God's act of creation (as the *actus purus*), modern quantum physics supports the notion that it is meaningless to talk of a time 'before' the Big Bang as time is only a property of matter as it presently exists. Aquinas' *actus purus* provides a way of understanding that as creator God is more than merely a first cause but the preserver who enables matter to continue to exist. As some scientists and theologians have argued, the universe seems to be so finely tuned to produce sustainable matter and life, that an underlying cause or principle which produces–orders–preserves is not at all unreasonable.

b) God's actions

The general term to describe God's actions in the world is **providence**. For Aquinas and theologians today providence simply means the way in which God provides for the world. More specifically it refers to the way in which God acts in human history. Aquinas had hoped to demonstrate how every aspect of the creation owes its purpose to God's active involvement. Unlike Aristotle and later **deists**, God is not merely a passive first principle of the universe but an active ever-present creator. Even so, many theologians today don't think Aquinas' primary and secondary causal distinction is adequate – God is still just an underlying cause however one looks at it. His theology does not lead to a loving active God as seen in the Bible but an impersonal abstract God of deism.

i) Process theology

Process theologians are among those who consider that although Aquinas' account of God has some merits (especially his 'preserving' role), his classical view of God and creation is nevertheless far too static and dualistic. While they agree that God influences events through secondary causes, they argue that Aquinas' one-way relationship doesn't allow for genuine human free will and the **indeterminate** way matter behaves, especially at a subatomic level. In other words, process theologians consider that Aquinas has placed too much emphasis on God's transcendence as controller of all causes and failed to give an adequate account of his immanence.

Process theologians argue that reality is a set of interconnected events or 'occasions'. These occasions take place because of other preceding 'occasions' and because there is a background organising principle. This principle is what is meant by God. God is also an event, but unlike other events he exists permanently. Process theologians resist the dualism of Aquinas which places God *over* matter (as they see it) and argue instead that God is in a **dipolar relationship** with the world. God doesn't order matter; rather he persuades, lures, encourages it (and us) to fulfil (or actualise) its potentials at any one moment in time.

- Dipolarity suggests that as a non-material being God depends on the material world in order to act, just as much as the material world depends on God as its non-material organising principle.
- Dipolarity echoes what Aristotle considered to be the form/matter relationship but without a *telos*.

Process thought offers a non-teleological account of God's relationship to matter. It redefines God's chief attributes so that transcendence is permanence not separateness, and omnipotence is his persistent and loving persuasion, not force or coercion.

Key words

Providence is God's action in the world generally (as creator) and specifically (in human history and miracles).

Deism is the belief that God is an ultimate cause or principle but that he plays no active part in the universe.

Key word

Indeterminate is a mathematical term to mean that there are any number of solutions to a problem.

Key word

Dipolar relationship in process theology describes the way God persuades rather than orders creation to fulfil its potentials.

Key thought

Process theology developed from the mathematical and philosophical ideas of A.N. Whitehead and in particular his book *Process and Reality* (1929). Other influential process theologians include Charles Hartshorne, John Cobb and Ian Barbour.

Key quote

'Both experience and history point to a God who acts not by coercing but by evoking the response of his creatures.'

IAN G. BARBOUR, *ISSUES IN SCIENCE AND RELIGION*, 463

Key people

David Hume (1711–76) was one of the most important philosophers of the eighteenth century. He was born in Edinburgh and educated at a time when Isaac Newton's natural science was influential in Scottish universities. He was sceptical of religion and miracles as seen notably in his essay *Of Miracles* (1742).

Key word

Capriciousness means to act in sudden and unexpected ways for no apparent reason.

ii) God's providence and miracles

According to Aquinas, God can perform acts which don't follow the normal expected course of events; in other words God can and does perform miracles. These are his direct acts in the world, independent from secondary causes. Aquinas describes three types of miracle:

- those which violate the laws of nature
- those which nature can do but not in that order
- those which normally happen in nature but without the operation of the principles of nature.

None of these pose particular problems for Aquinas as they do for many today – especially so-called 'violation' miracles. Aquinas defines a miracle as 'an event that happens outside the ordinary process of the whole created nature' (*Summa Theologiae*, 1a 110.4).

Violation miracles are not problematic from Aquinas' point of view as they illustrate another of God's *ex nihilo* acts. As the creation *ex nihilo* cannot have been contrary to nature (otherwise nature would not have been possible at all) then what might appear to us to be contradiction is in fact God drawing out the potential of nature another possibility. Neo-Thomists remind us that confusion arises only when God is treated as a cause like any other cause: God may act through secondary causes or without them – there is no contradiction.

On the other hand, **David Hume**'s criticism of violation miracles is influential. The core of Hume's argument is that all scientific knowledge is based on the principle of induction, that is for scientific law to be accepted it must be subjected to repeated testing. But as violation miracles are by definition unrepeatable and therefore untestable they remain at the very best highly improbable. For this major reason (he gives others) they cannot be accepted as a sufficiently rational basis for faith.

However, others have been less concerned with the causal problems posed by Aquinas than the moral and providential problem of God's **capriciousness**. If God has the ability to act directly in the world and not just through secondary causes, then why does he allow good people to suffer and bad to flourish? As Aquinas firmly rejected the place of chance (as all things ultimately depend on God) then the argument that God allows us to use our free will to determine our lives under his guardianship is not easily squared against acts of great evil when God might have acted.

c) Angels

The existence of the spiritual, non-corporeal beings that sacred Scripture usually calls 'angels' is a truth of faith. The witness of Scripture is as clear as the unanimity of Tradition.

(*The Catechism of the Catholic Church*, paragraph 328)

i) Angels and science

The existence and purpose of angels is probably not high up on the list of important theological issues. The *Catechism of the Catholic Church* confirms their significance as a matter of faith, but for many, Aquinas' argument for the necessity of angels in the chain of secondary causes is dismissed today as modern astronomy and subatomic physics can explain the invisible incorporeal world (i.e. a world beyond ordinary sense experience) in scientific terms and those who claim to have experienced or even seen angels are considered to be hallucinating or schizophrenic.

ii) Angels and the imagination

But there are some theologians who consider that in dismissing angels as fantasies of the mind we are also rejecting the vital place the imagination plays in human experience. Imagination cannot be easily dismissed by science for human imagination often plays a vital role in the way science progresses. Imagination need not be irrational but at the same time it extends beyond the rational and touches on the deeper experiences of human existence. Imagination is the basis on which the poet, novelist, artist and musician use images which resonate with human consciousness.

In religious terms the prophets of the Bible and afterwards were not making predictions about the future but transferring their deeper experiences of the divine into poetic images. These are not invented or made up but convey a reality which cannot be conveyed in scientific or purely rational terms. Perhaps the weakness of Aquinas' treatment of angels was just this; he was trying to be too rational.

Some of the existentialist theologians, notably **Rudolf Bultmann**, came close to realising this when they said that angels, demons and supernatural powers were *myths* conveying the sense that life is a constant battleground between the forces of good and evil, between angels and demons. But rather than allow the power of the imagery to continue to speak to us, Bultmann argued that angels and demons should be **demythologised** and stripped back to *human* experience and rejected as actual beings. Angels and demons belong to a pre-scientific view of the world which we no longer hold to be true.

On the other hand, as **Douglas Hedley** argues, if imagery is stripped away, then the power of the poetry to convey *real* insights into God and the world is inevitably lost. Angels are not just made up but are 'inspired images'; if God reveals himself to humans then it is reasonable that imagination provides the only really effective means for finite minds to encounter the infinite. Hedley quotes Paul Tillich who says of angels that they 'are the spiritual mirrors of the divine abyss'. In other words, angels express the depth ('the abyss') and range of God's being. Without angels and indeed demons, Hedley argues, the Christian drama of Jesus' life and death in his combat between

Key question

Is belief in angels irrational?

Cross-reference

See page 61 on Rudolf Bultmann.

Cross-reference

See pages 61–62 on demythologising.

Key people

Douglas Hedley (1961–) is a fellow of Clare College, Cambridge in theology and philosophy. His books include *Living Forms of the Imagination* (2008).

good (angels) against evil becomes no more than a teacher who unfortunately died for his beliefs. Using our imagination we can enter into the mindset of Jesus and see the world as he saw it; if we follow Aquinas' rational explanation of angels then we lose the poetry of religions experience and its dynamic revelation of God and the world.

Summary diagram

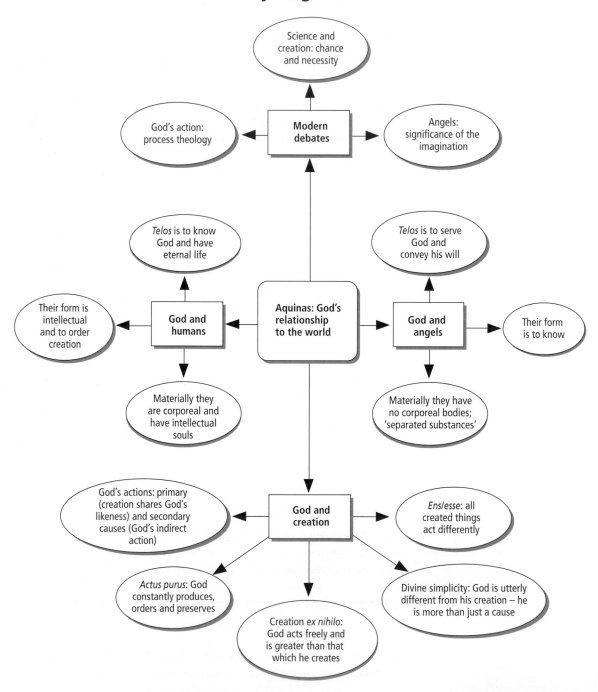

Study guide

By the end of this chapter you should be able to explain Aquinas' classical view of God, creation and angels based on Aristotle's four causes. In particular you should be to explain the *actus purus*, creation *ex nihilo* and primary and secondary causes. You should be able to analyse Aquinas' theology using the views of modern theologians, scientists and philosophers.

Essay questions

1a Explain Aquinas' teaching on God's action in the world.

As God is sole creator of the universe *ex nihilo* all matter is dependent on him for its existence. But God is more than first cause. The doctrine of divine simplicity suggests that, unlike everything else, there is no distinction between his *ens* and *esse* so he is continually acting and creating. Therefore, as the final cause of all matter he creates continuously in three ways: as producer, as organiser, as preserver. Therefore, as an omnipresent being God is constantly acting in the world. He can act in a general way because he is intelligence and matter is intelligible and he can do so indirectly through secondary causes. Sometimes he can do so directly via miracles.

1b 'God cannot act in the world without contradicting the laws of nature.' Discuss.

Those who agree with this statement might do so because if matter behaves according to its own laws then any action of God which isn't in direct conformity with these laws would be a contradiction. If God merely conforms to these laws then there might be little reason to include him except as a first cause. If God doesn't conform to these laws then Hume has already pointed out the problems of violation miracles.

On the other hand, God as creator is by nature the reason why all things exist and continue to exist. As the process theologians argue, God's preserving and ordering role need not be teleological. God acts by leading creation on without coercion, just as humans respond to God's direct love without losing their autonomy.

Further essay questions

2 a   Explain Aquinas' teaching on angels and their relationship to humans.

2 b   Assess the view that angels only exist in the imagination.

3 'Modern science supports Aquinas' view that the universe is here for a reason.' Discuss.

4 Discuss the view that classical theism leaves no place for genuine freedom.

Revision checklist

Can you give brief definitions of:

- formal and material causes
- immanence
- transcendence
- *ens* and *esse* of God
- divine simplicity.

Can you explain:

- God's *actus purus*
- God as primary and secondary cause
- why angels have formal cause but no material cause
- what it means for humans to be created in both the likeness and image of God.

Can you give arguments for and against:

- process theology's challenge to Aquinas' classical theism
- the view that Aquinas' theology of creation is undermined by modern science
- belief in angels is not irrational.

3

KNOWLEDGE OF GOD

Chapter checklist ✓

This chapter considers different ways in which we can know about the world and considers which of these best describes our knowledge of God: knowing God based on experience of the natural world or from revelation. The chapter then reviews John Calvin's two main ideas of God as Creator and Redeemer and his argument that knowing God is the basis for salvation. The chapter concludes by looking at some of the contemporary discussion of these ideas, in particular the debate between natural and revealed theology.

1 Natural and revealed theology

Key question ❓

What does it mean to 'know God'?

a) Knowing

In day-to-day life we use the word 'know' in several different ways. Consider the difference of usage in the following:

a) I know that 2+2=4
b) I know that Paris is the capital of France
c) I know of Peter Smith
d) I know Peter Smith.

Very briefly we might argue that: a) is logical knowledge based on the definition of what 2 means and what addition entails; b) is factual knowledge either based on a very well established report or first-hand experience; c) is very similar to the previous example and establishes Peter Smith's existence and maybe some of his characteristics; d) suggests personal relationship which is more intimate and complete than the previous example – it could be based on first-hand experience or much more detailed factual knowledge which only he has given me.

Given the ambiguities of knowing in these ordinary circumstances, what does it mean to say 'I know God'? For many it means that God's existence is logically true or that God's existence is a widely

Key word

Natural theology considers that God can be known through reason and observation of the natural world.

Key word

Revealed theology considers that God can be known only when he lets himself be known. This might be through a prophet, scripture, prayer, etc.

Key question

Is true knowledge scientific, philosophical or religious?

held fact. Demonstrating God's existence has long been of interest to philosophers of religion and to what theologians call **natural theology**. But the problem with this approach is that this kind of knowledge is often far removed from the kind of knowledge which religious traditions talk about when they speak of God.

For most religious believers knowledge of God is much closer to knowledge of Peter Smith in example d). It is also at this stage that different religions speak in specific ways. Judaism knows God as the giver of Torah and the one who establishes his covenant with Abraham, Isaac and Jacob; Christianity knows God in the person of Jesus Christ; Islam knows God in the Qur'an and in the example of the Prophet Muhammad. According to **revealed theology**, these statements are possible only because each religion claims that God has let himself be known in a special way.

But the fundamental problem for both natural and revealed theology is that, unlike all other forms of knowledge, the object, God, is uniquely different from any other object (in fact he is no object at all). Therefore, although the attractiveness of natural theology is that it offers a rational and reasonable *justification* for the existence of God, it also has to acknowledge that by definition God as an infinite being lies beyond reason. On the other hand, although revealed theology argues that what can be known of God is only that which he reveals of himself, it is much harder for it to offer any rational justification. For many this suggests that revealed theology is irrational and arbitrary.

b) True knowledge

At the heart of this debate is an ancient argument about what constitutes 'true knowledge'. True knowledge could mean hard, incorrigible facts about the world. Some associate this with scientific knowledge. But is this really true knowledge? It might be considered true insofar as it describes the physical properties of matter, but it is hardly knowledge in terms of understanding one's life and the skills associated with it to make it as worthwhile as possible. In the ancient world this second kind of knowledge is 'wisdom' and considered to be 'true knowledge'. The source for wisdom was oneself, because to 'know oneself' meant understanding one's place in society and in the world. For a very long time that is what philosophy was all about – the love (*philos*) of wisdom (*sophos*).

But there is a third possibility which is that true knowledge is knowledge of God. The question the third possibility poses is whether knowledge of God includes or excludes philosophy and science or relies entirely on what God reveals of himself to us – along the lines suggested in example d) above.

This is the task that John Calvin set himself and to which we now turn.

2 Calvin on knowing God as creator

PROFILE

John Calvin (1509–64) was born in Noyon, northern France. He was baptised Jean Chauvin but later adopted the Latin version of his name. He was an outstanding scholar, so much so that his father decided he should not become a priest, which was his original intention, but train as a lawyer.

In 1533, while at the University of Paris, Calvin seems to have undergone a sudden conversion to the **Protestantism** of Martin Luther (1483–1546) and to what he called 'teachableness'. Luther's Protestant movement was critical of the Church (by which they meant the Roman Catholic Church) considering that it had strayed from its origins in Christ. He also taught that the Church had become too powerful and that salvation should depend on personal faith. He argued that Christian authority should always begin with the Bible (*sola scriptura*) and that salvation is only through faith (*sola fide*) in God's justice or 'justification by faith' and not through good works, such as going on pilgrimages and giving money to the Church.

Facing persecution from the Parisian authorities, Calvin fled to Basel in Switzerland in 1535 where he wrote the first edition of his most influential book the *Institutes of the Christian Religion* (published in 1536). It was written to educate the 'unlearned' (ordinary people who did not know Latin, Hebrew or Greek) in the fundamentals of Christian teaching. Calvin always felt that theology was a process of learning and so the *Institutes* appeared in four further revised editions. From the second edition onwards it appeared in French (for the Protestant people of France) as well as in Latin.

During a chance visit to Geneva in 1538 Calvin met the Reformed Protestant preacher Guillaume Farel who persuaded Calvin to stay and preach **Reformed Christianity**. This was a highly significant moment. Geneva had just become a republic but was torn apart by many factions caused by the gap left by its Catholic past. However, Farel's and Calvin's attempts to reform the church–state relationship were unsuccessful and they were expelled in 1538.

From Geneva Calvin settled in Strasbourg and returned to academic life. But, encouraged by the reformers Martin Bucer and Philip Melanchthon, he learned how to be a very effective preacher as well as teacher and pastor. Under their influence he was keen that theology should be 'clear and orderly' just as God's creation is clear and orderly. The next edition of the *Institutes* was an attempt to do this, but it wasn't until the final fifth 1559 edition of the *Institutes* that he felt he had achieved this aim.

In 1541 Calvin returned to Geneva and was soon able to make it what he had always wanted it to be, a 'school of Christ'. He

Key word

Protestant was a termed coined in 1529 when six princes and 14 German cities protested against the restrictions placed on those who wished to belong to the Reform movements. It has come to refer to the churches and people who support the theology and practices developed during and after the Reformation.

Key thought

Reformed Christianity was formed by a group of Swiss reformers including Huldrych Zwingli (1484–1531) and Heinrich Bullinger (1504–75). Under Calvin its influence moved to Geneva. It distinguished itself from the German Lutheran Reformation because of its more radical theology which stressed total human depravity after the Fall; God's unconditional grace regardless of individual merit; and limited atonement for those whom God has chosen (the elect).

developed the *Institutes* to instruct pastors to read the Bible in its original historical context and to preach it according to the present situation. The *Institutes* were also aimed at ordinary men, women and children so they could test what the pastor said against their own understanding of Scripture. To help them do this Calvin found the Academy in 1559.

The legacy of the *Institutes* captures the Protestant belief that the individual's experience of God, not the Church, is the primary source of authority for faith. By 1559 Calvin was clear that knowledge of God (the means of salvation) comes in two related ways: revelation of God the Creator; and revelation of God the Redeemer.

a) *Sensus divinitatis*

Calvin's thesis is explicitly set out in the opening chapter heading of the *Institutes*, 'Without knowledge of the self there is no knowledge of God'. This is how he explains it:

> *Nearly all the wisdom we possess, that is to say, true and sound wisdom, consists of two parts: the knowledge of God and of ourselves. But, while joined by many bonds, which one precedes and brings forth the other is not easy to discern. In the first place, no one can look upon himself without immediately turning his thoughts to the contemplation of God, in whom he 'lives and moves' (Acts 17:28).*

(John Calvin, *Institutes*, I.I.1)

However, despite the chapter heading, Calvin's comments that it is not clear whether knowledge of self leads to knowledge of God or whether knowledge of God leads to knowledge of self. This is an ambiguity which runs throughout his theology. But one thing is clear: the kind of knowledge which Calvin has in mind is not scientific or purely rational (which he said 'flits in the brain') in an abstract philosophical sense but a form of wisdom. True wisdom means living a fulfilled life.

One way of reading this passage is from a natural theology perspective. Calvin suggests here and elsewhere that all humans have a *sensus divinitatis* – that is a natural inbuilt sense of God.

How does he support such a claim?

- **Universal Consent Argument**. A well-known argument suggested by the philosopher **Marcus Tullius Cicero** whom Calvin refers to, is that as so many people believe in God or the gods then God or gods must exist. This appears to suggest that all people have a sense of the divine and many come to realise that the object of this sense is God (or the gods). The argument could equally work today and we might add the research done by

Key question

Do all humans and human societies have an inbuilt sense of God?

Key word

Sensus divinitatis is the Latin phrase used by Calvin meaning a 'sense of God' or 'sense of the divine'.

Key quote

'There is within the human mind, and indeed by natural instinct, an awareness of divinity. This we can take beyond controversy.'

JOHN CALVIN, *INSTITUTES*, I.I.3

Key people

Marcus Tullius Cicero (106–43BC) was a Roman philosopher, statesman and orator. In his *De natura deorum* (*the nature of the gods*) he sets out his design argument for the existence of the gods using Stoic theology.

scholars into religious experience which appears to be ubiquitous (i.e. found in every culture).

- **Innate**. An idea Calvin develops from St Paul is that all humans have a natural or innate *disposition* to believe in God. In his *Letter to the Romans*, Paul says that knowledge of God is 'plain to them, because God has shown it to them', even if some choose to ignore it. Furthermore, Calvin's reference to Acts 17:28 (in the opening passage) is a classic Bible passage in support of natural theology where Paul argues that we all know of God unconsciously because God sustains all natural processes and enables us to live and thrive.

However, Calvin's position is not one which wholly endorses Cicero or Paul. Universal belief or experience of God does not demonstrate his existence. Innate knowledge of God is not *proved* to me because humans have a belief in God, because for Calvin even if no one believed in God, God would still exist. The argument Calvin offers is that these types of knowledge do not necessarily lead to *true* knowledge because true knowledge begins and ends with my encounter with God. As Paul Helm argues, the religious experience of others helps to *confirm* my knowledge of God but it does not provide it.

Calvin calls this relationship **correlation**. Put simply this means whatever we say of ourselves implies something about the nature of God and whatever we say about God implies something about the nature of humans.

b) Conscience

A second source of the knowledge of God is conscience. Conscience is our God-given faculty as creatures made in the image of God. As such, it is part of our moral choice-making processes which responds to God's will of what is right and wrong. Conscience also illustrates the principles of correlation and **accommodation**. The principle of accommodation is that God's revelation of himself is always given in a way in which finite minds can understand him.

- **Conscience is correlation**. Conscience literally means 'joint knowledge' between ourselves and God as witness whose presence gives a sense of moral judgement. In the presence of God's judgement people know whether they stand or fall.
- **Conscience is accommodation**. God has accommodated conscience at various stages by giving moral guidance. For example, Moses was given the Law at Sinai as summarised in the Decalogue; Jesus' teaching and the teaching of the Apostles developed the Law for a different stage in human history. But all have the same content – God's eternal will for man.

Key quote

'For what can be known about God is plain to them, because God has shown it to them. Ever since the creation of the world, his invisible nature, namely, his eternal power and deity, has been clearly perceived in the things which have been made.'

ST PAUL, *LETTER TO THE ROMANS*, 1:19–20

Cross-reference

Read Paul Helm, in *Engaging with Calvin*, Chapter 3.

Key word

Correlation, as used by Calvin, means that whatever humans say about themselves implies something about the nature of God and whatever we say about God implies something about the nature of humans.

Key word

Accommodation as used by Calvin, means that God limits and adapts his revelation so as to be best suited to human finite minds.

Key quote

Conscience 'is a certain mean between God and man, because it does not allow man to suppress within himself what he knows, but pursues him to the point of convicting him.'

JOHN CALVIN, *INSTITUTES*, III.XIX.15

- **No human power can override conscience**. Unlike Luther who argued that all people have a duty to obey the ruler, Calvin argued that a ruler or state may represent God's authority, but are subject to conscience first (*Institutes*, IV.X.5).

c) The creation as mirror of God

Key question

Does Calvin propose a design argument for God's existence?

Yet, in the first place, wherever you cast your eyes, there is no sport in the universe wherein you cannot discern at least some sparks of his glory. You cannot in one glance survey this most vast and beautiful system of the universe, its wide expanse, without being completely overwhelmed by the boundless force of its brightness. The reason why the author of the Letter to the Hebrews elegantly calls the universe the appearance of things invisible is that this skilful ordering of the universe is for us a sort of mirror in which we can contemplate God, who is otherwise invisible.

(John Calvin, *Institutes*, I.V.1)

Cross-reference

See pages 53–54 for discussion of the design argument.

The third related means of knowing God is the creation. This is the closest Calvin comes to presenting his version of the traditional **design argument**. In the passage above he says, as do many passages in the Bible, that the beauty and awesome nature of the creation lead us to consider it the work of God. However, unlike the classical arguments of Aquinas, Calvin is not so much proving the *existence* of God as demonstrating what the creation tells us about what we can know of the nature of God.

The argument also importantly includes the principle of accommodation which is what God reveals through the creation is appropriate to finite minds, but his essence nevertheless remains unknown to us. Using the biblical metaphor of a mirror, Calvin argues that what we know of God is a mirror or reflection of his invisible nature. Using a standard philosophical distinction he says that the creation is the *appearance* of God's nature but not his *essence*. It is then possible to form some idea of God's being (for example his love, power, justice and mercy) from his 'sparks of glory' imprinted on nature. What we learn about God would be like reading about the Queen from information released by her press officer to various newspapers. None of it would be wrong but each would be presented according to the style of the newspaper and would never quite tell us who the monarch really is as a person.

d) Scripture

The final source for knowledge of God as creator is the Bible or Scripture. This inclusion challenges a sharp distinction between revealed and natural theology. According to Calvin's theory of correlation, because the natural world reveals God's glory, it is only to be expected that Scripture equally reveals God's glory as experienced at various times by various prophets and writers of the

Bible, according to their situation and capabilities. More so than nature, Scripture offers deeper and 'clearer' knowledge of God.

However, the problem still persists that, as humans have finite minds, even scripture cannot provide us with comprehensive knowledge of God because as Paul says we only see God at first in a 'mirror dimly' (1 Corinthians 13:12). Therefore, although Scripture can often appear 'obscure' (a term often used by Calvin), the problem lies not with Scripture as objective revelation but our own subjective imperfection.

3 Calvin on knowing God as redeemer

Key question

Can knowledge of God only be through Christ?

Key word

Si integer stetisset Adam is the Latin phrase used by Calvin meaning 'if Adam had remained upright'.

In theory, knowledge of God the creator through the *sensus divinitatis*, conscience, creation and the Bible could even, allowing for finite human minds, bring humans into relationship with God. However, the argument for 'simple knowledge' completely overlooks one key factor which had preoccupied Augustine: the corruption of humanity due to the Fall. If, Calvin argues, Adam had remained upright (*si integer stetisset Adam*) then all would have known God and achieved a state of perfect happiness or blessedness. But, even so, Calvin says:

> *I speak only of the primal and simple knowledge to which the very order of nature would have led us if Adam had remained upright* (si integer stetisset Adam). *In this ruin of mankind no one now experiences God either as Father or as Author of salvation, or favourable in any way, until Christ the Mediator comes forward to reconcile him to us. Nevertheless, it is one thing to feel that God as our Maker supports us by his power, governs us by his providence, nourishes us by his goodness, and attends us with all sorts of blessings – and another thing to embrace the grace of reconciliation offered to us in Christ.*

(John Calvin, *Institutes*, I. II.1)

Key word

Regeneration in Christian terms is the process of renewal, restoration and recreation associated with baptism and other sacraments of the Church.

Cross-reference

See page 42 on true knowledge.

This passage clearly states the second aspect of his *duplex cognitio Domini* (the two-fold knowledge of God) the distinctive Christian knowledge of God the Redeemer as mediated by Christ. It is only this knowledge of God which brings humans into full and complete relationship with God. Knowing God in this way is, to use Calvin's language, to be **regenerated** – renewed, restored, recreated. **True knowledge** is salvation in Christ.

a) Christ the Mediator

We have already observed that Calvin doesn't make a sharp distinction between general and special revelation. Scripture, as special revelation, offers knowledge of God as creator but it is only the final and complete revelation in Christ contained in the

Key word

The **Trinitarian** view of God is central Christian teaching that God is one but reveals himself as three 'persons'; Father, Son and Holy Spirit.

New Testament which resolves any of the obscurities of the Old Testament.

This is one reason why the Bible should be read from a **Trinitarian** perspective:

- through God as Father the prophets and writers bear witness to his revelation
- through Christ as mediator clarity is given to God's promises
- through the Holy Spirit Christians are inspired, sustained and led in the process of interpretation.

However, even the knowledge of God mediated in Christ cannot tell us what God is in essence. The principle of accommodation means that Christ is the *image* or likeness of the invisible God (2 Corinthians 4:4) and he appears to us in a way that finite/sinful minds can understand. God becomes a human being because God accommodates himself to our actual physical condition. This is why Christ is said to be the mirror and mediator of the divine. As mirror he reflects those qualities (love, forgiveness, etc.) of God which would otherwise be hidden from us and as mediator he transmits God's essence in a way that is appropriate for us.

Key quote

'In their case the god of this world has blinded the minds of the unbelievers, to keep them from seeing the light of the gospel of the glory of Christ, who is the likeness of God.'

ST PAUL, *SECOND LETTER TO THE CORINTHIANS*, 4:4

b) Double grace in Christ

Therefore, to know Christ means that we are now in a position to understand God's judgement of sinners as his promise of blessing and hope of redemption. This is the *duplex gratia Christi* – the two-fold nature of grace in Christ:

- the grace of repentance produced through Jesus' death and resurrection
- the grace of justification in which humans are brought back into right relationship with God.

4 Contemporary discussion

At the heart of Calvin's theology there is ambiguity. Did he have a natural theology or is his theology entirely based on explaining revelation? Linked with this is whether he presented two quite different Gods: the God who, as creator, is a transcendent grand cause detached from the world and God the redeemer who is a personal loving being, closely involved immanently in the world.

The tension between these ambiguities has been the source of great debate amongst modern theologians, not least because knowing who and what God is covers a wide range of possibilities.

Key people

Emil Brunner (1889–1966) was
a Swiss Reformed minister and
theologian. He supported Barth's
neo-orthodoxy but was also
influenced by Aquinas' notion that
through analogy God can partially
be known through the creation.
This led to Barth's fierce rejection
in his essay *Nein!* (1938). Brunner's
defence in his essay *Nature and
Grace* and Barth's *Nein!* were
published together as *Natural
Theology* (1946).

Karl Barth (1886–1968) was
a Swiss Reformed minister
and theologian. Early on he
rejected liberal Protestantism and
developed what has sometimes
been called neo-orthodoxy – a
rejection of natural theology and a
revival of Reformed theology. His
greatest work is the multi-volume
Church Dogmatics (1932–67).

Key word

Point of contact is God's
revelation in the world which
provides humans with the first step
to knowing him. The idea was put
forward by Brunner and rejected
by Barth.

Key quote

'We shall not be able to avoid
speaking of a double revelation:
one in creation which only he can
recognise in all its magnitude,
whose eyes have been opened by
Christ; and of a second in Jesus
Christ in whose bright light he can
clearly perceive the former.'

EMILE BRUNNER, *NATURE
AND GRACE*, 26–27

a) Barth–Brunner debate

The questions Calvin raises became the focus of a celebrated
debate between two Reformed theologians **Emil Brunner** and
Karl Barth in 1934. Their debate illustrates some of the tensions
and ambiguities in Calvin's theology of knowledge, namely that if
humans are in a state of sin, how can they know and be prompted
to be open to God's grace unless God reveals himself generally in
nature? On the other hand, God's grace is not something we can ask
for and we can only know God because he chooses to let himself
be known. Brunner considered that Calvin's principle of correlation
allows general revelation as a **point of contact** with God, whereas
Barth argued that this was completely wrong. So, how can the two
men have taken such different views?

Brunner's argument follows Calvin's notion that God's general
revelation in nature (as experienced through conscience and *sensus
divinitatis*) as a point of contact enables humans to become aware of
God's commands and consequently their sinful state. But, Brunner
argued, this is not sufficient to achieve redemption which is *sola
gratia* (grace alone) as revealed in the person of Christ. Natural
theology offers 'the possibility of a discussion pointing toward such
evidence of the existence of God as we have'.

- *Imago Dei*. The image of God in humans after the Fall has been
  destroyed but only at the *material* (physical and emotional) level.
  At the *formal* (spiritual) level the *imago Dei* still exists otherwise
  humans would not be uniquely persons and different from
  animals. The formal image allows humans to be addressed by
  God. But the material image is completely sinful and corrupt.
- **General revelation.** God communicates through nature as it
  reflects his nature. But owing to sin, humans are blinded and
  incapable of receiving this communication of grace. Redemption
  is possible only in regeneration or renewal of life offered through
  Christ.
- **Conscience.** Conscience and the experience of guilt condemn
  humans and make them open to God's law.
- **True knowledge.** Through grace and renewal of the material image,
  knowledge of God is only available to the Christian who now 'has
  the true natural knowledge of God' (*Nature of Grace*, 27).

Barth's decisive *No!* or *Nein!* to Brunner comes as a shock. Barth's
view is that the only legitimate knowledge of God is when God
chooses to reveal himself to sinful man. It is therefore impossible for
any aspect of nature to prompt humans into a state of knowing God.

- **Formal image is purely formal.** Barth argues that Brunner has
  allowed the human material image to be sufficiently open to God
  that the formal self has leaked through and come to know God

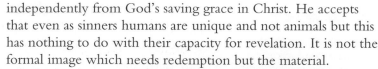

Key quote

'Even as a sinner man is man and not a tortoise.'

KARL BARTH, *NO!*, 79

Key quote

'Knowledge of the truly one and only God gains this meaning when it is brought about by this truly one and only God Himself. God is the one and only One and proves Himself to be such by His being both the Author of His own Being and source of all knowledge of Himself.'

KARL BARTH, *THE KNOWLEDGE OF GOD AND THE SERVICE OF GOD*, 19

Key people

Alvin Plantinga (1932–) is the retired professor of philosophy at the University of Notre Dame, USA. He argues that Christian belief can be subject to the same rigorous philosophical analysis as any other. As a Calvinist he begins with the notion that God can be held as a 'basic belief' along with other basic beliefs. He has written many books on this including *Warranted Christian Belief* (2000).

independently from God's saving grace in Christ. He accepts that even as sinners humans are unique and not animals but this has nothing to do with their capacity for revelation. It is not the formal image which needs redemption but the material.

- **No point of contact.** There is no point of contact, first because being human is all that God requires us to be for salvation and second, because God's grace cannot be in any way dependent or controlled by humans. God does not meet humanity half way; human depravity makes this entirely impossible.
- **Order of creation.** Barth concedes that, whilst natural theology might point to the *order* of creation, the order is not the basis for morality or salvation. God's moral commands as revealed in the Bible are entirely different from any human derived philosophical reason.

Many argue that Barth's emphatic 'no' was due to the rise of Nazism which liberal Christianity had failed to reject. The Nazi appeal to the natural order of society resulting in mass exterminations explains why Barth was so suspicious of reason and natural law. With this in mind, we can hear in a lecture given at the time why Barth argues that 'philosophies' are no more than humans dressing up in their own pomp and splendour and asserting themselves as the ultimate reality and authority:

> With the well-known ambition of a devoted father, man decks the children of his self-assertion with the same authority with which he has previously decked himself. These are the systems by means of which he proposes – at least in phantasy and fancy – to exercise his divine freedom and lordship. They might also be described as costumes, each one more beautiful than the other, which man dons in turn in his role as the one and only reality.
>
> (Karl Barth, *The Knowledge of God and the Service of God*, 18)

Calvin, as we have seen, was also suspicious and critical of philosophy, but the question remains whether Barth was right to have extended Calvin's theology even further. His critics consider that he has made revealed theology entirely irrational.

b) Reformed epistemology

The accusation is that natural theology offers sound reasons to believe in God whereas revealed theology does not. However, the Reformed theologian **Alvin Plantinga** considers that in fact it is the other way round. It is revealed theology which is reasonable and that, to use his particular phrase, Christian beliefs are 'warranted' or justified, whereas natural theology can never offer sufficient reason to believe in God and certainly no knowledge of who God is.

Plantinga's argument is rooted in Calvin's *duplex* argument and this way of thinking is generally referred to as **Reformed epistemology**.

i) Basic knowledge

The dream of scientists and philosophers alike is to begin with a piece of knowledge which is so completely certain that it cannot be doubted. Once this is established then all other claims can be based on this foundational idea. For scientists this foundation might be a basic law of physics; for philosophers such as Descartes it is an irreducible fact that I am a thinking being. However, such foundational epistemological claims are very hard to establish. Scientific knowledge changes; what was thought of as being a hard fact today turns out to be not entirely so tomorrow. Scientists nowadays often prefer to talk in terms of probabilities rather than certainties. In other words, it is unlikely that there can ever be a totally convincing foundation of knowledge, but it is still possible to have broad agreement (what Plantinga calls 'warrant') as to what is reasonable for a belief to be considered 'true'.

Basic knowledge is a belief which is held to be true because it just is so and it makes sense of many other experiences. The onus is on others to show that these basic beliefs would be better explained by other more reasonable (and therefore basic) beliefs about the world. Plantinga's argument is that certain Christian revealed truths are by this score basic.

ii) Sensus divinitatis

Like Calvin, Plantinga argues that there is no separate independent natural theology for the knowledge of God, but there is a general religious sense which makes it reasonable for Christians to make basic religious claims. These claims are not the product of reason (through philosophical arguments or the evidence of science) – Plantinga fiercely rejects natural theology – but the *sensus divinitatis*, the God-given faculty which enables humans to know God. Furthermore, Plantinga argues (along similar lines to Calvin), if there was no God then there would be no claims to know him; but as many people claim to believe in God then knowledge of God can be counted as basic knowledge.

However, basic knowledge is only available to the Christian because only Christ can remove sin which distorts or corrupts the *sensus divinitatis* and only the Holy Spirit can continue to help the believer to respond to the defect, in the same way as a pair of spectacles is necessary for defective eyes.

iii) Responding to the objector

A typical Christian might claim to know that God exists, that God speaks to him and that God forgives him. But according to the **atheological** objector there are many good reasons to suggest

Key word

Reformed epistemology describes the view held by some modern theologians and philosophers in the Calvinist tradition (eg. Alvin Plantinga, Nicholas Wolterstorff and Michael Rea) who believe that belief in God is a 'properly basic belief'. Epistemology is the philosophical study of knowledge and how we know things.

Key question

Is there anything you can know for certain which you can prove to be so?

Cross-reference

See pages 44–45 on the universal consent argument.

Key word

Atheological is Plantinga's term referring to those who reject theological claims as false.

that these theological beliefs are no more than wish fulfilment or conditioning of some kind. For example, they may be held to be contradictory (the existence of evil is incompatible with a good God). Religious experience may be explained as a neurosis or hallucination. Finally, religious claims (such as miracles) may merely lack sound evidence. Together these objections justify considering theistic knowledge as irrational. The conclusion of the objector is that the more basic belief is that God does not exist.

In response Plantinga argues that, although there can be no incorrigible proof of one's belief, there can nevertheless be good reasons to maintain it. In response to the defeater's atheological arguments, the theist believer may have to sift a whole range of strong and weak arguments for and against God's existence but it becomes quickly apparent that there is no totally convincing argument amongst the experts which proves or at the very least provides a strong *probability* that God does not exist or that he does not speak to people.

But this doesn't mean that the theist believer has to come up with a more substantial reason to defeat the defeater. As Plantinga says, 'All I need to do is refute this argument; I am not obliged to go further and produce an argument for the denial of its conclusion.'

iv) Criticisms

Key question

To what extent are the criticisms of Plantinga also criticisms of Calvin?

Reformed epistemology has generated a great deal of criticism within and outside revealed theology. The following are just a few of the points being made:

- His knowledge of God argument is not really basic. His claim that others have a sense of God is a form of natural theology which produces evidence to support his argument. This evidence is not basic but secondary.
- He assumes that Christian beliefs (such as the incarnation and the Holy Spirit) are true. A warrant for belief is only possible if they are true but he has given no reason to explain why they are so.
- The experience of the *sensus divinitatis* today better supports religious pluralism (that there are many kinds of religious experience) than Plantinga's position of Christian exclusivism (that only Christian revelation is true).
- His argument supports any firmly held beliefs believers consider to be basic. These basic beliefs could be those of non-Christian religions and atheism. They could be bizarre beliefs such as Father Christmas or the tooth fairy.

c) Natural theology

Key word

Fideism is the requirement that revelation is absolutely required for the human mind to know anything about God's existence or nature with certainty.

Despite the best efforts of Reformed epistemology there are many who consider that it falls into the error of **fideism**. The error of fideism is that by ruling out reason, there is no means of testing true or false beliefs. The Roman Catholic position stated at the First Vatican Council (1869–70) in the 'Dogmatic Constitution of Faith' outlawed fideism preferring instead a midpoint between the rationalism of natural theology and faith position of revealed theology. The great strength of natural theology is that knowledge of God is reasonable and can be held consistently with other non-religious scientific and philosophical views of the world.

i) Traditional design argument

Natural theology has, for centuries, often rooted itself in what has generally been called the **design argument**. Calvin's third argument is the biblically inspired notion that the creation reflects the glory of God which coupled with the *sensus divinitatis* appears to offer a powerful reason for considering that the world or universe is purposeful and designed only because God is its designer and creator. There are two traditional or classic versions of the design argument: the teleological and analogical.

The teleological version, as presented by Thomas Aquinas, argued that, as all things must have a final purpose (or *telos*) in order to exist, then as there is more order than disorder in the universe there must be something which guides all things to their end (*telos*). As Aquinas says, an archer guides an arrow to its target and this cosmic guide is what is meant by God.

The analogical argument is based on the relationship between things that we know are designed and created by a human craftsman and non-human things which display the same characteristics of design. From this relationship it is inferred than non-human things must also have a designer. Because the world appears to have design, the inference is that it must also have a cosmic designer which is what we mean by God. The argument famously put forward by **William Paley** can be summarised as follows:

- I know that all manufactured things (for example a watch) which have order, function, regularity and purpose have been created by a human designer-craftsman and are not the result of chance.
- The world (or universe) has order, function and purpose as can be seen in the intricate way all parts of it work together.
- Therefore, by analogy, the inference is that there must be a cosmic designer-craftsman of the world (or universe); which is what is meant by God.

ii) Hume's criticisms of the design argument

David Hume's criticisms of the design arguments in his *Dialogues Concerning Natural Religion* (1779) are important and extensive. Some of the many arguments he makes are:

Key word

Design argument or the argument for design infers that as the world everywhere shows signs of order and purpose then it must have a designer. That designer is God.

Key people

William Paley (1743–1805) was a Church of England priest, theologian and lecturer. He published his popular and influential *View of Evidences of Christianity* (1794) and *Natural Theology* (1801).

Key quote

'And what shadow of an argument can you produce from your hypothesis, to prove the unity of the deity? A great number of men join in building a house or ship, in rearing a city, in framing a commonwealth: Why may not several deities combine in contriving and framing a world?'

DAVID HUME, *DIALOGUES CONCERNING NATURAL RELIGION*, PART IV

Cross-reference

See the different types of knowledge statements on page 41.

Key question

Is dialectic theism compatible with Calvin's theology?

Key people

John Macquarrie (1919–2007) was Lady Margaret Professor of Divinity at Oxford University. He was particularly influenced by Heidegger and the existentialists and his theology is firmly grounded in the human experience of God. His *Principles of Christian Theology* (1977) influenced many generations of undergraduates.

Key word

Monarchian means the unity of God. It is also used negatively to refer to those who have reduced the place of the Son in the Trinity. by making Jesus an inspired prophet of God, not God himself.

Theism is the belief that God is more than a principle but can be experienced personally.

- **The analogy is false**. A watch is a mechanical and static device, whereas the world or universe is organic. It would be better to compare the universe with an orange. However, if we did that the argument would beg the question: if there is no obvious creator of the orange, then there is no obvious creator of the universe.
- **Epicurean thesis**. As all things require some kind of stability to exist then the universe can sustain some degree of randomness. This being so, then it is likely that an infinite universe over infinite time will develop patterns and order to give the appearance of design.
- **Like effects do not imply like causes**. Even if the universe has an apparent design (effect) the cause does not have to be attributable to a single design cause. The cause could be ourselves (humans like to see order and impose it on disorder); it could be a committee of gods.

Despite the weaknesses of Paley's analogy, design arguments persist because even current scientific thinking about the world from quantum physics to evolutionary biology depends on there being a very finely balanced arrangement of all processes. Some argue that God is the organising, sustaining principle of the universe.

However, even if a design-type argument is possible, has it provided sufficient reason for knowing God? Opponents of natural theology argue that, at the very best, natural theology points to the possibility of knowing that God *exists*, but that is an entirely different proposition from saying I know God who loves and forgives me. For this reason natural theology could only ever lead to the *deist* theoretical idea of God rather than an encounter with the living and active God of *theism*. As we have seen, it was partly for these reasons that Barth so adamantly rejected natural theology.

iii) Dialectical theism

John Macquarrie suggests that all the great religions have a 'blurry' distinction between natural and revealed knowledge. But natural theology offers a rational starting point for religion and gives it a framework from which important questions can be asked and considered in a philosophical manner.

The problem has been that the classical theists of the past (Aquinas and Paley for example) have tended to produce a **monarchian** and transcendent God which has very little to do with the living personal God as presented by religions such as Christianity. Macquarrie suggests that there is a better alternative ancient form of natural theology which he calls 'dialectical **theism**'. By this he means that God doesn't have to be either transcendent and detached from the world (as classical theism concludes) or immanent and part of nature (the view of pantheism), but both. Dialectic theism suggests that rationally transcendence is not possible without immanence and vice versa. For example, God is both being and nothing. As being, God is who he is but at the same time he is not a thing or item and he is more than a being. Likewise God is one and many. As one he is the unity of all things, the underlying being that holds all matter together but as many he expresses himself intelligibly to the world in the many ways in which humans understand him.

As for the question of the knowability of God, dialectic theology argues that God is both knowable and incomprehensible. As Calvin and Barth stressed, God who is wholly other and infinite is unknowable, hidden and incomprehensible yet as an expressive being God *can* also be known indirectly through analogy and symbols of human experience. Furthermore (as Calvin suggested in the opening of the *Institutes*), we already have an idea of this paradox when trying to know ourselves. As creatures who uniquely possess the image of God we are a kind of microcosm of creation itself: what we intuit about ourselves is also, at a deeper mystical level, an intuition or knowledge of God.

Macquarrie concludes, therefore, that there is and should be, a healthy dialectic between natural and revealed theology. Dialectic theism establishes the rational basis which Christian revelation literally fleshes out and brings to life. For example, dialectical theism argues for the paradoxical necessity of God being part of and yet set apart from the world. Christianity expresses this in historical terms as the incarnation of God in the person of Jesus.

Key quote

'It comes back to the question, what must God be, if he is to be both the focus of human worship and aspiration, and at the same time to be seen as a source, sustainer and goal of all that is? There is nothing in dialectical theism that would prevent the framing of a conception of God that would meet these conditions.'

JOHN MACQUARRIE,
IN SEARCH OF DEITY, 55

Summary diagram

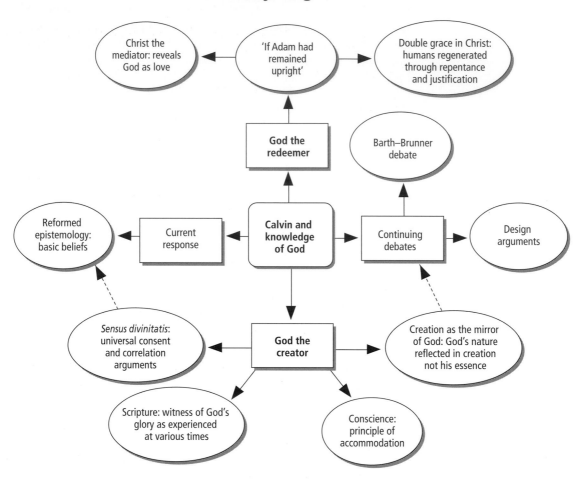

Study guide

By the end of this chapter you should be able to discuss what is true knowledge and whether this can only really be applied to God. You should be able to discuss critically Calvin's *sensus divinitatis* and in particular his ideas of correlation, accommodation and Christ the Mediator. You should have some knowledge of current scholars to develop your own views of natural and revealed theology.

Essay questions

1a Explain Calvin's teaching on God the Redeemer.

The essay might begin by explaining that Calvin argues that knowledge of God the Creator is not sufficient for salvation. True knowledge of God is the state of redemption in which a person becomes regenerate (a new being) and in our sinful state (due to Adam) this is not possible. This is why knowledge of God the Redeemer is at the same time knowledge of Christ as mediator. He is mediator of the image of God uncorrupted and as the 'mirror' correlates God's qualities of love and justice for us as finite minds to understand.

1b 'God can be known because the world is so well designed.' Discuss.

The argument might begin by referring to Paley's design argument which supports the idea that, as the world is beautiful and so well organised, it does provide a 'point of contact' between us as rational finite beings and God. Furthermore, we have a conscience and sensitive self which also suggests that the creation is so ordered that we can know God.

The essay might consider the position adopted by Barth that there is no point of contact because only the formal image of God can know God, since even if the world is ordered, our corrupted finite minds cannot apprehend God sufficiently for salvation. For example, Hume argued that based on logic, there is no reason why a designed universe should necessarily point to the existence of one God.

Further essay questions

2 a   Explain Calvin's teaching on God the Creator.
2 b   'Only Christians can claim to know God.' Discuss.

3 'Everyone has a sense of God, whether they know it or not.' Discuss.

4 To what extent is natural theology bound to fail?

Revision checklist

Can you give brief definitions of:

- the *sensus divinitatis*
- correlation
- accommodation
- Christ the Mediator
- fideism
- the world as God's mirror (or theatre).

Can you explain:

- what Plantinga means by basic knowledge
- why Barth so strongly rejected all forms of natural theology
- Calvin's teaching on sin and knowing God
- Brunner's 'point of contact'
- Macquarrie's dialectical theism.

Can you give arguments for and against:

- the claim that revealed knowledge of God is irrational
- the view that Calvin supports natural theology
- the view that the design argument does not provide knowledge of God.

4

THE PERSON OF CHRIST

Chapter checklist

This chapter considers the relationship between the historical Jesus and worship of him as the Son of God. It considers the scholarly debate over the past two hundred years about what kind of person Jesus was in historical terms and whether the Christ of faith preached by the early Christians is all that matters. The chapter focuses on James Cone's controversial presentation of Jesus as the black messiah and concludes by looking at responses to this and the problems of Jesus' uniqueness and relationship to culture.

1 Creeds and foundations

a) Jesus of the creeds

I believe in Jesus Christ, God's only Son, our Lord, who was conceived by the Holy Spirit, born of the Virgin Mary, suffered under Pontius Pilate, was crucified, died, and was buried; he descended to the dead. On the third day he rose again; he ascended into heaven, he is seated at the right hand of the Father, and he will come again to judge the living and the dead.

(Apostles' Creed)

Key words

Creed means belief and is a concise, formal and authorised summary of Christian belief and teaching. There are various creeds notably the Apostles' Creed (c. 390) and Nicene Creed (c. 374).

Kingdom of God is the Age to Come and in Jesus' teaching referred to a future transformation of this world.

Incarnation refers to God as Word (the second person of the Trinity) becoming fully human in the person of Jesus Christ.

Atonement means literally at-one-ment and in Christian terms is the process by which God reconciles the world to himself by removing the barrier of sin.

Parousia in Greek means 'arrival' and usually refers to the return of Christ at the coming of the Kingdom and final judgement. This is sometimes referred to as the Second Coming.

Key people

Friedrich Schleiermacher (1768–1834) see pages 80–81.

Key quote

'Christianity appeals to history; to history it must go.'

N.T. WRIGHT, *JESUS AND THE VICTORY OF GOD*, 11

Key quote

'But if there is no resurrection of the dead, then Christ has not been raised; if Christ has not been raised, then our preaching is in vain and your faith is vain.'

ST PAUL, *THE FIRST LETTER TO THE CORINTHIANS*, 15:13–14

Without the person of Jesus Christ, Christianity would be unable to make some of its most central claims. The various **creeds** developed over the centuries claim that:

- Jesus was a historical character and lived a fully human life and taught about the coming of the **Kingdom of God**
- he was God **incarnate**
- his crucifixion and resurrection were an **atonement** and established a new relationship with God and humanity
- at the **Parousia**, or Second Coming, he will judge the world.

All these statements are problematic philosophically, theologically and historically.

b) Testing the foundations

One way of testing the creeds is to investigate the historical foundations of Christianity. As Christianity grounds itself in an actual event two thousand years ago in a small country under Roman control, then it ought to be possible to test the evidence and consider what kind of person Jesus was.

In the nineteenth century, the theologian and philosopher **Friedrich Schleiermacher** suggested that the starting point ought to pose the same kinds of questions scholars had regularly asked about the figure of Socrates in Plato's dialogues. In his dialogues Socrates is presented as Plato's master, and his words reported as the ones he actually spoke. But how do we distinguish between Socrates the man as reported by the historian Xenophon, and Socrates the philosopher as Plato presented him? Schleiermarcher asks:

> *What can Socrates have been, in addition to all Xenophon says he was, without contradicting the characteristic qualities and rules of life that Xenophon definitely declares to have been Socratic — and what must he have been, to give Plato the impulse and justification to portray him as he does in his dialogues?*

(Friedrich Schleiermacher, *Lectures on the Life of Jesus*)

Perhaps there is no difference between Xenophon's Socrates and Plato's Socrates. But Schleiermacher's point is that even if Plato is elaborating and developing Socrates' words, they are still grounded in the historical figure. But would it matter if, in fact, Plato had made up Socrates' words and ideas to suit his own idea of Socrates according to his own situation? Some argue that for a living tradition to work, the *idea* is what matters more than the original moment. But the objection to this view is that unless the idea is firmly grounded in actual historical events then people will elaborate it so much that over time it becomes distorted and unacceptable.

Key people

Gottold Lessing (1729–81) was a playwright, art critic and philosopher who developed a rational approach to Christianity. In his play *Nathan the Wise* (1779) he depicts religion as he considers it ought to be, that is rational, moral and tolerant but lacking anything supernatural.

Key word

Lessing's Ditch is the principle of the 'proof of power' that unless a Christian claim can be rationally justified then it should be discarded. In Lessing's words, 'That, then, is the ugly great ditch which I cannot cross, however often and however earnestly I have tried to make that leap.'

Cross-reference

Read pages 47–48 on Calvin's view of Christ.

Key question

How necessary is it to know about the historical Jesus?

The latter point was made by **Gotthold Lessing**. Lessing argued that if the life and teaching of Jesus is to be the foundation for a person's life, then there has to be a clear distinction between what is clearly elaborated or made up and what Jesus may reasonably have said and done. The key idea for Lessing is 'reasonableness'. In what is referred to as '**Lessing's Ditch**', Lessing argued that when a moment in Jesus' life, as recorded in the Gospels, reaches a point which is contrary to reason (such as, miracles, demons and angels), the 'ugly great ditch' of irrationalism should not be crossed.

Lessing poses a problem which we have already considered in the previous two chapters, namely the relationship between faith and reason or revealed and natural theology. So, in making judgements about the person of Jesus, a great deal depends on what scholars think are the appropriate tools to do the job. Lessing suggested the key tool should be reason according to what is scientifically and historically plausible. This is why Christianity is untenable because of its belief in the historical event of Jesus' resurrection and without the resurrection, as St Paul argued, Christian belief is empty. Once all these things are removed what is left is Jesus the teacher of tolerance.

On the other hand, the Reformers and notably Calvin considered that a purely historical or rational understanding of Jesus would never reveal Jesus the Son of God. With faith, Calvin argues, we see Jesus as the pure mirror or reflection of the divine which is necessary in order to know God.

> *Christ, then, is the mirror wherein we must, and without self-deception may, contemplate our own election.*
>
> (John Calvin, *Institutes*, III.XIV.5)

But the problem with the view of Calvin and others, as Tom Wright eloquently argues, is that history is treated as an icon; as an icon it is like a picture which tells a story but which need not be tested against reason. As Wright points out, this can lead to an anti-historical and sentimental presentation of Jesus such as we see in Victorian pictures of Jesus where he is depicted as the blue-eyed, fair-haired friend to adoring followers.

2 The Jesus of history and Christ of faith

Key people

Albert Schweitzer (1875–1965), a German theologian, physician and musician, was a lecturer in theology at Strasbourg University where he published controversial ideas about Jesus. He also worked as a doctor and missionary in Africa.

In 1906 **Albert Schweitzer** published his influential book *The Quest of the Historical Jesus*. Schweitzer's great survey concluded that the quest to discover the historical Jesus resulted in two views.

- The first view was represented by scholars such as J.S. Reimarus (1694–1768), whose research revealed that Christians had invented Jesus as God's son when in fact he was a Jewish reformer who then

Key word

Messianic secret describes the number of occasions in Mark's Gospel where Jesus says he is not the messiah. These were added after Jesus' death by the Gospel writer to explain why Jesus was not considered to be the messiah in his lifetime.

Key thought

The Quest refers to the various scholarly attempts to discover the historical Jesus.

Key people

Tom Wright studied and taught at Oxford University, was consecrated Bishop of Durham and in 2010 was appointed professor of New Testament and early Christianity at St Andrew's University, Scotland. He is considered to represent an academic conservative theology and has written many popular as well as academic theological books. These include his trilogy *The New Testament and the People of God* (1992), *Jesus and the Victory of God* (1996) and *The Resurrection of the Son of God* (2003).

Key people

Rudolf Bultmann (1884–1976) was a Lutheran and a highly influential professor of New Testament at Marburg University. His project was to rediscover the earliest roots of Christianity before it became absorbed and adapted by Jewish and Greek culture. His many influential books include *The History of the Synoptic Tradition* (1931), *The Gospel of John* (1941) and *Primitive Christianity* (1949).

Key word

Kerygma in Greek means 'preaching' and is used by scholars to refer to the earliest message of Christianity.

became a political fanatic, failed and was executed. His disciples made up the resurrection and hoped God would bring about the end of the world.

- The second was represented by scholars such as William Wrede (1859–1906) who claimed that the gospels are almost entirely the invention of the gospel writers. Wrede said that the author of Mark's Gospel made up a **messianic secret** where Jesus frequently tells people *not* to say he is the messiah to give a pseudo-historical reason why he was never considered to be a messiah in his lifetime. This is also Schweitzer's view. Schweitzer concluded that Jesus had thought of himself as a Jewish prophet announcing the apocalyptic end of the world – which of course never happened – but his earliest followers developed his idea and gave it new meaning as circumstances changed.

The Quest began with Reimarus and ended with Schweitzer in 1906, but in 1953 Ernest Käsemann (1906–98) revived interest in the Quest and triggered a movement called the 'New Quest'. The New Quest argued for the possibility of history for knowing the person of Jesus based on the 'criterion of dissimilarity', i.e. a saying of Jesus which cannot be found in Judaism and later church traditions is probably authentic. More recently **Tom Wright** has developed what he calls the 'Third Quest'. Its 'criterion of similarity' argues that when placed in their Jewish setting, the Gospels tell us a great deal about the person of Jesus which is not inconsistent with the Jesus whom Christians worship.

i) The Christ of faith: Rudolf Bultmann

In many ways Bultmann follows in the steps of the Reformers – the Jesus of history is less important than the Christ of faith. Bultmann remains highly sceptical that we can know for certain anything about the Jesus of history because all we can know with a degree of certainty is the **kerygma** or preaching of Jesus' followers after his death. Bultmann developed a system where by analysing the gospel one could see how the kerygma had developed. Therefore, by stripping away these developments it is possible to get back to the very earliest stages to within earshot of the historical Jesus but not actually Jesus himself.

In the quest for the historical Jesus (or the earliest kerygma), Bultmann also developed what he called **demythologising**. He argued that in the times before science could offer a rational explanation of the world, humans used metaphors to express their deepest spiritual, philosophical and psychological experiences. These might be expressed in terms of angels, demons, miracles and apocalyptic images but were frequently treated as objective facts. Jesus would also have thought and expressed himself using these myths. However, their true meaning can be recovered once the myth is removed and the original

Key word

Demythologising is the process by which ancient myths or metaphors used to express deep religious and philosophical experiences of the world are stripped of their imagery (which has falsely been treated in objective factual terms) to recover their original existential experience.

Key quote

'I do indeed think we can know almost nothing concerning the life and personality of Jesus …'
RUDOLF BULTMANN,
JESUS AND THE WORD, 8

Cross-reference

See Bultmann, *Primitive Christianity*, page 110.

Key quotes

'Jesus proclaimed the message. The Church proclaims *him*.'
RUDOLF BULTMANN,
PRIMITIVE CHRISTIANITY, 110

The Gospels 'do not tell of a much admired human personality, but of Jesus Christ, the Son of God, the Lord of the Church, and do so because they have grown out of Christian worship and remain tied to it.'
RUDOLF BULTMANN, *THE HISTORY OF THE SYNOPTIC TRADITION*, 373

Key people

E.P. Sanders (1937–) was professor of New Testament at Oxford University and then Duke University. His influential books investigate the relationship of Paul and Jesus to Judaism. His books include *Jesus and Judaism* (1985) and *The Historical Figure of Jesus* (1993).

experience recovered and re-understood by us today. Demythologising and sorting out the development of the kerygma reveal the following:

- **Jesus the teacher**. Largely from Jesus' parables and key sayings, the historical Jesus was a teacher teaching people who despaired of this world to turn away from 'darkness' or sin and trust in the truth of God and his kingdom. The novelty of his preaching was 'his sense of the utter nothingness of man before God'. Jesus taught that God's judgement was not just an end-time event but something we encounter all the time in our everyday experience when we are alienated from God's love.
- **Christ the divine messiah**. After his death the early Jewish Christian church proclaimed Jesus as the divine 'Messiah' who would come again and bring judgement and salvation from heaven. The shift, as Bultmann puts it, was that 'Jesus proclaimed the message. The Church proclaims *him*'.
- **The heavenly revealer**. In the next stage outside Palestine, Christianity in the Greek thinking world had to adapt its message. Jesus was presented in many different ways, sometimes using very abstract terms such as the '*Logos*' or Word and sometimes as a Greek heavenly 'Man'; a supernatural hero who will subdue the powers of darkness and establish truth and light. John's Gospel, of all the gospels, best represents Jesus in this Greek or Hellenistic sense as the 'light of the world' (John 8:12) 'the way, and the truth, and the life' (John 14:5). In some strands Jesus is thought to have pre-existed his earthly life as the eternal Word of God (John 1:1) and the eternal reflection of God (Hebrews 1:3).

To conclude, for Bultmann and those who share his approach is that the early Church was inspired by the powerful ongoing experience of the risen Christ. It is their reflections on this which are the basis and cornerstone of Christian faith rather than the historical Jesus, of whom very little can be known.

ii) The Jesus of history: E.P. Sanders

Another group of scholars suggests that the Jesus of history and the Christ of faith are two entirely separate ideas because the world of reason and empirical study is entirely different from the claims of faith. Whatever we can know of the historical Jesus reveals a man who must have operated within the constraints of history and the laws of science. To claim anything else is to move outside the rational realm. **E.P. Sanders** for example, as an influential New Testament scholar, claims that as a historian he must not move into the world of theology in his quest to establish the historical Jesus because to do so is to fall into a **category mistake** and confuse history with faith claims. However, unlike Bultmann, Sanders thinks that we can have a pretty good historical picture of who Jesus was

Key word

Category mistake occurs when factual statements are confused with value judgements, or historical knowledge is confused with faith knowledge.

Key quote

'Jesus saw himself as God's last messenger before the establishment of the kingdom. He looked for a new order, created by a mighty act of God.'

E.P. SANDERS, *JESUS AND JUDAISM*, 319

when placed in his Jewish setting; but historical analysis does not conclude that Jesus was unique. Even if he taught an inspirational message we simply don't have enough information about other prophetic figures of the time to make that kind of evaluative comparison. Sanders argues that:

- Jesus saw himself 'as God's last messenger before the establishment of the kingdom'.
- He considered that the Temple would be renewed and the twelve tribes of Israel would be reassembled.
- Like other charismatic leaders of his day, his vision of society was that there would be a major reversal in society where the poor, meek and lowly would have leading places.
- He was a popular figure among the ordinary people who were attracted to him because of his healings – some even thought he would be like other great figures from Israel's past as a 'son of God'.
- His miracles, teaching on non-violence, hope for outcastes, eschatological hope or teaching of God's grace make him substantially different from others at the time, but these are not sufficient to make him unique.

History, in fact, has difficulty with the category 'unique'. Adequate comparative information is never available to permit such judgments as 'uniquely good', 'uniquely compassionate' and the like. It is, rather, a fault of New Testament scholarship that so many do not see that the use of such words as 'unique' and 'unprecedented' shows that they have shifted their perspective from that of critical history and exegesis to that of faith. We can accept with argument Jesus' greatness as a man, but we must stop well short of explaining his impact by appeal to absolutely unique personal qualities.

(E.P. Sanders, *Jesus and Judaism*, 320)

3 James Cone on the black messiah

Key quote

'The heart of the problem was the relation of the black religious experience to my knowledge of classical theology.'

JAMES CONE, *GOD OF THE OPPRESSED*, 5

PROFILE

James Cone was born in 1938 in Fordyce, Arkansas, and grew up in the segregated town of Breadon. Both his parents were social activists and members of the African Methodist Episcopal Church. His strong political views and gift for fiery preaching and lecturing were inspired by his father's courage in his campaign to desegregate the local school (even when threatened with lynching) and his mother's gift for public speaking, especially in church. He studied at Philander Smith College and gained his doctorate from Northwestern University in 1965. Most of his academic life has been spent at the Union Theological Seminary in New York City

Key quote

'Being black in America has little to do with skin color. To be black means that your heart, your soul, your mind, and your body are where the dispossessed are.'

JAMES CONE, *BLACK THEOLOGY AND BLACK POWER*, 151

where, in 1977, he was appointed to the Charles A Briggs chair of systematic theology.

Four years after completing his doctorate he published his first book, *Black Theology and Black Power* (1969), which helped launch black theology. His central thesis is that Black Power is 'Christ's central message to twentieth-century America' and that means a 'complete emancipation of Black people from white oppression by whatever means Black people deem necessary'. In his next book *A Black Theology of Liberation* (1970) Cone developed the use of 'white' to denote the failure of the USA politically, theologically and philosophically. His attendance at the Ecumenical Association of Third World Theologians (EATWOT) in 1976, which brought together theologians from Africa, Asia and Latin America, enabled him to expand his American version of black theology to include other racially oppressed groups worldwide.

His theology is self-consciously contextual. This means that it draws on a variety of different experiences and influences as well as explicitly Christian sources (such as the Bible). Black American experience from slavery, church, blues, spirituals, and stories are treated as important revelatory sources of God's continued involvement in human history. White theology, Cone argues, has become too remote and too abstract. Even so, Cone is still indebted to the theology of Paul Tillich, who argued that theology always emerges and reflects the culture of its day, and Karl Barth who provided him with the idea that God's revelation always counters human rationality. By calling Jesus the 'black messiah' Cone wanted to present him as a historical figure whose struggles against oppression were political as well as religious.

The other influences on him were Malcolm X, the black Muslim activist, and Martin Luther King. In his book *Martin & Malcolm & America: A Dream or a Nightmare* (1991) Cone argues that Malcolm X's strongly separatist message for America was the appropriate means for achieving King's vision of the 'beloved community', but that King's call to reconciliation would never change the racist mindset of America. The civil rights movement is not enough; Cone has constantly argued that black people should find their own identity and not just imitate white life style and the white churches.

a) The Christ of faith is the Jesus of history

Jesus Christ is the subject of Black Theology because he is the content of the hopes and dreams of black people.

(James Cone, *God of the Oppressed*, 30)

The Jesus of history and the Christ of faith distinction is, Cone says, a serious error. The historical Quest has its place because it clearly demonstrates that the early Christians did not invent the idea of

'Christ', as Bultmann suggests, but were inspired to continue the revolutionary view of society and personal communion with God which Jesus taught and embodied in his life and resurrection. In other words, the Christ of faith is not something added to the Jesus of history but the very same thing and completely necessary for the continuing place of Jesus in black people's lives.

Again, Cone is critical of the Bultmann-type view because it turns Christ into a subjective idea or a philosophical concept. This is not what Christianity believes. Christianity is a historical religion because it claims that God is actually involved in human history and no more so than in the person of Jesus Christ. Black theology reasserts that in the person of Jesus, God is revealed as the one who sides with the oppressed against injustice.

It is because Christianity is historical that all theology is contextual. Every generation responds in its own way to the person of Jesus, and every culture develops a theology which speaks from the condition in which humans find themselves. It is inevitable that Jesus will be presented in very different ways in the different cultures in which he is experienced.

What Cone objects to in 'white theology' is its tendency to speak as if there is only *one*, universal and objective Jesus which only the enlightened (white) theologian knows about, independent of experience. Cone's suspicion is aimed at those white theologians who have tried to fit Jesus into a particular idea or category such as Lessing's 'wise man' or Schweitzer's failed apocalyptic prophet. Jesus does not fit into any category because his life and teaching challenged culture; it was not systematic or philosophical but subversive.

b) The black messiah

The starting point, therefore, for black theology is historical. The experience of black people is suffering and oppression which enables them to identify with Jesus' suffering and his hope of justice. This is why Jesus can also be called the 'black messiah'; in the New Testament the writers give Jesus many titles which express who he is and what his purpose is. These include 'the Good Shepherd', 'Son of David', 'the Messiah' and so on, adding the new title 'Black Messiah' is merely continuing an ancient tradition. Blackness, though, is an ambiguous term. Sometimes Cone uses it metaphorically to refer to Jesus' suffering in solidarity with the oppressed, at other times it does quite literally mean that Jesus was not white.

The black community is empowered because of the black Christ and through him it has become a 'black community in defiance'. Jesus offers salvation because of his complete identification with the poor, the oppressed and the marginalised. Through an encounter with the black Christ, black Americans are freed to do what they have to in order to affirm their humanity.

i) Jesus' Jewishness

Cone asserts 'He *is* black because he *was* a Jew.' What does he mean by this? Cone means that white theologians tend to overlook that Jesus came from a particular ethnic background, a particular religious tradition and a particular culture. All these factors reveal a God who liberates an oppressed people. In the Old Testament the **Exodus** is the model through which God acts in history to free an enslaved people and it is only by understanding Jewish history that we can make sense of the central theological idea in which God makes a covenant with his people. Jesus represents a new exodus and fulfilment of the covenant hope.

ii) Cross and resurrection

The cross is not just a symbol. For black people it has particular resonance as the 'lynching tree' when slave masters hanged their slaves for so-called misbehaviour. Jesus also died on the cross because of a gross miscarriage of justice; he also was treated as a slave to be disposed of. Cone fears that the cross has lost its power; white theology has underplayed quite how shocking an event it was. Yet the story does not finish there – if it did, Jesus' role as liberator would have been a failure and have no continuing meaning for the oppressed ever since. One only needs to visit a black church to realise that Jesus is not treated as an idea but as a very real, living and tangible presence. This means that black theology *must* be political. Cone says,

> It is in the light of the cross and the resurrection of Jesus in relation to his Jewishness that Black Theology asserts that 'Jesus is black'. If we assume that the Risen Lord is truly present with us as defined by his past history and witnessed by Scripture and tradition, what then does his presence mean in the social context of white racism?

(James Cone, *God of the Oppressed*, 124)

iii) Blackness as participation

In stressing Christ as God's son, Christians in the past and present have fallen into what is known as **docetism**, the belief that Jesus may have *appeared* human but was not fully so. It is perhaps one of the dangers of considering Jesus only from the Christ of faith perspective. Cone firmly rejects all forms of docetism because docetism undermines the historical reality of Jesus who fully participates in the human condition. That is why Cone says,

> Christ's blackness is both literal and symbolic. His blackness is literal in the sense that he truly becomes One with the oppressed blacks, taking their suffering as his suffering and revealing that he is found in the history of our struggle, the story of our pain.

(James Cone, *God of the Oppressed*, 125)

Key word

Exodus is the liberation of the Hebrew slaves from Egypt led by Moses.

Key quote

'If Jesus' presence is real and not docetic, is it not true that Christ *must* be black in order to remain faithful to the divine promise to bear the suffering of the poor?'

JAMES CONE, *GOD OF THE OPPRESSED*, 125

Key word

Doceticism is the view that Jesus as a divine being only appeared to be human. Docetism is rejected by mainstream Christianity because it suggests that if Jesus was not fully human, then his death for the sins of the world is false.

It is through his actual suffering and death that God is able to reconcile his people to him. Atonement is the process of healing, giving the oppressed a sense of dignity and value as people created in the image of God and why, Cone says, Christ has to be truly black.

iv) Gospel for the oppressed

Key quote

'Indeed, if Christ is not *truly* black, then the historical Jesus lied.'

JAMES CONE, *GOD OF THE OPPRESSED*, 126

To his white critics who accuse Cone of making the gospel message too focused on one people at the expense of Jesus' universal gospel message of salvation, Cone replies, 'I contend that there is no universalism that is not particular'. As we have already noted, the gospel has always been particular because it has dealt with concrete historical events from the exodus to Jesus' life and death. Blackness is therefore a symbol which reminds Christians that the gospel is about God who always sides with the oppressed. Jesus' very first sermon begins, 'he has appointed me to preach good news to the poor. He has sent me to proclaim release to the captives' (Luke 4:18), and so Cone concludes:

> The 'blackness of Christ', therefore, is not simply a statement about skin color, but rather, the transcendent affirmation that God has not ever, no not ever, left the oppressed alone in struggle. He was with them in Pharaoh's Egypt, is with them in America, Africa and Latin America, and will come in the end of time to consummate fully their human freedom.

(James Cone, *God of the Oppressed*, 126)

4 Contemporary discussion

a) Uniqueness, exclusivism and culture

Key word

Jesus Seminar was founded by Robert Funk and John Crossan in 1985. Scholars debate and then vote on which sayings of Jesus from the Gospels and the *Gospel of Thomas* (not found in the New Testament) they think are authentic and then publish the results.

The aim of Reimarus was to undermine Christianity by showing that from a historical point of view Jesus was no different from many other deluded religious people of his time. In their various ways every Quest scholar has reinforced the view that Jesus was so sufficiently unusual as to be unique, i.e. to be God's son. Although not intended to debunk Christianity, one of the purposes of the **Jesus Seminar** is to challenge the popular Christian American view of Jesus and to demonstrate that not only are many of his teachings not actually his but those which are authentic don't reveal an uniquely different person.

Cross-reference

See pages 62–63 for Sanders' presentation of Jesus the Jew.

We have already noted Sanders' presentation of **Jesus the Jew** and his conclusion that as uniqueness is a value judgement, it is not the role of historians to comment on what is a matter of faith.

i) Uniqueness and the resurrection

In some ways Cone shares Sanders' view that being Jewish means that Jesus in not unique. The advantage of calling Jesus the 'black messiah', for Cone, is that it removes the usual problem which other religions have with Christianity when they claim that God exclusively revealed himself in Jesus and allows genuine dialogue with the religions of the Third World countries. By calling Jesus black, Jesus is not associated with white, imperialist ideology. Blackness is a reminder that Jesus was a particular person, living at a particular time of a particular racial and gender type. Particularity is not the same as exclusiveness; for if God acts in the world then it must necessarily be particular. As Cone argues, the term 'black messiah' is not a permanent title, its metaphorical power is for a particular people. In this way he follows in the footsteps of Bultmann and others, for by demythologising the titles given to Jesus of the New Testament he can then reinterpret them today in the light of black experience.

> But the validity of any christological title in any period of history is not decided by its universality but by this: whether in the particularity of its time it points to God's universal will to liberate particular oppressed people from inhumanity. This is exactly what blackness does in the contemporary social existence of America. If we Americans, blacks and whites, are to understand who Jesus is for us today, we must view his presence as continuous with his past and future coming which is best seen through his present blackness.
>
> (James Cone, *God of the Oppressed*, 125)

However, Cone's significant reference to 'continuity' of the historical Jesus with the present has led many scholars today to re-assess the historical significance of the resurrection. Among liberal theologians and historians, the resurrection has usually been considered to be a metaphor of hope, or an invention of the early Church, but many contemporary Quest theologians argue that the historical Jesus really did think God would raise him up after his death and that it would be quite wrong to ignore this aspect of his teaching. As Markus Bockmuehl says, there is simply too much evidence to 'bracket it out' as belonging to the Christ of faith. In other words, the resurrection is a fundamentally important part of the way Jesus understood his life.

The question is whether the resurrection makes Jesus unique and whether this leads to exclusivism of the kind which Cone was hoping to avoid. As Cone has argued the resurrection is the reason why black churches can reasonably consider Jesus to be a living presence as 'the way, the truth, the life', but it is unclear whether ultimately this excludes most Christians from salvation.

Cross-reference

See *The Cambridge Companion to Jesus*, page 117.

Key quote

'The Son of man must suffer many things, and be rejected by the elders and the chief priests and the scribes, and be killed, and after three days rise again.'

JESUS IN *MARK'S GOSPEL* 8:31

ii) Culture

Despite Cone's insistence that the Jesus of history and Christ of faith are one and the same, his equal insistence that theology is a product of the culture in which it is developed poses a dilemma. If Christianity is a product of its time, then equally it cannot make universal claims – the point **Reimarus** made in his study of the historical Jesus.

On the other hand, when theologians have attempted to make Jesus a timeless, universal figure they have so removed his distinctiveness that he is not the person Christians worship but a person of general interest. The criticism of Cone is equally true of all contextual theologies popular today. Schweitzer warned: 'The historical Jesus will be to our time a stranger and an enigma'.

It is for this reason that modern Reform and Lutheran theologians such as Barth and Bultmann continue to support the Christ of faith, as Christ is not dependent on culture but challenges and transforms it from outside.

b) Liberation

Cone and the liberation theologians argue that the chief characteristic of the historical Jesus was his strong sense that in his teaching, actions, death and even resurrection, God would liberate Israel. Liberation however is not exclusive to the liberation theologians. Tom Wright as a 'third quest' theologian, and many others, consider that the prophet-liberator is strongly supported by our knowledge of first-century Judaism.

i) Christ the liberator

Even though some scholars are cautious about leaping from Jesus the Jewish reformer and liberator to the Christ who liberates humans from sin, for others there is no leap. For them the historical Jesus knew that his life was more than merely political but had deep religious significance.

One such scholar, **Jaroslav Pelikan**, concluded his book *Jesus Through the Centuries* (1985) with reference to Dostoevsky's great novel *The Brothers Karamazov* (1880), where, in one passage, a character imagines that Christ returns to earth to find himself condemned by the Grand Inquisitor, the representative of the established Church. The point Pelikan draws from this passage is that the various historical presentations of Jesus as reconstructed by the quest theologians since the eighteenth century, have almost all undermined the reason why Jesus was crucified, which was to liberate humans from their own oppression. Like Cone, Pelikan considers that the Jesus of history and of faith continues to challenge all institutions, especially institutionalised Christianity.

Cross-reference

See page 60 on Reimarus.

Key quote

'The historical Jesus will be to our time a stranger and an enigma.'
ALBERT SCHWEITZER, *THE QUEST OF THE HISTORICAL JESUS*, 397

Key people

Jaroslav Pelikan (1923–2006) was Sterling Professor of History at Yale University. He is best remembered for his five volumed *The Christian Tradition* (1973–1990) .

Key people

Burton Mack is a member of the Jesus Seminar. His book *A Myth of Innocence: Mark and Christian Origins* (1988) argues that the few sayings of Jesus which can be considered authentic suggest that he was a wandering Jewish Cynic.

Key word

The **Cynics** were an ancient Greek philosophical movement who taught that the good or virtuous life should be lived in accordance with nature and not by social convention.

Cross-reference

See pages 134–135 on liberation theology.

Key question

Does history really support the presentation of Jesus the liberator?

ii) Not a liberator but a Cynic

Burton Mack argues in a similar way to Bultmann that we simply cannot know what Jesus thought and what his intentions were. In his analysis, the Jesus of history which emerges closely resembles the wandering **Cynic**, wise men whose parables and aphorisms were designed to challenge their audiences and make them question their values. Jesus' social experiment was not as God's chosen one to establish his kingdom on earth, but to offer a new wisdom. Mack follows in the footsteps of Wrede and Bultmann when he claims that the Jesus who fights against demons and challenges the priests is an invention of the early Church who needed more than a teacher of radical wisdom to suit their situation.

So the question is, if Jesus was only teaching people to establish a new order of society on earth, then the power of Cone and the other liberation theologians' claim that God was actually siding with the oppressed in the person of Jesus is considerably reduced. In fact, it almost completely undermines **liberation theology**.

c) In whose image?

In a famous passage in his *Quest*, Schweitzer observed that when scholars tried to reconstruct the Jesus of history, what they saw at the bottom of the well of history was not the reflection of Jesus but themselves. Perhaps it remains a truism that we read into history the things which most concern us. For example:

- **Bultmann**. Bultmann was powerfully affected by the existentialism of Kierkegaard and Hiedegger and their view that humans have to create their own sense of being by leaping into the unknown. So, Bultmann's Jesus is an existential teacher whose words not actions are what matter; his Jewishness is almost totally irrelevant. One can see that Jesus' timeless message which touches on every day human experiences of doubt, worries about meaning, the dread of death were especially relevant brought on by world wars in the mid-twentieth century.
- **Jesus Seminar**. This group of largely American second-quest theologians appear to use rigorous methods for establishing the historical Jesus but their agenda is really to challenge the conservative evangelical Jesus with its emphasis on his atoning death. Their Jesus is a teacher who often speaks in cryptic terms to provoke. The Seminar's Jesus reflects the academic life as a teacher who is more interested in ideas than action. Very few of Jesus' actions are considered and the idea that Jesus considered his death to be a sacrifice is largely rejected.
- **Cone**. Cone's Jesus is, in contrast to the Jesus Seminar, a man of action, who sides with the oppressed and whose death is a result of the corrupt society in which he operates. But Cone's emphasis on

Jesus' Jewishness is not because it places him in a religious tradition, but reflects his ethnic origins. Jesus is 'black' because he belongs to an ethnically oppressed group. Cone's black Jesus reflects the black power movement's suspicion of white liberals and especially white liberal Christians who have used Jesus as a general principle of love and reconciliation, not as a revolutionary activist.

It is difficult to know whether it is ever possible to escape the image problem and it is one reason why many, such as Martin Kähler and James Carlton Paget, are critical of most Quest enterprises:

> *Martin Kähler argued the Quest was a futile exercise as the gospels themselves welded together faith and history. He argued that the Quest was 'in the end a subjective exercise, in which scholars created fifth gospels that had more to do with themselves than with the gospel proper'.*

(James Carlton Paget, in *The Cambridge Companion to Jesus*, 145)

Summary diagram

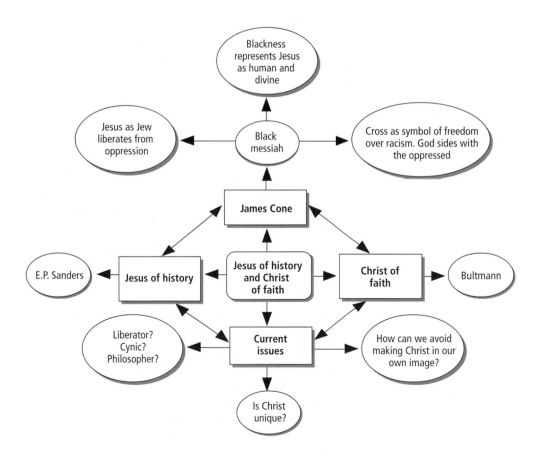

Study guide

By the end of this chapter you should be able to explain the various views scholars hold on the Jesus of history/Christ of faith relationship. You should be able to explain what Cone meant by Jesus as liberator and black messiah and why he rejects the history/faith distinction as being too subjective. You should be able to explain why Cone argues that Jesus' Jewishness is fundamental to Christianity's social, political and spiritual reforms.

Essay questions

1a Explain why some scholars think there is a difference between the Jesus of history and the Christ of faith.

The essay might begin by explaining that, for many scholars, the claims made in the creeds that Jesus died for the sins of the world or to reconcile humans to God are not historical but theological or ideas developed on reflection after Jesus' death by the early Christians. Reference could be made to Bultmann's argument that the Christ of faith emerged through the powerful experience of the resurrection. The essay might go on to explain how many of the Quest theologians concluded that Jesus was just a prophet or Cynic teacher and that as his predictions of the Kingdom did not happen the early Christians developed 'messianic secrets' or even the resurrection itself. The essay might conclude by looking at E.P. Sanders's warning that the move from Jesus the Jew to belief in Christ is a philosophical error.

1b 'If Jesus died a failure then Christianity should also have died out.' Discuss.

Some might agree that in historical terms Jesus might have died a failure because he believed that the Kingdom was soon to arrive but it didn't, or that he expected a reform of society which didn't happen. The essay might reason that Christianity may well have died out had it not been for the imagination of some early Christians, notably Paul and the Gospel writers, who could see in Jesus' life a more important idea or message which they superimposed on the historical facts.

Alternatively, as James Cone argues, Jesus was not a failure in moral and spiritual terms because even during his life time his followers became aware of God's actions challenging the social structures of the time, siding with the poor and marginalised. The resurrection wasn't an invention but a powerful religious experience which formed the basis of the kerygma.

Further essay questions

2 a Explain what James Cone meant by calling Jesus the 'black messiah'.

2 b Assess the view that calling Jesus the black messiah tells us more about Cone than Jesus.

3 'Only by knowing who the historical Jesus was can we test the truth of Christianity.' Discuss.

4 'Christianity stands or falls depending on whether the resurrection is a historical moment.' Discuss.

Revision checklist

Can you give brief definitions of:

- kerygma
- docetism
- incarnation
- quest.

Can you explain:

- Lessing's Ditch
- messianic secret
- demythologising
- the meaning of 'black' in Cone's 'black messiah'.

Can you give arguments for and against:

- the ideas Jesus represents are more important than what he did historically
- there is still a need to know more about the historical Jesus
- the Resurrection is the most important event in Jesus' life.

Chapter checklist ✔

In this chapter the question of what it means to interpret a text is introduced and how this has been developed by scholars in terms of biblical exegesis and eisegesis. The chapter goes on to consider what is meant by biblical authority and then focuses on the hermeneutics of Schleiermacher. The final section surveys contemporary discussion, in particular fundamentalism and liberalism.

1 The Bible and truth

a) Interpretation

Key question

Is the interpretation of a piece of writing the same as having a conversation with someone?

Is there a correct way to interpret the Bible? What is interpretation? Interpretation is a surprisingly complex task and one which we do all the time – not just with texts but with music, art and in everyday conversation with others. But some suggest the interpretation of texts, or the written word, is significantly different from how we interpret words in a conversation because the text becomes detached from the author and the words are no longer entirely the author's property. However, in all these examples, interpretation is primarily an *intermediary* task of communication. This is how Morgan and Barton define in it:

> *Interpretation is an intermediary task performed by rational human beings to make communication possible in difficult cases. In interpreting we first understand the human utterance and then elucidate it for ourselves or someone else.*

> (Robert Morgan with John Barton, *Biblical Interpretation*, 1)

This definition suggests a number of important ideas. Interpretation:

- is carried out by rational human beings. Interpretation is not random or purely subjective.
- is done in difficult cases. That is, for example, when a text could have more than one meaning, where there is ambiguity, where more information is needed.

- requires understanding first, elucidation second. This requires the interpreter to place himself or herself sympathetically in the mindset of the text itself and *then* to explain, clarify or unpack the ideas in his or her own words.

This may seem obvious. But already we have seen there is a difference between how one interprets a conversation and text, because in conversation there is direct communication with the author of the spoken words. The question of authorship and his relationship to the text is a key issue for hermeneutics. **Hermeneutics** is usually defined as the *art* of interpretation because it is more than merely a mechanical process and requires subtle insight and sympathy.

The Bible poses its own particular interpretation problems: it is an ancient set of texts, written in very different circumstances by mostly unknown authors in Hebrew (Old Testament) or Greek (New Testament) in pre-scientific times where values were very different from our own.

But, whatever one might think about the Bible, it has acquired authority. For countless millions of people down the ages the Bible is a source of knowledge and truth. One of the tasks of Biblical hermeneutics is not just to elucidate the meaning of the text but also to consider how the gap between the past and the present can be bridged.

b) The problem of authority

The word 'authority' comes from the word 'author'. When we recognise authority we are saying that those words, those commands, those instructions originate from that person as the *author* and we treat them differently from other general words. For example, often in the Gospels Jesus is recording as having 'spoken with authority', unlike the scribes and Pharisees; the people acknowledge the power and significance of his teaching and now choose to follow his instruction.

Recognition of authority is ambiguous. Its negative meaning is that obedience to authority must be blind and at the expense of reason and autonomy. In its positive use obedience to authority is a sign that a person has acted out of considered trust. Since the beginning of the twentieth century Christian fundamentalists and conservatives have argued that obedience to the authority of the Bible is to live in utter respect of God's commands. The fear amongst fundamentalist and conservative Christians is that once we allow ourselves to make critical interpretation of the Bible, we have made ourselves the source of authority.

But is that really so? Even those who think they are simply carrying out what the Bible commands do so because, in fact, *they* have made an interpretation which *they* have chosen to act upon. As

Key word

Hermeneutics is the art of interpreting a text.

Key question

Why is obedience to authority problematic?

Key quote

'What is this? A new teaching! With authority he commands even the unclean spirits and they obey him.'
MARK'S GOSPEL 1:27

Key people

George Pattison (1950–) is the Lady Margaret Professor of Divinity at Oxford University. He has writen widely on Heidegger, Dostoyevsky and Kierkegaard.

Key quote

'If the apostle or the preacher tells me I must believe in Jesus if I am to be saved, and that he can offer no proof for this other than his own word that it is so, how can this be anything other than an attempt to stop me functioning as a free and responsible agent?'

GEORGE PATTISON, *A SHORT COURSE IN CHRISTIAN DOCTRINE*, 25

Key words

Exegesis means 'reading out of the text'. Meaning is located in the text and is there simply waiting to be read.

Eisegesis means 'reading into the text'. Meaning is not fixed by the text but is a relationship between the reader's own agenda and experiences and the text itself.

George Pattison comments, in order for the words of the author or community to mean anything, a creative autonomous willingness to participate in the communication of the author's words is required. The problem is that too often conservative believers become dazzled by their sense of obedience to authority and give up their ability to think properly for themselves:

> *The very power of the original voice seems to rob those who surround him of their freedom to think and act for themselves.*
>
> (George Pattison, *A Short Course in Christian Doctrine*, 24)

Many argue that the authority of the Bible rests on the fact that it positively encourages autonomous reflective judgements about meaning. As Paul Tillich frequently argued, the Bible allows us to *encounter* God; it offers us many pointers and directions in which God might be reflected upon and considered. In fact, one might go further and say that without autonomy the experience of God lacks depth because the alternative is blind faith, which is not faith at all. As the Christian existentialist Kierkegaard often remarked, authentic faith results from not being seduced by authority. Faith does not occur merely because you tell me the Bible is true but because I choose to embrace its ideas.

Yet despite the very different starting points of the Christian fundamentalist and liberal Christian existentialist, the Bible remains a foundation. Even for non-believers the Bible has value because it has inspired great art, music, drama and literature. As this brief introduction has illustrated, so much depends on how the Bible is to be interpreted and understood.

c) Exegesis and eisegesis

Between them, the two terms exegesis and eisegesis cover the range of possible ways in which the Bible can be read and interpreted. The relationship between the two is often subtle and of particular interest to hermeneutics. In brief, the distinction between the two is:

- **Exegesis** means 'reading out of the text'. Meaning is located in the text and is there simply waiting to be read. Exegesis might involve knowing the meaning of the word in its historical context, providing historical information of customs, events and current ideas.
- **Eisegesis** means 'reading into the text'. Meaning is not fixed by the text but is a relationship between the reader's own agenda and experiences and the text itself. Eisegesis takes into account the gender, racial and political status of the reader and the way the text can be interpreted according to these biases.

i) Exegesis

In modern hermeneutics, exegesis falls into two kinds: synchronic and diachronic. In simple terms synchronic interpretation means that a particular text should be studied in its final form as it appears in the Bible and diachronic interpretation is interested in the history of the text as it developed and achieved its final form. In each area, critics (i.e. scholars) have developed specialised techniques of interpretation.

Key words

Synchronic and **diachronic exegesis.** Synchronic interprets the biblical text in its final form. Diachronic investigates the text as it has developed historically over time.

- **Synchronic exegesis**. Discourse critics look at the way the text has been organised, the use of language, its structure and so on. Narrative critics look at: the way the plot is constructed; the development of characters; the perspective of the author (often in the Bible implied by the text); the relationship of a particular story with what happens before and after; and the role of the narrator. Some exegetes like to take a feminist, political or psychoanalytical approach to the narrative and see what this reveals. Finally, some critics take a deconstructionist view of the text and analyse what has not been said, or what has been left out, or what appears just below the surface of the narrative. This view tries to free the text from the reader.

Cross-reference

For a very clear account of exegesis read David Holgate and Rachel Starr, *Biblical Hermeneutics*, pages 44–85.

- **Diachronic exegesis**. Diachronic approaches look at the many ways a text can develop historically over time. Textual critics analyse the transmission of the manuscripts from their original language (Hebrew and Greek) and work out what has been added, changed or miscopied. Grammatical critics are interested in the meaning of the words in their original languages and historical setting. Form critics look at the genre or type of literature a passage conforms to and its purpose. Some form critics then try and explain how and why the original form or genre has developed into a new form before it reached its final state. Source critics investigate what sources or texts were used to create the present text. For example, Luke and Matthew both seem to have used a now lost source scholars call 'Q'. Redaction critics investigate how the text has been edited into its final form and the bias or theological interests of the editor. Reception critics look to see how the text has impacted on readers down the ages.

Key question

How far can we read into a text?

ii) Eisegesis

Texts are works in process, rather than fixed by their original author. Thus the meaning of the text depends on the reader as well as the writer.

(David Holgate and Rachel Starr, *Biblical Hermeneutics*, 88)

As this statement from Holgate and Starr suggests, eisegesis is the process whereby the reader becomes involved in the text, it is the moment for most people when the text comes alive. Eisegeis begins with the particular experience and interests of the reader and shares much in common with the reception critic's interest as to how the text actually affects its readers in their particular context. Again, there are many ways in which scholars have analysed eisegesis:

- **Reader response criticism**. Critics or scholars consider the text is like a music performance – without an audience it would mean little in itself. Seen in this way the reader of the text actually supplies vital elements such as imagination and creativity which fill in the gaps missing in the text itself.
- **Gender and sexuality criticism**. Feminist critics argue that a gender-free reading of a text is not only impossible but leaves out many issues about the text which have been overlooked by other methods. Feminist theologians have highlighted biblical passages which pose very awkward questions about religion and sexuality.
- **Ethnicity and race criticism**. Critics here such as black theologians bring experience of slavery and discrimination and consider how the Bible is to be read in terms of its ideas of election, attitudes to race, survival and so on.
- **Social context criticism**. Critics here include notably the liberation theologians of Latin America whose experience of poverty, social deprivation and corruption has led to very new ways of engaging with the Bible. Gutiérrez, for example, argues that having a grasp of the social sciences (such as Marx) precedes reading the Bible because then there can be a proper meaningful dialogue with it.

Cross-reference

Read pages 63–64 on James Cone and black theology.

Cross-reference

Read pages 111–116 on liberation theology and Marx.

One of the great strengths of eisegesis is that it closes the gap between the Bible as an ancient text written over two thousand years ago and experience today. To those who say 'the Bible is out of date' the eisegesis critics' reply is that this would be like a young person saying that he cannot talk to an older person because he belongs to a different generation. In fact, we might say it is because he belongs to a different generation that the conversation becomes interesting as differences are explored and discussed and, after a while, what seemed like a gap disappears.

On the other hand, eisegesis, by itself, when applied to biblical texts can be far too subjective as it allows almost any interpretation. In practice, therefore, eisegesis needs exegesis just as much as exegesis needs eisegesis.

d) Propositional and non-propositional revelation

Authority and interpretation of the Bible also depend on an important distinction often made between propositional and non-propositional revelation. Propositional revelation suggests that the Bible makes true statements or it says what it means. Non-propositional revelation suggests that the Bible indirectly makes true statements because its words are human and limited to human experience. Superficially, those who hold a propositional view of the Bible give it far higher authority than those who consider the Bible to be the product of its time. Hence, the Reformers could claim *sola Scriptura* – only scripture as authority. In practice, the distinction is not so easy to make.

i) The apophatic way

The apophatic or 'negative way' suggests that as God is greater than anything, then it follows necessarily that nothing can be said about God from the human perspective. God is, to use a popular phrase, the 'cloud of unknowing'. However, if God were totally unknowable then of course his existence would be irrelevant. God reveals himself to humans but in ways which are in essence mysterious, profound and beyond language. Those who follow the apophatic way enjoy the paradox between what can and cannot be known of God. The Bible is, therefore, a repository of many kinds of response to God and although rational interpretation will help clarify meaning, the deeper mysteries will remain. Interpretation of the Bible means that every person in every age encounters the mystery of God in their own way.

ii) The cataphatic way

The cataphatic or 'positive way' presents God's attributes as things which can be known. Calvin, for example, argued that even though God is, in essence, unknowable, his revelation through his prophets and other inspired writers of the Bible **accommodates** itself to human minds and therefore proposes certain and positive truths which faith acknowledges and responds to. Some go further and argue that propositional truths are not just found in the Bible but also in the traditional Creeds and teachings of the Church and Confessions of the Reformers.

iii) Liberal/conservative theology

The propositional/non-propositional distinction is therefore important for the way in which the Bible should be interpreted. Superficially, at least propositional revelation appears to support the conservative (and fundamentalist) Christian tradition which treats the Bible at face value as the revealed Word of God. Non-propositional revelation favours liberal Christian theologians because of its emphasis on the Bible as a historical record of human religious experience.

But, in fact, the conservative/liberal view of the Bible does not fall neatly into propositional/non-propositional distinction.

Barth, who is considered a conservative theologian, follows the apophatic tradition because as God's revelation is always beyond human comprehension the Bible can only be a *witness* to God's Word, it cannot be in itself God's Word. Yet, it is also the greatest source we have of God's Word as it inspired its human writers.

Key word

Apophatic way is derived from the Greek meaning 'to show no'. Apophatic theology therefore talks in terms of what God is not, i.e. God is unknowable, God is not evil, God does not occupy time and space.

Cross-reference

Read page 45 on Calvin's principle of accommodation.

So, we might conclude that, although the Bible is properly non-propositional, we should nevertheless treat it propositionally.

iv) Problems

Many questions are raised by the propositional/non-propositional distinction. For example:

- How does one judge between the quality of God's revelation from one historical event to another or from one person to another?
- How does one judge 'true' revelations from false ones? If propositions are tested against human reason, does this suggest that revelation is essentially non-propositional because revelation is being re-expressed in human terms?
- How does one test the historical reliability of propositions in the Bible especially if they appear to contradict each other?
- Given the wide range of literary genre and styles in the Bible (history, law, poetry, legend, story, myth, etc.), whose interpretation is to be trusted as accurate?

2 Friedrich Schleiermacher on hermeneutics

Key quote

'Schleiermacher is one of those rare figures in the history of theology whose thought, while greatly influential (as his was over the next two centuries) continues to spark new discoveries in a later age.'

ESTHER REED, *THE DICTIONARY OF HISTORICAL THEOLOGY*, 509

PROFILE

Friedrich Schleiermacher (1768–1834) was born in Breslau, in Silesia (modern-day Wrocław, Poland). His father was a Reformed pastor. He was sent to a Moravian pietist school at Niesky and then trained for the Christian ministry at Barby. During this time he became dissatisfied by pietism with its over-emphasis on Jesus' sacrifice. He therefore went to study philosophy and theology at Halle university and he studied the great romantic writers of his day: Schiller and Goethe. This led him to be very critical of Kant, especially his ethics which he felt gave little place to the experience of the individual and his place in history. In 1796 he moved to Berlin as a full-time pastor but he was also writing extensively on a wide range of topics – ethics, religion, poetry and philosophy. He completed his *Principles for a Critique of all Previous Ethical Theories* in 1803.

In 1804 he was made professor of theology and university preacher at Halle but left in 1807 to lecture in Berlin and was one of those who helped found the university there in 1810. He taught in Berlin until his death in 1834. He was renowned as a stimulating and provocative preacher, as the translator of Plato's works into German and a gifted lecturer in philosophy as well as theology.

However, it was his perceptive, rigorous and imaginative treatment of theology which has earned him the title 'The Father of Modern Theology' particularly in two publications. In his *Brief Outline on Theology as a Field of Study* (1811, 1830) he argued that the purpose of theology is practical; that it is to serve members of the church in their common life. To achieve this theology has to be historical by going back and clarifying the tradition in terms of contemporary ideas. One of its functions therefore is hermeneutics, the precise and systemic process of interpretation of the Bible, the creeds of the Church and Christian ethics. This came to fruition in his most popular and influential book *Christian Faith* (1821–22, 1830–31). Religion, he argued, cannot be subsumed into popular culture as it has its own distinctive core experience, the 'feeling of absolute dependency'. This is true in all religions but Schleiermacher argued that what makes Christianity very special is the historical event of Jesus whose life was one of perfect 'God-consciousness'. It is this which the early authors attempted to capture in their writings and which the Church subsequently expressed in its formal doctrines; it is the role of the theologian to interpret them for each new generation according to the cultural norms of the time. In *The Christian Faith* Jesus is presented as the one person who has had perfect 'God-consciousness' and it is on this which the Church has subsequently based its doctrines.

Schleiermacher is also known as the 'Father of Hermeneutics'. In his lectures (published as *Hermeneutics and Criticism*) he set out the rules which should be used for systematic interpretation of any text and then considered how these might then apply to the New Testament. His ideas have deeply influenced contemporary philosophers such as Hans-Georg Gadamer and Paul Ricoeur.

a) Religious knowledge

To begin with, the fact that all doctrines and precepts developed in the Christian Church have universal authority only through their being traced back to Christ, has no other ground than His perfect ideality in everything connected with the power of the God-consciousness.

(Frederick Schleiermacher, *The Christian Faith*, 93.5, 384)

Religious knowledge is personal and immediate consciousness – a moment of 'piety' or 'exaltation' of God as Infinite. As religious propositions can only be conveyed in language, the role of hermeneutics is to unlock the original experience. As the mind organises these different experiences and expresses them in different styles or genres, then it is vital to get these right otherwise utterances which are supposed to be poetic, for example, might be wrongly understood as history. The Bible reflects a wide range of genres from poetry to history, from legend to prophecy.

But Schleiermacher is conscious that, as the human mind so quickly organises experiences into doctrines or formal teachings (what he calls 'dogmatic propositions'), it may be impossible to ever know the original historical moment in which a feeling of absolute dependency was experienced. But not all is lost: enough of the original experience can be conveyed through language so that Jesus' original communication or preaching is still powerful enough in the Church's teaching to convey his message authentically.

> *The whole work of the Redeemer Himself was conditioned by the communicability of His self-consciousness by means of speech, and similarly Christianity has always and everywhere spread itself solely by preaching. Every proposition which can be an element of the Christian preaching is also a doctrine because it bears witness to the determination of the religious self-consciousness as inward certainty.*
>
> (Frederick Schleiermacher, *The Christian Faith*, 16.2, 77–78)

b) Hermeneutical circle

Schleiermacher described hermeneutics as the 'art of understanding'. It is 'art' because it is not just a philosophical or scientific exercise but one which also requires imagination, intuition and empathy. Although his theory of hermeneutics was developed to apply to any text, its significance for Christians is that reading the Bible properly brings the reader into proper relationship with the text and ultimately the moment of exaltation.

i) The process of interpretation

> *The people [Jews] answered, 'His blood be on us and our children!'*
>
> (Matthew 27:25)

For generations this passage from Matthew's Gospel has been taken to mean that the Jews accepted their guilt in Jesus' crucifixion. This is no trivial matter – the passage has authorised the persecution of the Jews, even their murder. But is this what the passage actually means? To answer this properly, Schleiermacher argued, we would have to place this passage in its historical context, as well as its context in the whole of Matthew's Gospel and in comparison with the other gospels. Only then can we be in a position to judge what was originally intended. Although he never used the phrase, this process has been called the **hermeneutical circle**. It is a process ('circle') which constantly asks: how much prior knowledge do I need to have of a text in order to interpret it? What function does the text have in 'correcting' or modifying that knowledge? When can an interpretation be considered true?

Schleiermacher established two processes of hermeneutics, the grammatical explanation and the psychological explanation.

Key question

Is the careful use of a dictionary all that is necessary to know what a text means?

Key question

Can a passage only be understood if the whole text is read?

Key quote

'The vocabulary and the history of the era of an author relate as the whole from which his writings must be understood as the part, and the whole must, in turn, be understood from the part.'

FRIEDRICH SCHLEIERMACHER, *HERMENEUTICS AND CRITICISM*, 24

Key word

Hermeneutical circle is the process of interpretation which reads a text in its widest possible context.

- **Grammatical explanation** focuses on the words in the text. First, all words must be given precise definitions as intended by the author and his original audience. Second, every word must be analysed in relationship to the others in a sentence, paragraph, chapter and so on.
- **Psychological explanation** focuses on the theme which motivates the author and which runs throughout the text and, indeed, other works the author may have written. Here, we are looking to see what makes *these* words special because the author has now created something new. Interpretation requires that we place ourselves in his or her shoes (the 'divinatory method') and then compare this text to other similar texts in order to see what makes it new ('the comparative method').

In summary, Schleiermacher is aware that all too often our interpretations are ones which we have been brought up to believe rather than what the text itself says. Later writers, notably Ricoeur, call this the **hermeneutic of suspicion**.

ii) Interpretation as conversation

> *One can think of the issue in general as follows. There is a particular appeal in conversation if two people dealing with whatever it is come to a sphere which they have in common and is immediately familiar so they bring in things from it when the occasion arises. A text of this kind takes in a conversation, for the secondary thoughts are only ever taken from an area shared by the writer and the readers, from an area where the writer can presuppose that it can be made just as easily present to his readers as it is to him.*

(Friedrich Schleiermacher, *Hermeneutics and Criticism*, 129)

Schleiermacher likens the hermeneutical circle to a *conversation*. Just as in a conversation with a stranger when one begins with simple questions about where they live and what they do, the conversation then moves on to deeper questions about what they like, what they think about various issues and so on. So it is with the reader and the text. The reader works systematically through these kinds of questions until there is some sense in which the text ceases to be a set of words but offers up its meaning.

iii) Knowing the author

The text therefore has to be treated as one would treat communication between persons. Unlike some modern philosophers, such as Ricoeur, for Schleiermacher it is of importance to know who the author or authors of the text are, just as in the same way that as we get to know a person it helps to know their background (who their parents are, where they went to school, etc.). In fact, he argues that we should know the author better than he knows himself. And just as a relationship would

Cross-reference

See on page 88 on the hermeneutic of suspicion.

be bound to fail if one was to use a biology book to know how to behave, so the use of a dictionary to look up words can only have general use, but could cause great misunderstanding if used for specific passages.

c) Biblical interpretation

Having established the process of reading *any* text, Schleiermacher's next task is to apply the process to the Bible and in particular the New Testament. Although in theory biblical hermeneutics should be no different from any other forms of hermeneutics, it becomes quickly apparent there are a number of specific issues which modify the process. Here are a few:

- The New Testament is written in Greek, so we must assume the writers thought in Greek terms even if they were translating their ideas from Hebrew.
- In order to perform the hermeneutic circle, therefore, the Greek version of the Old Testament (the Septuagint) has to be used even though it may not supply an exact meaning of the word.
- We don't always know who the authors were of the New Testament – especially the Gospels and even some letters which are attributed to Paul. The Gospels are more than merely biographies but this is not enough for us to get a sense of what the theme or purpose of the author was. It is therefore the role of the reader to supply what is missing and add the 'secondary thoughts' which may be implied by the text but not stated explicitly.

Key quote

'In the assertion that we must become conscious of the language area as opposed to the other organic parts of the utterance also lies in the fact that we understand the author better than he does himself.'

FRIEDRICH SCHLEIERMACHER,
HERMENEUTICS AND CRITICISM, 33

3 Contemporary discussion

Biblical interpretation today has developed in three often overlapping ways, which might be termed: fundamentalism, conservatism and liberalism. In practice, none of these terms is particularly accurate and can be misleading.

a) Fundamentalist biblical theology

The term fundamentalism was coined in the USA in the early twentieth century at a time when many felt that the traditional fundamentals of Christian belief (such as Last Judgement, heaven and hell, the divinity of Christ and his Second Coming) were being treated by liberal theologians more as metaphors than actual events. Since then, fundamentalism has come to refer to any group of Christians who believe that personal salvation can only be secured through a literal belief in the Bible. What is meant by literalism is that the Bible reveals the *true* Word of God; its author is God who inspires humans to write.

Key question

If the Bible is God's word, should it be read literally?

Key words

Creationism is the belief that the Bible and not evolutionary science offers the correct view of how the world was created.

Biblical inerrancy means that the Bible is without error or fault.

Key quote

'Scripture is without error or fault.'
THE CHICAGO STATEMENT (1978)

In more recent times fundamentalism has been particularly associated with **creationism**, a movement mostly found in the USA which believes that as the Bible is **inerrant**, scientific evolutionary theories about the origins of the universe are often wrong and misleading.

- **Creationism**. A reading of Genesis 1–3 indicates the purposefulness of a creation designed by God. Evolutionary theory is wrong because the idea of chance fails to explain why nature functions so well; fossil evidence does indicate that animals and plants breed true to their kind (Genesis 1:11). As the great flood (Genesis 6–9) subsided, it layered the earth – it would be quite wrong to think these represent different evolutionary periods or epochs of geological time.
- **Historicity**. Humans are not related to chimps, even though modern genetics indicates they are both similar. According to the Bible humans were created specially (Genesis 2:7–23, Romans 1:20). The human race has originated from the *historical* characters of Adam and Eve, racial difference is due to God's punishment at Babel (Genesis 11:8–9).
- **The supernatural**. Because archaeological evidence has frequently supported biblical accounts, miracles stories are treated as historical events and as proof of the authority of the Bible.

There are many criticisms of fundamentalism, not least that it treats the Bible as if it is to be read in only one way, when many parts of it are intended to be read as poetry, song, legend and so on. But besides this, fundamentalism contradicts itself in the following ways:

- **Problem of harmonisation**. Fundamentalist theories often have to be very elaborate to explain or harmonize contradictory stories. For example, some say Jesus had *two* ascensions to heaven (compare Luke 24:50–53 which takes place on the day of his resurrection and Acts 1:3–11 which takes place 40 days after his resurrection). But this solution not only causes more historical problems (why does the rest of the New Testament seem unaware of two ascensions) but misunderstands the theological significance of what ascension means (the idea of completion and revelation of God's glory).
- **Use of the Old Testament**. If in Luke 24:27 the risen Jesus *interprets* the Old Testament for the disciples does this mean that the Old Testament cannot be read literally but interpreted? This makes fundamentalism inconsistent.
- **The logic of biblical inspiration**. A favourite fundamentalist text is 2 Timothy 3:16 which claims biblical authority because all Scripture is inspired. But if this passage is Scripture and inspired, then its only authority is itself. It is hardly satisfactory to accept the inerrancy of the Bible simply because it says so. In short, this

Key question

Does it matter if the Bible presents conflicting views?

Key word

Tautology is when the same thing is said twice using different words making it redundant or unnecessary.

Key word

Scepticism is the position which tends to doubt what others hold to be true.

Key word

Allegory is where a character or event in a text symbolically represent another deeper, spiritual, philosophical or political idea.

Key quote

'All scripture is given by inspiration of God, and is profitable for doctrine, for reproof, for correction, for instruction in righteousness.'

2 TIMOTHY 3:16

is a **tautology** along the lines of 'The Bible is true, because the Bible says so'. As we discussed at the start of this chapter, the Bible's authority rests on the ways humans have experienced it and recognised its worth.

b) Conservative biblical theology

Conservative theology occupies the middle ground between the literalism of fundamentalism and what it considers to be the historical **scepticism** of liberalism. For example, Jesus says, 'If your right eye causes you to sin, pluck it out and throw it away' (Matthew 5:29). But why in practice do very few fundamentalists take this literally? The conservative response is that different *types* of literature must be read in different ways and even the fundamentalist literalist knows this. In this case it has to be balanced against Jesus' command to love oneself, so to 'pluck out' is a metaphor for repentance.

In the early Church, problems such as this were solved by taking an **allegorical** approach to scripture. The justification was based on Plato's philosophy that as this world is a reflection of the heavenly realm, then the stories in the Bible should be read as pointers to the spiritual realm. However, by the medieval period the method was often so over employed that even straight historical events were given allegorical meaning. The reformers, notably Luther, encouraged more rigorous exegesis taking into account the different types of literature.

Conservative hermeneutics covers a wide range of exegetical methods from those who treat the Bible as propositional revelation to those who take the apophatic approach and interpret it as a profoundly inspired witness of God's word but not the Word of God as such.

i) God-inspired events: John Bright

Some theologians suggest that God reveals himself in events to which humans respond. This view allows for some human interpretation and the use of language appropriate to the time in which it occurred. This very popular view (between the 1940s and 1960s) called 'biblical theology' made much use of modern scholarship and archaeology. John Bright's influential *History of Israel* (1959) argues for the historical accuracy of the Old Testament and the *uniqueness* of Israel's history as a witness of God's actual involvement in human affairs. The criticism of Bright's theology is that he tended to stress some historical parts of the Bible more than others and that he saw the whole Bible in Christian terms of salvation rather than objective historical scholarship.

ii) Developing revelation

Many conservatives consider that the use of critical literary and historical **exegetical** methods developed by liberal scholars do not

Cross-reference

Read page 77 on different types of exegesis.

necessarily undermine the basic notion that scripture is inspired. Scholars have for a long time agreed that the book of Isaiah is composed over a long period of time and is probably three books in one, for example.

Developing revelation strengthens the notion that God is active in human affairs consistent with their condition at different stages of history. If history is Spirit-led, as creation is described as being the product of God's Spirit (Genesis 1:2), then the Spirit continues to be part of the historical process. For example, Genesis 1:1–2:4a is usually treated as being composed around 586BC during the Exile, whilst Genesis 2:4b–end is much earlier probably being written around 960BC. The writers use different names for God and describe the creation in very different ways. Both views offer different insights into God according to their situations: Genesis 1 stresses the majesty of God who orders matter, whereas in Genesis 2 God is intimately presented as a potter who creates humans out of love. As the Bible is both the words of men and the Word of God then both views are equally necessary and provide a breadth of insight.

d) Liberal biblical theology

Liberalism is a slippery notion but in the world of hermeneutics it has come to refer to those critics who begin by reading and interpreting the Bible like any other book (or set of texts). This is the approach of Schleiermacher and we have seen how his hermeneutical method tries to ensure that the Bible is interpreted as carefully as any other piece of ancient literature.

i) A liberal-conservative paradox

There are some scholars who appear to be liberals but on closer analysis are not so. This is especially so in the case of **Rudolf Bultmann**. At first Bultmann's hermeneutical methods appear radical; he argues that the language of the New Testament should be demythologised, so that what looks like objective descriptions of hell, angels, demons and so on are just first-century metaphors or myths before there was adequate scientific knowledge to describe the world. Once this is understood then these **myths** can be seen to represent deep human experiences of the word, so that stripped of their false objectivity modern readers can experience the original moment.

But in other ways Bultmann, like Barth, is really quite conservative. The New Testament and in particular the Gospels, aren't historical accounts of Jesus' life but rather *witnesses* of the impact he had on the early Christians. Bultmann developed his version of form criticism so that the layers of early Christian *tradition* could be stripped back to the earliest kerygma or preaching of the Church. What Bultmann finds is that every layer makes the

Key question

Should the Bible be read like any other book?

Key quote

'Man's knowledge and mastery of the world have advanced to such an extent through science and technology that it is no longer possible for anyone seriously to hold the New Testament view of the world – in fact, there is no one who does.'

RUDOLF BULTMANN, *KERYGMA AND MYTH*, 4

Key word

Myth is a story which conveys deep human experiences of the meaning of the world and our place in it.

Cross-reference

Read pages 61–62 on Bultmann, Jesus and the kerygma.

Cross-reference

Read pages 61–62 on Bultmann and the Christ of faith.

Key people

Paul Ricoeur (1913–2005) was brought up a devout French Protestant. As an academic philosopher he developed his interest in language and interpretation and published many influential works including *Freud and Philosophy* (1965) and the three-volume *Time and Narrative* (1984–88).

Cross-reference

See pages 83–84 on the problem of authorship.

Key word

The **hermeneutic of suspicion** questions the underlying political and psychological motives which often form interpretations.

Cross-reference

See pages 122–124 on liberation theology and the hermeneutic of suspicion.

same proclamation that Jesus is Lord, even though, as Christianity developed, each community used very different terms to express this.

ii) New hermeneutics

Schleiermacher's pioneering work on hermeneutics opened the door for a whole new kind of philosophy. The impact of more recent hermeneutics on biblical interpretation has been especially fruitful in overcoming the sense of alienation which many feel when dealing with an ancient text.

Paul Ricoeur has developed Schleiermacher's hermeneutical circle to focus far more on the way the reader engages with the text regardless of when it was written and by whom. For him the power of the hermeneutical circle is that the symbols of the text also work by pointing outside the text to the world itself. In other words, interpreting a text is at the same time a way of understanding the world. The implications for biblical hermeneutics are important.

- As we often have very little knowledge of who wrote the various parts of the Bible, Ricoeur's disregard of the author answers Schleiermacher's problem.
- By disregarding history Ricoeur closes the time gap between when the Bible was written and its readers. Ricoeur argues that every reader has the ability to suspend the present and enter into the biblical world with a 'willingness to listen' without judgement.
- At the same time the reader adopts a 'willingness to suspect'. Ricoeur's **hermeneutic of suspicion** causes the reader to question his own motives for reading a particular biblical text or to question the interpretations of others (notably the official interpretations of the Church). Marx, Freud and Nietzsche have each provided invaluable ways of questioning the way the text is approached. Marx might help the reader question the economic and class bias of the interpretation. The **hermeneutic of suspicion** has become an invaluable tool for **liberation theologians** which allows the poor to interpret the Bible themselves.
- The 'vow of disobedience' adds a new dimension to the hermeneutical circle. Whereas for Schleiermacher it meant seeing the text in the context of other texts as a type of conversation, Ricoeur's circle is more combative. The conversation isn't just to get to know the text but to 'interrogate' it (as he puts it) and to pose it questions and to see how it responds. His approach removes the false piety and reverence with which some Christians read the Bible. The Bible is a sparring partner whose answers may not always be attractive but force decisions about the nature of existence and faith.

Key quote

'Myth, then, can no longer be defined in opposition to science. Myth consists in giving worldly form to what is beyond known and tangible reality. It expresses in an objective language the sense that man has of his dependence on that which stands at the limit and at the origin of his world.'

PAUL RICOEUR, *PREFACE TO BULTMANN*, 387

This is why there is a circle: to understand the text, it is necessary to believe in what the text announces to me; but what the text announces to me is nowhere but in the text. This is why it is necessary to understand the text in order to believe.

(Paul Ricoeur, *Preface to Bultmann* in *The Conflict of Interpretations*, 386)

Ricoeur is cautious about Bultmann's use of demythologising. Although Bultmann is right that in demythologising the text is interrogated, but to strip away myth is to forget that this was the only way in those days that deeper ideas of good news could be announced to the listeners (or readers). Bultmann hoped that demythologising would make the original preaching or kerygma speak to us today, whereas in fact, by ridding it of its metaphorical language he strips it of almost all religious significance.

Summary diagram

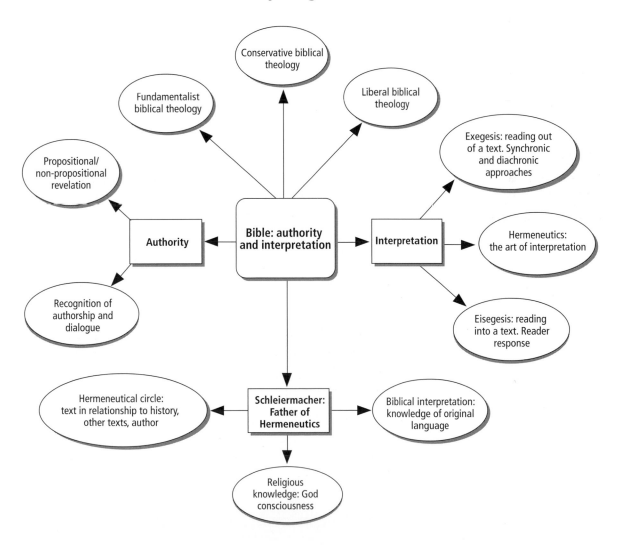

Study guide

By the end of this chapter you should be able to explain what is meant when it is said that hermeneutics is 'the art of interpretation' and what problems biblical interpretation poses for exegesis. You should also understand Schleiermacher's central teaching on hermeneutics and why it is rejected by contemporary biblical fundamentalists and many conservatives.

Essay questions

1a Explain why there are different views about the authority of the Bible.

The essay might begin by explaining that authority comes from the word 'author' so that when the authority of the Bible is recognised, what is meant is that its words, instructions and rules are ones which require our respect. When Jesus 'spoke with authority' even the other teachers of the time had to reconsider their positions. The debate over the authority of the Bible rests on how much interpretation is permitted. Fundamentalists argue that as the author of the Bible is God's inerrant Word, then Christians have no option but to follow it. Liberals, on the other hand, consider that blind obedience to the authority of the Bible leaves no room for conversation, dialogue and communication. Conservative Christians think that liberals don't take the authority of the Bible seriously enough and allow for many texts to have symbolic meanings.

1b 'The Bible has authority even if it is historically inaccurate.' Discuss.

The argument might begin by questioning the relationship between historical accuracy and authority. Some might argue that the Bible is not intended to be historical in the sense of a record of events. If, for example, Genesis 1 is myth or poetry, then as myth it has authority but not if it is history because our knowledge of the world today contradicts it.

On the other hand, the argument might consider that when and where the Bible was written is irrelevant. What matters, as Ricoeur suggests, is that the text speaks to us if we have a 'willingness to listen'. If we do this then what is odd or strange about an ancient text is not that it is old but that we have yet to engage with it fully. The Bible has authority because of its continuing power to provoke.

Further essay questions

2 a Explain the difference between exegesis and eisegesis.
2 b Assess the view that the Bible only makes sense to people of
     faith.

3 'Schleiermacher wrongly placed too much emphasis on knowing
   the author of the biblical text.' Discuss.

4 'There is no correct way to interpret the Bible.' Discuss.

Revision checklist

Can you give brief definitions of:

- authority
- apophatic way
- propositional revelation.

Can you explain:

- the difference between synchronic and diachronic approaches
  to interpreting the Bible
- Schleiermacher's hermeneutical circle
- Ricoeur's hermeneutic of suspicion
- why interpretation is an 'intermediary' task.

Can you give arguments for and against:

- knowing who the author is of a biblical text
- fundamentalist reading of the Bible
- treating the Bible in non-propositional terms.

6 THE BIRTH OF LIBERATION THEOLOGY

Chapter checklist

The chapter begins by looking at the emergence of liberation theology in the late 1950s after 500 years of Spanish and Portuguese colonialism in Latin America. It goes on to consider the influence of Vatican II on the Catholic bishops meeting at Medellin in 1968. The principal ideas of Marx are outlined and the chapter concludes with liberation theology's early critique of development and dependency.

1 Historical situation

View of Rio de Janeiro and statue of Jesus on the Corcorado Mountain

> *Like all theologies, liberation theology is the product of a particular historical moment; unlike some theologies, liberation theology is fully aware of this fact.*
>
> (James Nickoloff, *Gustavo Gutiérrez: Essential Writings*, 5)

Liberation theology was not invented but rather grew out of the political and pastoral situation in Latin America during the 1960s

Key word

Contextual theology considers that the role of theology is to reflect and articulate Christian ideas in response to a particular historical situation or experience.

Key question

How did a conservative Church develop a radical theology?

and 1970s. In responding in particular to the plight of the poor politically and spiritually, liberation theology is self-consciously a **contextual theology**. What this means is that theology is not a pre-packaged set of ideas but the means by which theologians *reflect* on a situation in the light of experience and within the Christian tradition. To use the language of liberation theologians: the first step is to side with the oppressed against injustice, the second step is to reflect theologically. However, in a continent where the Roman Catholic Church has traditionally defined what theology is, liberation theology's radical approach is often seen as subversive and dangerous by both the Church and the state.

For centuries, since colonisation, Latin America has been strongly Catholic and conservative. So, how and why has liberation theology developed?

a) Colonisation of Latin America

After 1492 when the continent was discovered by Europeans from Spain and Portugal, the indigenous people were forced into a new culture which included the adoption of Catholicism. In 1493 Pope Alexander VI divided the continent into different countries between Portugal and Spain and charged their monarchs to convert the population to Catholicism. This was done in a particularly bloody and violent manner – not helped by Spain's vigorous dealings with the Protestants during the Reformation. The result was a sharply divided class society. The poor indigenous people tended to live in the countryside separately from the European colonisers who grew rich exporting the natural resources (tobacco, meat, leather). In this divided society peasants did not meet Church officials but developed their own form of popular Catholicism.

b) Independence

Even though independence was achieved from Spain and Portugal in the years 1808–24, the culture of slavery and landownership by the rich did not disappear. Independence was gained by the rich elite who wanted freedom to trade with Britain. In other words, Latin America had not really gained its own cultural and economic autonomy and was still locked into a European mindset.

By the 1830s although the Catholic Church had by now recognised the new countries, many bishops had vacated their dioceses which the Church was unable to fill (very few clergy and bishops were from Latin America and over 80 per cent came from Europe). Without strong traditional Church presence the liberal progressives supported economic development and exported goods, which they did by confiscating land from Catholic religious orders and indigenous Indians to use for their own agricultural exports. During this time Protestant missionaries from the USA had infiltrated the continent bringing with them a very conservative form of Christianity which many of the peasants found extremely attractive. Liberal progressives also encouraged these missionaries because it opened up further trade links.

c) Catholic renewal in the 1950s

With the rise of Protestant evangelical Christianity, communism and secularism, the Catholic Bishops of Latin American or **CELAM** called their first major conference in 1955 to address the situation. But they were also disturbed by the increasing social problems with the dramatic rise in very poor **bairros** tacked onto the new expanding cities. The contrast between rich and poor had never been more obvious.

The Conference raised a wide range of social and theological issues. In essence, the bishops asked whether it was possible to develop a radical theology from a conservative church.

Key words

CELAM stands for *Consejo Episcopal Latinoamericano* or Latin American Episcopal Conference.

Bairro is Portuguese for 'neighbourhood' and often refers to the shanty town or favela areas occupied by the poor.

- **Role and attitude to clergy**. With so few parish priests and scattered parish villages, village communities were used to acting independently. The people had already come to the conclusion that if God is a God of grace, then the priest was not necessary for salvation. Besides which there was often a great mistrust of clergy who were seen to be no different from corrupt local officials or those who worked in rich schools and universities. Increasingly, clergy themselves felt guilt at their hypocrisy and double standards.

- **Communism**. Cuban and Brazilian communist revolutions in the 1960s demonstrated clearly that the people supported communist and atheist revolutionary change. If, at grassroots level, the people were abandoning their Catholic faith in favour of communism, then clearly the Church had lost touch with its grassroots members.

- **USA and development**. The revolution in Cuba (1959) inspired similar guerrilla movements in Venezuela, Guatemala and Peru. The reaction of the USA under President Kennedy was to provide development aid to governments and military support to meet the new threat of communism. The Church hierarchy supported the governments and a form of **development** which, rather than addressing the issue of the poor, simply reinforced centuries of **dependency** on external northern European powers.

Cross-reference

Development and dependency are discussed on pages 103–104.

- **Radical Christian voices**. Outside the Church hierarchy Catholics were calling for radical change. The Brazilian President Juscelino Kubitschek (1955–60) described the situation of social injustice as a sin against Christ and demanded a reform of landownership of the rich. Paulo Friere's radical approach to teaching peasants combined Christian and Marxist ideas to enable the poor to become self-sufficient and resist exploitation. Amongst many clergy there was the realisation that poverty was not the result of laziness or the will of God but structural – woven into the very fabric of a corrupt society.

For all these reasons the CELAM conference indicated that it was not enough for the Church to attend to people's spiritual welfare and leave their political needs to the state; the logic of the Christian gospel actually demanded a reversal – people first, theology second.

2 Birth of liberation theology

Key thought

The **Second Vatican Council**, held between 1962 and 1965, was opened by Pope John XXIII and closed by Pope Paul VI. Its aim was progressive by addressing questions of modernity such as the Church's relationship with other Christian traditions and world religions; reform of worship; the role of bishops; progress and the secular world. It is generally referred to as Vatican II.

Key question

To what extent did Vatican II help create liberation theology?

Key words

Orthopraxis means right action. **Orthodoxy** means right teaching.

Key quote

'In ringing phrases the bishops called for Christians to be involved in the transformation of society.'

PHILLIP BERRYMAN, *LIBERATION THEOLOGY*, 23

The 1955 CELAM meeting, the influence of the **Second Vatican Council**'s and Pope Paul VI's encyclical letter *Populorum Progressio* in 1967 (which pointed out the dehumanising tendency of capitalism), laid the foundations for the emergence of a self-conscious theology of liberation. But political theology was in the air and formed the basis of many council agendas. In 1966, for example, the World Council of Churches meeting at Geneva addressed the topic of 'Christians in the Technical and Social Revolutions of our Time'.

a) Medellin, Columbia 1968

In 1968 the meeting of the Second Latin American Bishops' conference was held in Medellin, Colombia, where 130 Latin American Catholic bishops met. The conference concluded with a second plenary meeting of CELAM.

Although the term 'liberation theology' was not used, there was wide use of the term 'liberation'. The theme of the conference, 'The Church in the Present Transformation of Latin America in the Light of the Council', was to consider the implications of the Second Vatican Council from 'the perspective of the poor'.

The briefing papers marked a break with the past. They looked at the economic conditions, cultural situations and the political life of Latin America first, *then* the place of the church and *then*, briefly, theology. It was the first time in which the term **orthopraxis** was used in contrast to **orthodoxy**. Orthodoxy or 'right teaching' refers to the traditional teaching of the Church, whereas orthopraxis or 'right action' is action for social justice.

Medellin reinterpreted the modernising elements of Vatican II in the light of the Latin American situation. The bishops argued that Vatican II had failed to give sufficient analysis of the *poor* in sociological and theological terms. Its frequent use of economic and political language was very different from usual Church councils.

For instance:

- Medellin spoke specifically of the 'situation of sin' manifested as 'institutional violence' due to 'grave structural conflict'.
- The bishops considered the need for 'sweeping bold, urgent and profoundly renovating changes'.
- The council recognised the need for education at grassroots level to 'enable people to become agents of their own advancement'.
- Often the language of Medellin praised the revolutionaries more than the traditionalists or **developmentalists**.
- They commended **base communities**, small co-operative people-run communities as opposed to the role of traditional churches.

But there was much ambiguity at Medellin. Sociological and political language such as 'development' and 'liberation' were widely used but not clearly defined. The bishops' notion of revolution was still essentially traditional and European; there was not a strong endorsement for the poor to fight for their rights. But even so, as Berryman concludes, Medellin was hugely important, it was a 'magna carta', a charter for the poor.

b) Gustavo Gutiérrez

In an encyclopedia which allowed only one sentence to the subject, it would not be wrong to say that liberation theology began in 1969 and that its founder was Gustavo Gutiérrez.

(Alistair Kee, *Marx and the Failure of Liberation Theology*, 131)

It was shortly after Medellin that two theologians, Gustavo Gutiérrez and Hugo Assmann published their full-length books on liberation theology. Of the many influential liberation theologians none have been more associated with the movement than Gutiérrez.

At Medellin the bishops had asked: who are the poor? It was to this question that Gutiérrez made his own distinctive contribution. The poor are those who occupy, as Gutiérrez famously put it, the 'underside of history', the aspect of history that is forgotten or missed but which in fact occupies the larger part of human existence. Gutiérrez argued that in order for the Church to function properly as a church, it must grow *out* of the people by making itself the 'church of the poor'.

Gutiérrez defined the poor in three ways. The poor are those who are:

- **dehumanised** through lack of material goods (i.e. *not* poor in spirit)
- **open to God** just as the faithful people of Israel are described in the Old Testament as the inheritors of God's covenant
- **committed in solidarity** so that others might become rich spiritually.

Cross-references

See page 103 on developmentalism.

See Chapter 9 on base communities.

Cross-reference

See Phillip Berryman, *Liberation Theology*, 24.

Key people

Gustavo Gutiérrez (1928–) is a Peruvian Catholic priest and theologian who lives and works with the poor in Lima. His book *A Theology of Liberation* (1971) was foundational in the development of liberation theology.

Key question

To what extent has liberation theology been a new Reformation?

Key people

Phillip Berryman (1938–) was a Catholic priest serving in a bairro in Panama City in the 1960s. In 1973 he resigned from the priesthood but worked with the American Friends Service Committee from 1976–80 and through them was able to keep in touch with the Latin American church. His book *Liberation Theology* (1987) resists the idea that liberation theology is Marxist.

Cross-reference

See pages 151–159 for more detail on other theologies of liberation.

Key thought

In order to consider Berryman's question, read pages 43–44 on Calvin and the Reformation.

Key thought

Hereafter, reference to northern Europe will also include North America.

c) A new Reformation

With its emphasis on the authority of ordinary people reading and interpreting the Bible for themselves, its challenge to traditional church structures and hierarchy, liberation theology has an agenda which sounds very much like those of the Protestant Reformation. Like the Reformation, it aims to work from the actual experiences of the people and their historical situation. So the question which **Phillip Berryman** poses is whether liberation theology can carry out a reformation without causing the schisms which resulted in the Protestant Reformation of the sixteenth century.

i) Reform of society

A reformed theology aims to be the means for bringing about change in the world. From Latin America liberation theology has spawned many more **theologies of liberation**, each theology dealing with a specific social need. For instance, a black theology of liberation has developed specifically in the USA and in addition there are African liberation theologies, Asian liberation theologies, feminist theologies and gay theologies. Their connecting identity is the desire to liberate an oppressed people or class of people from the exploitation caused by the oppressive structures of society. However, what makes liberation theology contentious is that although the notion is firmly rooted in the Christian tradition, analysis and application frequently utilise radical non-theological sociological, political and economic analyses.

ii) Reform of traditional theology

Liberation theology challenges established white, middle class and northern European ways of doing theology. Liberation theology has developed because conventional theology as taught at university, studied at school or even preached in the churches has failed to engage with the real world. Theology in this conventional sense deals with universal ideas which can be imposed 'top down' by Church authority. Liberation theology, on the other hand, is 'bottom up' and emerges from context and experience.

iii) Challenge to northern European dualisms

Criticism of traditional theology has also led liberation theologians to a critique of northern European culture. Their criticism can be summed up as a challenge to northern European and North American dualism. Dualism just means that a distinction can be made between two related categories, but here it essentially distinguishes matter from spirit in a number of different ways.

For example:

- **Science and religion**. Northern Europe has given priority to science and reason as the basis for society and placed religion in a separate private sphere. For liberation theologians science and religion are equally part of public life. Many of the so-called conflicts between science and religion are non-issues for liberation theologians. The origin of the universe and the probability of miracles, for example, by no means undermine what it means to live a religious life. For the poor what matters are issues of justice, human welfare and solidarity.
- **Materialism and spirit**. Mind–spirit dualism in northern Europe gives superficial priority to matter over spirit. But liberation theologians argue that materialism properly understood considers matter to be a manifestation of spirit (both human and divine). Liberation theologians argue that, whereas northern European 'spirituality' wants to escape the world, their own form of materialism is rooted in the physical historical world.

Liberation theology is therefore a bottom-up theology. It begins with the poor and ends in the world; it is critical or **suspicious** of any institution (Church, schools, universities, seminaries) which look to northern Europe as a justification for their existence.

iv) A theology of action

Liberation theology is primarily a theology of **praxis** or action. The idea of praxis, as derived from Marx, is far more than just doing or acting. Praxis is a critical or reflective process which moves from theory to action and from action to theory. Gutiérrez calls this movement first and second acts. The 'first act' or 'step' is commitment to the poor, the 'second act' or step is critical reflection in light of the Christian gospel. Both together constitute 'doing theology'. Theology, for many Europeans, simply means understanding Christian teaching as laid down by the Church. Whilst liberation theologians take these seriously they also suggest that 'orthodoxy' (right teaching) is probably less important than 'orthopraxis' (right action). The proper relationship between the two is **dialectical** – in other words there is a creative tension between action and teaching where each inform and modify the other.

Liberation theology is more than moral action; it is a 'critical reflection' (Gutiérrez) on all central Christian beliefs. To do this, liberation theology takes the experience of the poor and peasant worker as seriously as that of the priest or bishop. Put in this way liberation theology is a radical theology which challenges all forms of hierarchy and traditional views of authority.

Cross-reference

Read pages 88–89 on hermeneutic of suspicion.

Key word

Praxis is a critical or reflective process which moves from theory to action.

Key word

Dialectic describes the creative tension between conflicting ideas or states which resolves into a synthesis. The synthesis might then find itself in conflict with a new state of affairs.

3 Marxism

Key people

Che Guevara (1928–1967) was an Argentine Marxist who played a key role in the Cuban Revolution led by Fidel Castro. His language of martyrdom, redemption of the oppressed and revolution was absorbed by many theologians. He was executed after a failed revolution in Bolivia.

Key word

Capitalism is the belief that human societies flourish best when operating in a free competitive market motivated by profit.

Key people

Karl Marx (1818–83) was born in Trier, which was then part of German Rhineland. Although his father converted to Christianity from Judaism for social reasons, his grandfather was a much respected rabbi. At university he came under the influence of a radical group of Hegelians, the 'young Hegelians', and through them developed his atheism and later his analysis of economics. He was aided financially and academically by Frederich Engels (1820–95) and they collaborated on many works. Marx fled Paris in 1849 and settled in London where he wrote and worked as a journalist. His influential writings include *The Communist Manifesto* (1848) and *Capital* (1867–83).

In April 1982 four hundred people met in Santiago for an international conference on 'Christians for Socialism'. Amongst those liberation theologians who attended were Hugo Assmann and Gustavo Gutiérrez. The conference condemned Christian 'third way' democracy and pressed for a more radical change through the convergence of politics and Christianity. The language of the conference was strongly indebted to Marxist ideas.

As the Santiago conference illustrates, Marxism is important for two reasons in the study of liberation theology. First, the small communist groups, inspired by the Cuban Revolution, stirring up the poor to revolt against governments gave voice to popular Marxist ideas. Language of revolution, ownership and class war were in the air and liberation theologians used them and were inspired also by the charismatic figure of the Cuban Revolution, **Che Guevara**. Second, the Marxist sociological analysis of society provides a powerful tool which liberation theologians have adapted for their own purposes.

Segundo, for example, represents one strand which finds in Marxist-type socialism a way of thinking which challenges the **capitalist** mentality that has caused so much harm in Latin America. Whilst he does not share the Marxist or communist goal, he considers its analysis of production and ownership to be essential in dealing with a society which has discarded the poor.

So what characterises Marxist language and ideas? The following are some of **Karl Marx**'s key ideas.

a) Alienation and exploitation

Many of Marx's ideas were a development of his study of **Hegel**. From Hegel, Marx developed two key ideas which he regarded as the fundamental reasons why humans fail to be happy and fulfilled. Individuals are often alienated from themselves, each other and society and therefore vulnerable and open to exploitation. The result is a dehumanised and tragic society.

i) The master–slave relationship

One of the powerful metaphors Hegel used to describe this situation and which shaped so much of Marx's early thought is that of the master–slave relationship. In brief, the analogy is that:

- In the initial state of the master–slave relationship, master and slave live in a kind of harmony because the master rules and the slave obeys.
- The slave obeys because he gives up his humanity and allows himself to be exploited by the master.

Key people

Friedrich Hegel (1770–1831) was a highly influential German philosopher and one of the founders of German Idealism. He developed his own form of dialectic whereby ideas and history develops through thesis (the initial state), antithesis (the opposite state) and synthesis (the resolution of thesis/antithesis). His influential writings include *The Phenomenology of Spirit* (1807) and *Elements of the Philosophy of Right* (1821).

Key words

Bourgeoisie and **proletariat**. Bourgeoisie are all those who own the means of production and proletariat are the workers who have no ownership or direct control over production, according to Marx

Key quote

'The depreciation of the human world progresses in direct proportion with the increase in value of the world of things.'

KARL MARX, *ECONOMIC AND POLITICAL MANUSCRIPTS*, IN DAVID MCLELLAN, *KARL MARX: SELECTED WRITINGS*, 86

Key word

False consciousness describes how a person or people may hold a view of the world which they consider to be true when in fact it is fundamentally false.

- Master and slave are alienated from each other.
- Once it enters into the consciousness of the slave that the master only has power over him because he *acts* as a slave, the slave realises that he, too, has power. If he ceases to be a slave, then the master's power becomes ineffective.
- In the power struggle which follows, master and slave both give up their former positions and cease to be slave and master but humans.
- Slave and master are reconciled to each other, mentally, spiritually and physically – at least for the time being.

In Marx's version, master and slave are represented in society by **bourgeoisie** and **proletariat**, owners of production and workers.

The history of all hitherto existing society is the history of class struggles … Society as a whole is more and more splitting up into two great hostile camps, into two great classes directly facing each other: Bourgeoisie and Proletariat.

(Karl Marx and Fredrick Engels, *The Communist Manifesto I*, in David McLellan, *Karl Marx: Selected Writings*, 246)

Whereas for Hegel revolution takes place because God as Spirit is part of the processes of change, Marx considered that all change is material due to historical forces of nature and humans, not God. But in other respects Marx agrees with Hegel that change or dialectic is caused by a struggle of opposites, and even then the synthesis or result may be unstable – alienation may only be temporarily resolved.

ii) Means of production

One of the primary causes for exploitation and alienation is ownership of the means of production. As Marx argues in the *Communist Manifesto*, in a capitalist society when what matters is production of goods, everyone becomes dehumanised. This is particularly so for the worker because he has no power to control production and is merely 'an appendage of the machine'. Working in the factory he has no creative input into what he makes; he is alienated from the product and hates his work. Finally, even when he receives his wages, the bourgeoisie still manage to exploit him because they own the shops where he spends his money on goods and his lodgings where they charge him rent.

b) False consciousness

In his early writings Marx considered that one of the primary causes of alienation is religion. Following the argument of Ludwig Feuerbach (1804–72), God is no more than a projection of deep-seated human desires such as justice, love and hope. Whilst for

Feuerbach God is an important aspect of human consciousness, organised religion can be very destructive. Religion objectifies these desires as 'God' and forgetting it has done so then makes God a supreme power which humans then have to obey. As long as humans believe that God is an *actual* being, they are suffering from false consciousness, alienated from real desires.

Marx agreed with Feuerbach but he went further. Not only is religion a source of alienation but so is the very idea of God. Marx had no time for Hegel's idea that God as Spirit is part of the process of reconciliation of broken human relationships. In the following famous quotation Marx argues that religion 'is the opium of the people', a comforting but false consciousness, the primary source of alienated humanity; being truly human is to be part of the material world free from all such illusions.

> *The foundation of irreligious criticism is this: man makes religion, religion does not make man. Religion is indeed the self-consciousness and self-awareness of man who either has not yet attained to himself or has already lost himself again. But man is no abstract being squatting outside the world. Man is the world of man, the state, society.*

> (Karl Marx, *Deutsch-französische Jahrbücher*, in David McLellan, *Karl Marx: Selected Writings*, 71)

ii) Historical materialism

Another element which Marx took over and adapted from Hegel was his view of history. Hegel's idea was that history is a process, a process of dynamic change where matter and God as Spirit in harmony with human minds (or spirit) is gradually working towards a state of harmony. But the process as we have seen from the master–slave example is one of tension or dialectic. Dialectic suggests that there are often moments in history of great human flourishing and creativeness, only to be replaced by decay and suffering, to be replaced again by a better stage.

Marx also shares Hegel's optimistic notion that each stage of history usually improves on the last. However, as a materialist he rejects Hegel's God as Spirit and instead sees history (much as Darwin had described the natural world) as the 'blind' working of the material forces of nature over which humans can have some influence. Through dialectical class struggle, feudal societies have made way to capitalist societies which will eventually give way to socialism to be followed by communism. Each stage depends on the previous epoch of history and improves on it. Marx observed that each historical era only gives way under considerable resistance and needs an intellectual catalyst, such as himself as an intellectual prophet, to be able to see what is happening in history and steer it in the right direction.

Key quote

'The abolition of religion as the illusory happiness of the people is the demand for their real happiness. The demand to give up the illusions about their condition is the demand to give up a condition that requires illusion.'

KARL MARX, *DEUTSCH-FRANZÖSISCHE JAHRBÜCHER*, IN DAVID MCLELLAN, *KARL MARX: SELECTED WRITINGS*, 71

Key question

Why does Marx have an optimistic view of history?

Key word

Historical materialism is Marx's central idea that the material forces of nature and human societies have a dialectical relationship. Matter and human minds are in constant tension.

Key quote

'In reality and for the practical materialist, i.e. the communist, it is a question of revolutionizing the existing world, of practically attacking and changing existing things.'

KARL MARX, *THE GERMAN IDEOLOGY*, IN DAVID MCLELLAN, *KARL MARX: SELECTED WRITINGS*, 190

Cross-reference

See page 98 on praxis.

Cross-reference

See Karl Marx, *Economic and Philosophical Manuscripts*, in David McLellan, *Karl Marx: Selected Writings*, 97.

c) Praxis and reversal

As a moral philosopher Marx was a consequentialist. If a better society could be achieved using non-communist means, then it would be justified because of the greater freedom and happiness enjoyed by all. But Marx also realised that a revolution of this kind wouldn't be sufficient to change the deeper underlying *structures* of society. Just as human minds create their environment, environments shape and create human minds. The means of change necessitate a fundamental restructuring of economic and social attitudes. In Marxist terms, what is needed is an active process whereby ideas are directly applied politically and economically. This is what is meant by **praxis** or the process of putting ideas into action by making structural changes to society.

> *The materialist doctrine concerning the changing of circumstances and upbringing forgets that circumstances are changed by men and that it is essential to educate the educator himself.*
>
> (Karl Marx, *Theses on Feuerbach III*, in David McLellan, *Karl Marx: Selected Writings*, 172)

d) Private ownership of property

In the *Communist Manifesto* Marx and Engels wrote that: 'The communist revolution is the most radical rupture with traditional property relations'. For Marx and other writers, the ownership of private property had come to represent the essence of a corrupt society. Ownership of land gives individuals power over others; it can lead to war; those without property and land are dispossessed and dehumanised. In short, private ownership is the source of alienation. Abolishing private ownership of property in its most complete form is the means by which humans can rediscover their natural sociability, as 'the genuine solution of the antagonism between man and nature and between man and man'.

e) The final state

Marx did not spend much time describing what the final state or *telos* of history would be like once the dual aberrations of exploitation and alienation had been removed. It would, though, be an existence of *real* freedom and real happiness. It would be free from false ideologies, including religion, politics and economics. Although Marx rejected Hegel's spiritual view of the final state, he does nevertheless have a form of 'religious' utopia where humans would live in harmony and cooperation. This is the communist epoch.

4 Development and dependency

Key word

Development describes the process of improving the quality of human lives by raising living standards through an increase in incomes and levels of food production, along with growth in medical services and education.

Key question

Why is liberation theology so critical of development?

Key word

Dependency theory describes how an external dominant political power causes a weaker political power to become dependent on it as in a master–slave relationship.

Key word

Developmentalism is a negative form of development which has led to dependency. The term is used by Latin American liberation theologians.

From the middle of the nineteenth century onwards, the USA established special trading and economic privileges in South America. In exchange, the USA offered military protection against insurgents. But Latin American priests and bishops have increasingly questioned this. This form of **development** has come at a cost. As Cardinal Paulo Evaristo Arns of São Paulo, Brazil said in 1985 at a conference on debt, debt should not be repaid at the cost of the poor.

Latin American theologians have questioned the very idea of development – at least as it has been practised in northern Europe. The conventional view had been that development was necessary because of 'backwardness'. But Latin American commentators argued that adopting this view had done nothing to alleviate poverty for hundreds of years. Exports had not brought wealth and social justice for all, only the rich had prospered.

They argued instead for a new notion of development which would replace the older language of 'advanced' and 'backward' with 'dominant' and 'dependent'. Liberation theologians picked up Pope Paul VI's theme of *Populorum Progressio* (On the Development of Peoples) (1967) which set out the Vatican's agenda on social teaching, but they rejected its assertion that development must be consensual not revolutionary because revolution 'produces new injustices'. On the contrary, the liberation theologians argued that for development to really work, revolution is necessary to overcome the core problem of dependency.

Dependency theory suggests that aid from the USA and elsewhere does not ultimately improve Latin American society because the external dominant political power creates a slave mentality, spiritually and physically. At an obvious level it means that trade often fluctuates wildly as multinational companies invest in Latin America seeking cheap labour and, then, when the markets change, they withdraw. But at a more subtle level, the elite of society follow the trends and fashions of the dominant powers. They are also trapped by capitalist values. Many liberation theologians argue that the dialectical social sciences (such as Marxism) offer the necessary means of breaking the cycle of dependency by offering a radically new (or revolutionary) way of thinking about development.

One change to development is that it must be dissociated from northern European capitalism. **Developmentalism**, as liberation theologians have negatively termed this kind of development, is consumer led, based on the idea that the greater market choice leads to a happier society. But it is just this kind of developmentalism which has caused Latin American problems for so long. It has glossed over the real causes of poverty by treating poverty as an unfortunate by-product of capitalism. This is why, as

Gutiérrez argues, genuine development has to begin by changing consciousness.

> *Attempts to bring about the changes within the existing order have proven futile. Only a radical break from the status quo, that is, a profound transformation of the private property system, access to power of the exploited class, and a social revolution that would break this dependence would allow for the change to a new society, a socialist society – or at least allow that such a society might be possible.*

> (Gustavo Gutiérrez, *A Theology of Liberation*, 65)

The change in consciousness, Gutiérrez argues, must be external as Hegel suggested by breaking the master–slave relationship; it must be historical as Marx argued; it must tackle the deeper psychological problems as suggested by Freud; and finally, it must seek spiritual freedom as Jesus preached. Ultimately, the challenge is to *reverse* dependency and find a truly liberated model of what he calls 'integral development' which genuinely values the poor based on the radical application of Christian love.

Summary diagram

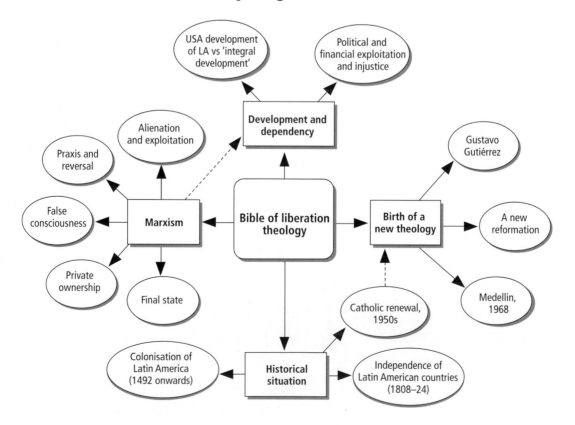

Study guide

By the end of this chapter you should be able to explain the historical, political and religious context which gave rise to liberation theology in Latin America. You should also be able to explain the key Marxist ideas and liberation theologians' criticism of northern European practice of development.

Essay questions

1a Explain how liberation theology came into being in Latin America.

The essay might begin by explaining the roots of liberation theology in the continent's colonial past, in particular in the nineteenth century when a rich land-owning elite developed their trade with Europe and the USA supported by clergy and the hierarchy of the Church. The rich–poor divide was one of the major areas of concern in the first meeting of CELAM (1955) and especially the lack of priests in the bairros. The bishops were conscious of the problem of dependency, capitalism, exploitation of the poor and the failure of the Church to provide for the needs of the people. The CELAM meeting at Medellin (1968) marked the birth of liberation theology inspired by the liberalising social reform of Vatican II. The term 'liberation' was widely used to tackle the 'structures of sin'. Gutiérrez articulated Medellin's theology.

1b 'All theology is contextual.' Discuss.

All theology is contextual in the sense that theology is the means of interpreting the central ideas of Christianity according to the situation and prevailing ideas of the time. For example, Augustine used Plato and Aquinas used Aristotle when formulating their ideas. Liberation theology argues that as God acts in history, then any moment of history is appropriate for theology to rethink its language and ideas.

On the other hand, if theology was all contextual, there would be no central, universal and timeless truths. Theology would become fragmentary and relative. Theology may re-express Christian beliefs but the ideas themselves cannot change.

Further essay questions

2 a Explain Marx's teaching on historical materialism.

2 b 'Marxism is a type of religion.' Discuss.

3 To what extent is Gutiérrez right that capitalist models of development always lead to exploitation?

4 'Theology should always begin with the poor.' Discuss.

Revision checklist

Can you give brief definitions of:

- bairro and favela
- CELAM
- dependency
- underside of history
- false consciousness
- Vatican II.

Can you explain:

- why Gutiérrez was critical of development
- what liberation theologians meant by dependency
- the difference between orthopraxis and orthodoxy
- Marx's teaching on alienation and means of production.

Can you give arguments for and against:

- private ownership of property
- liberation theology as a 'new Reformation'
- history as progression.

Chapter checklist ✓

The chapter begins by considering the meaning of a
'preferential option for the poor' and how this is applied
through first and second act praxis. The second part of the
chapter looks at the way Marx has been used by various
liberation theologians and the debate which this has caused.

1 Preferential option for the poor

Key words

Puebla state is situated in Mexico
and was the location of the third
meeting of the CELAM in 1979.
The meeting there is usually
referred to simply as 'Puebla'.

**Preferential option for the
poor** is the Christian duty of
the privileged to side with the
poor in solidarity and act against
exploitation.

The meeting at **Puebla** has been described as 'a serene affirmation
of Medellin'. The theme was 'The Evangelisation of Latin America
in the Present and in the Future'. It developed as a central idea from
a notion which Gutiérrez had helped to establish – the **preferential
option for the poor**. The first thing to notice about the phrase is
that it is not aimed at the poor but those who are in a privileged
position to act in solidarity in the battle against exploitation. The use
of 'preference' is aimed at all Christians (especially church leaders
and teachers) who are not poor and therefore have the power and
means to place the poor first. The 'option' means that solidarity
is a free act where the privileged learn to be poor by discarding
any feelings of arrogance and superiority. In this way the Church
becomes what it was always intended to be – radically egalitarian.

*We affirm the need for conversion on the part of the whole church to
a preferential option for the poor, an option aimed at their integral
liberation.*

(Puebla, *Final Document*, number 1134)

a) The people's church

Key word

Integral means essential, vital and
fundamental.

By using **integral** with 'liberation' Puebla clearly stated that the
essential duty of the whole Church is the task of not just dealing
with internal sin but the external economic conditions which have
created the social structures of sin and injustice. Puebla therefore
developed the controversial notion of the people's church or

iglesia popular. It was controversial because it recognised that for many of the poor the official church was no more than an extension of the state, an institution which was the source of their alienation and exploitation. The call for an *iglesia popular* challenged the very essence of the Church's authority on moral and spiritual teaching; Puebla called for a reform because the gospel, as preached by Jesus Christ, wasn't to form an institution but was to be found in solidarity with the poor. In a Marxist way of thinking, what was being asked for was a *reversal* of official consciousness and a new way of doing theology.

b) Theological motivations for a preferential option

Cross-reference

See Leonardo and Clodovis Boff, *Introducing Liberation Theology*, 44–46.

The Boff brothers outline five theological motivations which justify the preferential option for the poor:

- **Theological motivation**. The God of the Bible is a living God who is immanent in the world and involved in human history. God hears 'the cry' of his people (Exodus 3:7) and seeks justice. When the church imitates God it must hear the cry of the poor and seek justice.
- **Christological motivation**. Jesus sided with the poor and acted in solidarity with those who had been marginalised by society.
- **Eschatological motivation**. The moment when God judges the world will be based on whether a person has sided with the poor according to Jesus' parable of judgement (Matthew 25:31–46).
- **Apostolic motivation**. After Jesus' death the first apostles organised a general levy on all Christian groups to raise money for the poor. They did not distinguish between Christian and non-Christian poor.
- **Ecclesiological motivation**. All Christian members of the Church should, as a matter of faith and commitment, seek the transformation of society.

Key question

Why should Christians side with the poor?

Key quote

'All need to make the option for the poor: the rich with generosity and no regard for reward, the poor for their fellow poor and those who are even poorer than they.'

LEONARDO AND CLODOVIS BOFF, *INTRODUCING LIBERATION THEOLOGY*, 46

2 First and second act praxis

a) First act praxis

Key thought

The main areas of classical theology are set out in Part 1 of this book.

A preferential option for the poor is, in the first instance, not a *theological* endeavour but a *human* project. Liberation theologians do not reject the classical concerns of theology such as the existence of God, God's action in the world, knowledge of God, the nature of Christ and so on but consider that the dangers with this kind of theology is that it can become too otherworldly and detached from the messy, complicated process of living as human beings.

Key word

Pre-theological in liberation theology is the stage prior to any theological reflection when acting in solidarity with the poor is more important than official Christian teaching.

First act praxis is **pre-theological**; it does not begin with doctrine or the official teaching of the Church, but with the simple realisation that injustice and human exploitation are wrong. First act praxis begins when Christians act in solidarity with the poor, live alongside them as humans and learn which conditions have led to this situation. So, as Leonardo and Clodovis Boff describe in their book *Introducing Liberation Theology* (1986), a preferential option begins with a 'preliminary stage' where church workers and theologians might act through:

- **restricted visits** to the base communities/pastoral work
- **alternating** scholarly work and pastoral visits
- **living permanently** by living alongside the poor.

Key quote

'Being a theologian is not skilfully using methods but of being imbued with the theological spirit.'
LEONDARDO AND CLODOVIS BOFF, *INTRODUCING LIBERATION THEOLOGY*, 23

Although this is not a theological stage, it would be wrong to say that this lacks theological *motivation*. Those who opt for the poor do so because they already have a theological view of the world which recognises that God in Christ chose to be part of the human condition and to bring joy out of suffering.

The much-quoted passage from the New Testament is Jesus' parable of the Sheep and the Goats (Matthew 25:35–46) when he praises those who have acted spontaneously from faith by feeding the hungry and giving water to the thirsty.

b) Second act praxis: the mediations

Cross-reference

Gustavo Gutiérrez, *A Theology of Liberation*, 55.

Although second act praxis is the most theoretical aspect of liberation theology, its origins are practical and pastoral. Gutiérrez comments that theology 'rises at sundown'; it is a process of critical reflection after pastoral action has been carried out. He goes on to say, 'Theology does not produce pastoral activity; rather it reflects on it'. In the 1950s parish priests were already developing their own strategies to provide practical care for the poor. The pastoral process of 'seeing, judging and acting' is the foundation of the three mediations. A **mediation** is a distinctive phase of theological praxis; the mediations form the heart of liberation theology.

Key word

Mediation is a distinctive phase of theological praxis.

i) Socio-analytical mediation: seeing

Liberation theologians argue that all theology is contextual. Theologians have always combined Christian and non-Christian ideas to address their audiences: Augustine was indebted to Platonism and Aquinas to Aristotle. In the case of liberation theology, in a situation of gross economic and social injustice, Christian theologians require the services of sociologists and economists to analyse the situation in order to ask the question, 'Why is there oppression and what are its causes?'

Cross-reference

Leonardo and Clodovis Boff, *Introducing Liberation Theology*, 25.

At the time when the liberation theologians of Latin America were developing their theology, a scepticism of capitalism and development naturally led to a suspicion of any economic system which supported the free markets of northern Europe and the USA. These systems were seen to be the fundamental causes of poverty and injustice. The first mediation, therefore, favours a socialist or even Marxist critique of the economic situation. Some theologians have explicitly used Marx, while others have used his language but not necessarily all his thinking. For the Boffs, Marxism has provided a useful 'instrument' or 'companion along the way' for analysing the causes of poverty and injustice.

For example, using a Marxist way of thinking, the Boffs suggest there are three explanations for poverty:

- **Empirical poverty** is the result of vice, laziness and ignorance. The Boffs reject this analysis of poverty because the solution to this way of thinking of poverty is usually through aid or charity and that simply treats the poor as objects of pity not persons.
- **Functional poverty** is the result of backwardness. This view is typical of a liberal capitalist who tackles poverty through loans and progress (or development). Even though this view recognises *collective* responsibility to solve the problem, in a capitalist world it is a primary cause of dependency – it fails to deal with the root of the problem.
- **Dialectical poverty** is the result of oppression. Marxist or socialist analysis realises that poverty is the result of exploitation, exclusion from the process of production and priority of capital over labour. Tackling poverty requires revolutionary and radical confrontation with oppressive conditions.

The socio–analytic mediation also broadens the notion of the poor to refer to all those who are **infrastructurally oppressed**. Seeing poverty as oppression focuses on a class of people who are poor and marginalised because of deep–seated social prejudices and discrimination such as racism, ageism and sexism. The **superstructurally oppressed** are not, in the first instance, of primary concern to the liberation theologian. For example, the rich black football star who suffers racial prejudice within his profession is not in the same position as the poor indigenous Latin American whom society consciously or unconsciously marginalises in every way.

ii) Hermeneutical mediation: judging

Once they have understood the real situation of the oppressed, the theologians have to ask: What has the Word of God to say about this? This is the second stage in the theological construction – a specific stage, in which discourse is formally *theological.*

(Leonardo and Clodovis Boff, *Introducing Liberation Theology*, 32)

Key words

Infrastructural oppression arises from the basic organisational beliefs of society which are biased against certain types of people because of their race, class, age or sexuality.

Superstructural oppression occurs in the organisation of institutions arising from the basic (or infrastructural) beliefs of society.

Key question

Why is hermeneutical mediation necessary if a person is already motivated by being a Christian?

Key quote

'Liberative hermeneutics reads the Bible as a book of life, not as a book of strange stories … Liberative hermeneutics seeks to discover and activate the *transforming* energy of the biblical texts … rereading of the Bible stresses its historical context in order to construct an appropriate – not literal – translation into our own historical context.'

LEONARDO AND CLODOVIS BOFF, *INTRODUCING LIBERATION THEOLOGY*, 34

Cross-reference

Read Chapter 8 for a more detailed analysis of liberation and biblical hermeneutics.

Cross-reference

See page 125 for an explanation of conscientisation.

Key question

Should theologians use Marx even though he is an atheist?

The hermeneutical stage is the most explicitly theological moment in the process. Having analysed the socio-economic reasons for oppression in a particular situation, the task is then to reflect on it from a specifically Christian perspective. As the Boffs put it 'What has the Word of God to say about this?' The primary source for the Word of God is the Bible. Liberation theologians are not fundamentalists but nor are they sceptics; the Bible offers insights from many moments in history that can be reinterpreted according to the present historical situation.

Reading the Bible as a dialectical process between the Bible and the experience of the poor produces new interpretations of the biblical texts. Allowing the poor to interpret the Bible also enables them to become aware of its challenges and their own spiritual and political situation. So, as the Boffs comment, the primary aim of the liberation theologian is to favour *application* rather than *explanation* of texts; the role of the professional theologian is therefore to provide scholarly assistance but not ready-made answers.

The favoured texts of the Bible are: Exodus, the Prophets, Gospels, Acts and Revelation. Some also use the books of Maccabees and the wisdom literature of the Old Testament such as Proverbs, Job and Wisdom.

iii) Practical mediation: acting

Liberation theology is far from being an inconclusive theology. It starts from action and leads to action … And so, yes: liberation theology leads to action: action for justice, the work of love, conversion, renewal of the church, transformation of society.

(Leonardo and Clodovis Boff, *Introducing Liberation Theology*, 39)

The first moment of action comes when siding with the poor in solidarity. Having analysed the situation socio-economically and become **conscientised** through theological reflection, we are obliged, in the final state, to act. Action requires dialectical change not just reform. As their own subjects, the poor are empowered as persons (and not non-persons) to bring about economic and material liberation from oppression.

3 Liberation theology's use of Marx

Few liberation theologians would disagree with Marx's famous saying:

Philosophers have only interpreted the world in various ways; the point is to change it.

(Karl Marx, *Theses on Feuerbach XI*, in David McLellan, *Karl Marx: Selected Writings*, 173)

The debate is to what extent liberation theologians have used Marx (or Marxism) in the socio-analytic mediation as a means of analysing the conditions which have caused structural poverty and oppression. Whilst some such as Leonardo Boff, Clodovis Boff, José Miguez Bonino, Juan Luis Segunda and José Miranda have all explicitly used Marx as a tool for analysis, others, such as Gustavo Gutiérrez and Jon Sobrino, are far more guarded. Over time, Gutiérrez made it clear that Marx and Christianity could *not* be combined, even if they share some common ground:

> *At no time either explicitly or implicitly have I suggested a dialogue with Marxism with a view to a possible 'synthesis' or to accepting one aspect while leaving others aside.*

(Gustavo Gutiérrez, The Truth Shall Make You Free, 63)

Even so, in their critique of capitalism and the need to find a social science which has the power to analyse structural oppression, Marx and Marxism provide a powerful starting point for liberation theologians.

a) The influence of Marx

Cross-reference

Read pages 99–102 on Marx's central ideas.

Liberation theologians and Marxists agree that even though human life is intrinsically good, it is also human nature which has been the source of human misery. Yet the two differ greatly in their analysis of why this is the case: traditional Christianity has explained the paradox in terms of sin, while Marxist analysis focuses on material and historical conditions. But for liberation theologians the two are not mutually exclusive; indeed, for many liberation theologians Marx forces Christianity back to the material world of humans which is where theology should always begin.

Cross-reference

Read pages 8–10 on Augustine on sin.

Almost no liberation theologian would argue that Marx is essential for Christianity, for if that were the case then it would suggest that Christianity has been defective until Marx. However, after that theologians have varied enormously in the way they have used Marx. There are those who make explicit use of Marx and those who use him only to analyse the economic situation. More radically there are those who find his language and general concepts useful for a rethinking of many basic Christian ideas. In other words, Marx is a useful *instrument* for doing theology; as the Boffs comment, Marx is a useful 'companion' along the way, but there is only one teacher, Jesus Christ.

Key quote

'Contemporary theology does in fact find itself in direct and fruitful confrontation with Marxism.'

GUSTAVO GUTIÉRREZ, *A THEOLOGY OF LIBERATION*, 53

i) Historical materialism and reversal

Cross-reference

See page 101 on historical materialisation.

It is Marx's central idea of **historical materialism** which establishes liberation theology as a contextual theology by reversing traditional top-down with a bottom-up theology. As Marx argued, once we see how the material base is created (the infrastructure), then we

Key quote

'Therefore, it uses Marxism purely as an *instrument*. It does not venerate it as it venerates the gospel. And it feels no obligation to account to social scientists for any use it may make – correct or otherwise – of Marxist terminology and ideas, though it does feel obliged to account to the poor … Marx (like any other Marxist) can be a companion on the way (see *Puebla* paragraph 544), but he can never be *the* guide, because 'You have only one teacher, the Christ (Matthew 23:10).'

LEONARDO AND CLODOVIS BOFF,
INTRODUCING LIBERATION THEOLOGY, 28

Key quote

'Blessed are the meek, for they shall inherit the earth' (Matthew 5:5); 'The Kingdom of God is not coming with signs to be observed; nor will they say "Lo, here it is!" or "There!" for behold, the kingdom of God is in the midst of you.'

(LUKE 17:20–21)

Key people

José Porfirio Miranda (1924–2001) was born in Mexico, ordained into the Catholic priesthood, studied economics at Munich university and theology in Frankfurt and later in Rome. He was a professor of economics, philosophy, law and biblical exegesis at various universities in Latin America. His books include *Marx and the Bible* (1971) and *Communism in the Bible* (1981).

Cross-reference

Read page 102 on Marx and private property.

can see how the human superstructures are formed and then finally we are in a position to understand how to distinguish reality from projected human ideas.

Many liberation theologians also claim to have materialist theology and to embrace reversal. A major reversal is that theology should begin with the condition of the poor as the underside of history rather than abstract doctrines such as the nature of God. A bottom up theology which begins with actual human experience of suffering, alienation, joy and hope reveals the reality of the Kingdom of God. Seen in this way, Christian historical materialism points to many unexpected reversals – the last will be first; the Kingdom of God is a transformation of material society, not heaven; the meek not the powerful will inherit the earth.

ii) Critique of capitalism

Marxist analysis is most noticeable in the base community when applying the first mediation to a given situation and society's structures in general. Through Marx the theologian is able to discern: who are the oppressors; who owns the means of production; the ideologies which have reinforced the situation of exploitation. In essence, all these criticisms can be traced to the inherent unfairness of capitalism which always creates an exploited underclass (or proletariat).

Liberation theologians often present Marx in the same prophetic tradition (stretching from the eighth century BC prophets to Jesus) which attacked the social and economic conditions that exploited the poor. Liberation theologians share the basic Marxist idea that as humans are designed to work and be productive (Genesis 1:28), then failing to own the means of production is a major cause of alienation and exploitation.

José Porfirio Miranda begins his biblical hermeneutics by using the Marxist suspicion of private ownership of the means of production. For Marx, private ownership of land is the root cause of injustice because it creates in the mind of the owner the idea that he also owns the lives because they are also *objects*. This illustrates Marx's principle set out in the first *Theses on Feuerbach* that alienation and oppression are caused when humans falsely objectify the world and then treat it as their own possession.

This important Marxist insight, Miranda argues, brings our attention to the same idea which is at the very heart of the Bible. The idea has become buried through centuries of theology and it has taken Marx to uncover it, but the point is that the biblical view is *older* and richer and more radical than Marx. It is a constant refrain of the prophets to be wary of objectifying the material world by creating God in our own image. Miranda's argument begins with Marx but moves on.

Key quote

'The chief defect of all hitherto existing materialism (that of Feuerbach included) is that the thing, reality, sensuousness, is conceived only in the form of the object or of contemplation, but not as sensuous human activity, practice, not subjectivity.'

KARL MARX, *THESES ON FEUERBACH*, I

Key quote

'You shall not make for yourself a graven image, or any likeness of anything that is in heaven above, or that is in the earth beneath … you shall not bow down to them or serve them.'

EXODUS 20:4–5

Key quote

'The God who does not allow himself to be objectified, because only in the immediate command of conscience is he God, clearly specifies that he is knowable exclusively in the cry of the poor and the weak who seek justice.'

JOSÉ MIRANDA, *MARX AND THE BIBLE*, 48

- **Human nature**. Marxism has underestimated the insight of the biblical writers that capitalism since the start of human civilization is due to the subjective *human* condition – not just external causes. In describing the fallen aspect of human nature the Bible gives a much fuller reason than Marx as to why humans oppress and exploit others.
- **Idolatry**. The second of the Ten Commandments warns against idolatry – that is treating God as a thing or object. The abandonment of this commandment has been the fundamental reason why capitalism and materialism (as exemplified in private ownership) have become idols to be worshipped especially in industrialised Europe. To counter this, theology needs to recover the **negative theological** view that as God is wholly different from the material world he cannot be known and must not be objectified – which is what idealism has done.
- **Knowledge of God** The Bible therefore offers a middle way between materialism and idealism. Marx may have pointed in this direction but it is the biblical writers who understood it better. Although God cannot be known in himself, he can be known where good is done. The constant call of the prophets is that knowledge of God comes through establishing justice which is always out of love for one's neighbour. Conversely, as St Paul argues, God's judgement is known through conscience where there is injustice.

iii) Praxis and alienation

Marxist suspicion of all forms of ideologies as a source of false consciousness is directed especially towards institutions. As institutions tend to objectify ideas, they subordinate and alienate humans from the real processes of production. In a continent where various powerful institutions have justified their existence and alienated the poor, the liberation theologians have found in Marx a powerful tool to criticise the Church as an institution which has traditionally given the means of religious production to priests and bishops and kept the poor and oppressed at arm's length.

Using Marx as a critique of the Church, was a primary reason why, in 1984, the Vatican condemned Leonardo Boff in particular for his uncritical use of Marxism and silenced him from writing for a year. In his *Church: Charism and Power*, Boff had argued that:

- The hierarchy of the Church is not how the Church was first envisaged, but the one created when it became the official religion of the Roman empire.
- If the Church had taken seriously the biblical teaching of the prophets it would not have developed its ruling class model hierarchy.

Cross-reference

Read page 144 on Boff and base communities.

Key question

Does the use of violent revolution simply cause more oppression?

Key people

Camilo Torres (1929–66) is perhaps the most famous Colombian Catholic priest who joined the communist guerrilla group ELN in their active resistance against the government. Although by the time he came to fight he was no longer a priest, he still regarded his actions in a priestly way. As he said, 'I took off my cassock to be more truly a priest.' He was killed in his first combat experience, when the ELN ambushed a Colombian Military patrol.

Key people

Leonardo Boff (left) was born in Brazil and was ordained a Catholic priest in 1964. He studied at Oxford, Louvain, Würzburg and Munich and was professor of systematic theology at the Institute for Philosophy and Theology at Petropolis, Brazil. His book *Church: Charism and Power* (1981) was the primary reason why Cardinal Ratzinger summoned him to Rome in 1984 and imposed a year's silence on him. In 1992 he left his priestly ministry and Franciscan religious order. More recently he has focused his interests on ecological matters and in 2001 was awarded the alternative Nobel prize in Stockholm. His many publications include *Jesus Christ Liberator* (1972) and *Ecology: Cry of the Earth, Cry of the Poor* (1995).

Boff's analysis of the Church is a reminder of Marx's eleventh *Thesis on Feuerbach* that praxis is the first act and should precede theology. In practice, as in Marx, the relationship between orthopraxis and orthodoxy is dialectical – ideas give rise to action as much as actions develop the ideas themselves. The **base communities** most closely resemble the kind of church where praxis is free from hierarchy.

iv) Revolution and solidarity

In the Marxist material view of history, circumstances evolve to provide moments with those who can read the signs of the time know they should seize and force history to move on to the next stage. Revolution is necessary because there will always be those reactionary forces who resist change and who therefore impede progress. In Marx, revolution does not begin with the oppressed but those 'prophets' or philosophers who can interpret the world and by acting in solidarity with the oppressed organise change. Marx's notion was that the only way of changing the deep-seated situation of exploitation was through 'despotic inroads' (i.e. violence) if other methods failed. Only then, as Hegel put it, can the master–slave relationship be reversed and a new stage in history achieved.

The 'preferential option for the poor' is therefore a Marxist idea insofar as it is the rich, or those who own the means of production, who are in a position to side with the power and force the Church and society in a 'class struggle' to the next stage. Siding with the poor is another example of reversal, whereby those who are rich are prepared to give up one way of life for the gospel. In Jesus' teaching, the kingdom of God is not an abstract utopia but, as Boff calls it, a 'topia' – a transformation of actual existing social conditions.

Liberation theologians have certainly been persuaded that the capitalist status quo will not change merely by tinkering with the system, but most are reluctant to use 'despotic inroads' to bring about change. The exception is the iconic figure of **Camilo Torres**. Torres argued that words without action are empty and if this meant revolution, even violence, then it was a sign of faith to be involved. As a priest, his decision to join the guerrillas was instantly shocking, daring and inspirational.

Key quote

'The duty of every Catholic is to be a revolutionary. The duty of every revolutionary is to make the revolution.'

CAMILLO TORRES

Cross-reference

Philip Berryman, *Introduction to Liberation Theology*, 21.

Key people

Joseph Ratzinger (1927–) was born in 1927 and was professor of theology at various German universities. In 1981 he was appointed Prefect of the Congregation for the Doctrine of Faith (whose role is to protect the Catholic faith against errors in teaching and doctrine). In 2005 he was elected Pope and took the name Benedict XVI.

Key question

Could liberation theology operate without the use of a Marxist analysis of society?

Key quote

'Taken by itself, the desire for liberation finds a strong and fraternal echo in the heart and spirit of Christians.'

INSTRUCTION ON CERTAIN ASPECTS OF THE 'THEOLOGY OF LIBERATION' III

Key word

Reductionism means to explain something in more basic, usually physical, terms. Reductionist arguments are often in the form 'X is nothing but …'.

If the Marxist problem is closely analysed, I believe that an affirmative answer is possible. Dialectical and historical materialism in the mental process of Marxists appears to be so useful for revolutionary methods that it can be considered quite objective … with firm decision and without timidity, we should enter into this collaboration …

(Camilo Torres, speech in 1964)

But as Berryman comments, 'By no means did all, or even a majority, of priests and sisters become radicalised'. Of Argentina's 5,000 priests at that time, only 800 might have been considered radical.

b) Liberation theology is too Marxist

In 1984 the Congregation of the Doctrine of the Faith issued its *Instruction on Certain Aspects of the 'Theology of Liberation'* (or *Libertatis Nuntius*) chaired by Cardinal **Joseph Ratzinger**. The core of the *Instruction* was an outspoken critique of Marxism and, by extension, liberation theology. At first the *Instruction* is less hostile and speaks of 'theologies of liberation'. It is sympathetic to those theologies which use the term 'liberation' to mean that justice should prevail in defence of the weak but it is extremely critical of other radical liberation theologies which have made 'insufficiently critical' use of Marxism. This was probably an indirect reference to Leonardo Boff and Gustavo Gutiérrez, who had both been reprimanded by Ratzinger.

As stated in its introduction the aim of the letter was:

to draw the attention of pastors, theologians, and all the faithful to the deviations, and risks of deviation, damaging to the faith and to Christian living, that are brought about by certain forms of liberation theology which use, in an insufficiently critical manner, concepts borrowed from various currents of Marxist thought.

(*Instruction on Certain Aspects of the 'Theology of Liberation'*, Congregation of the Doctrine of the Faith)

Although positive about the place of liberation in Christian theology, the *Instruction* was critical of the way the liberation theologians had limited its usage in the following ways:

- Liberation is at the heart of Christian theology, but it is a liberation from 'the radical slavery of sin'.
- There are many kinds of freedom; liberation theologians tend to stress only the political kind.
- Liberation theology has placed too much emphasis on temporal or political liberation – it fails to look sufficiently at human sin.
- Liberation theology is **reductionist**. By interpreting sin in terms of social structures, it equates salvation with praxis and revolution, not God's grace.

- Liberation theology makes truth exclusive only to those who practise a certain kind of praxis.
- The Kingdom of God is mistakenly taken to mean *human* struggle, whereas redemption is only through God's grace.

The recognition of injustice is accompanied by a pathos which borrows its language from Marxism, wrongly presented as though it were scientific language.

Instruction on Certain Aspects of the 'Theology of Liberation', VII.12

c) Liberation theology is not Marxist enough

My criticism has been that it is not Marxist enough. Or rather liberation theology, far from using Marx's philosophy 'in an insufficiently critical manner', has not cared deeply enough or dared to apply it in a sufficiently careful and comprehensive manner … in fact resistance to Marx is the cause of its failure.

(Alistair Kee, *Marx and the Failure of Liberation Theology*, 211, 257)

Key people

Alistair Kee (1937–2011) was, until his retirement in 2002, professor of religious studies at Edinburgh University. His many publications include *Marx and the Failure of Liberation Theology* (1990) and *The Rise and Demise of Black Theology* (2006).

Alistair Kee's thesis is that the Vatican's criticism that liberation theologians have used Marx too much but in an insufficiently critical manner is almost entirely wrong. In his view the problem is that even those theologians who have used Marx critically, have done so without ever really tackling Marx's fundamental premise that the criticism of religion as a false objectification of reality is equally a criticism of *all* other ideologies. In other words, beliefs or ideologies about the world which appear to be universal, fixed and objective are really no more than human projections produced under particular historical circumstances. Kee's point is that liberation theologians cannot just select the bits of Marx they find helpful and avoid the basic premise on which they are built.

At first Kee's argument appears contradictory. Why would liberation theologians embrace Marx's atheism which considers that religion is the primary source of alienation and false consciousness? The answer is that despite his atheism, Marx's historical materialism relies on a strongly spiritual sense in which each historical stage gives way to the next driven by an *idea* of a better world. Marx may have tried to justify this in purely biological or material terms, but evolutionary biology does not support his claim; this is because his historical materialism is in fact an ideology. So, in fact, Marx and Christianity are not so very different; the difference is that Christianity accepts that it is an ideology: history is not just determined by material forces but also by God.

However, the value of Marx's historical materialism, which Christian theology should take much more seriously, is that every new historical stage requires a radical re-assessment of its beliefs

Key word

Secular is concerned only with non-religious matters.

and ideas. If Christianity is to survive as a radical force in the next stage, its task now is to consider how it is to tackle the mindset of the present age of **secular** capitalism. Sadly, Kee concludes, liberation theology is far too conservative and traditional to meet this challenge; that is why it has failed.

i) Failure to accept the basic premises of historical materialism

A fundamental premise of historical materialism which Marx developed from Hegel is that there is a logical sequence or 'supersession' of historical stages which cannot be skipped. Marx argued that socialism can only be achieved once society has secured a sound capitalist base. Therefore, the failure of liberation theology has been to reject northern European capitalism by skipping from peasant feudalism to socialism. Although liberation theologians may be right that capitalism comes at a moral and spiritual cost, by accepting the premise of historical materialism, they are denying the poor the means of economic growth which capitalism offers and from which socialism will emerge.

ii) Failure to apply reversal fully

The heart of Kee's criticism is that liberation theologians have in practice failed to allow the poor and peasants to apply Marx's reversal to religion itself. Even those theologians who profess to use Marx do not allow the poor to read Marx because he is an atheist. In other words, they just have to accept that these theologians know best. In reality then, theologians may write radical theology, but in practice they perpetuate the kind of superstitious false-consciousness which Marx thought made religion backward and dangerous.

> *The peasants might not understand the basic philosophical or epistemological error, but they can be assured by someone who does that when it comes to religion Marx is suddenly an incompetent fool who knows nothing about the subject. How comforting it is to have a consultant on such matters!*

(Alistair Kee, *Marx and the Failure of Liberation Theology*, 262)

iii) Failure to tackle secularism

Key quote

'Liberation theology has failed the academic community, but more importantly it has failed the very people to whom it is committed.'

ALISTAIR KEE, *MARX AND THE FAILURE OF LIBERATION THEOLOGY*, 266

By being selective and omitting Marx's principle of reversal of religion, liberation theology has failed intellectually. It is not possible to use Marx only as an instrument for socio-economic analysis and omit his doctrine of reversal. By doing so, liberation theology has lost the opportunity to tackle the greatest challenge to human existence in a capitalist and liberal age: secularism. Although Marx personally professed to be an atheist, this does not mean that his notion of reversal necessarily rules out human spirituality. A more radical progression, even in Marxist terms, would be to suggest that in the dialectic historical progress the next stage after secular capitalism would be the reversal of capitalism with socialism and secularism with spirit.

Summary diagram

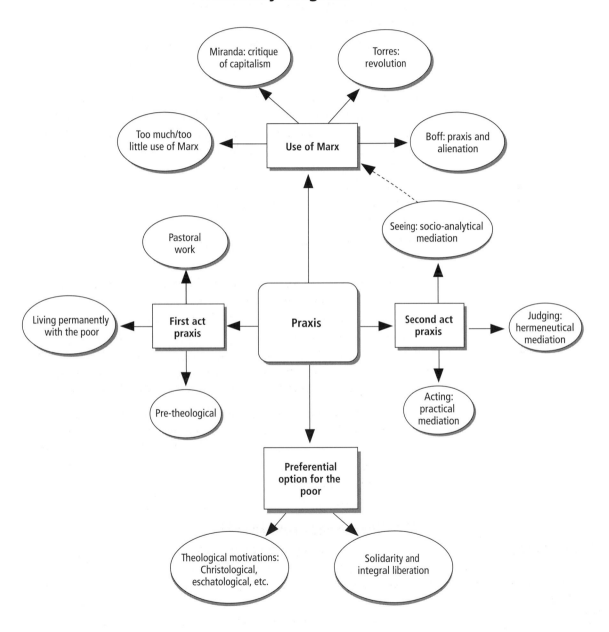

Study guide

By the end of this chapter you should be able to explain what is meant by first and second praxis, the use of Marx by various liberation theologians as an instrument for analysis and the debate which this has caused.

Essay questions

1a Explain the three mediations.

The essay might begin by explaining that the mediations form part of the process of praxis where people (theologians and the poor) begin by dealing with a situation of injustice and exploitation and end in action. At the pre-theological stage all that is required is solidarity. At the second stage (second act) the first mediation is to analyse the causes of injustice and poverty (the socio–analytic mediation) especially infra-structural conditions; the second mediation is the most consciously Christian stage of reflection which asks how the prophets, Jesus' teaching or the early Christians would deal with this issue (hermeneutical mediation); the final practical mediation is the one of action as modified by the previous two mediations.

1b 'The mediations don't help the poor, they just help theologians.' Discuss.

It might be agreed that, despite allowing the poor to drive praxis, the mediations are intellectual processes which are governed by theologians. Reference might be made to Kee's argument that the people are more radical than theologians allow, yet they are not allowed to read Marx or implement the revolutionary reversals suggested by Jesus' teaching on the Kingdom.

On the other hand, the mediations are a process which enable the poor to become their own subjects. The theologian is necessary to guide and provide education where necessary, but the meditations successfully place the process of theological praxis back into the hands of the people. The base community movement is evidence for this.

Further essay questions

2 a   Explain how liberation theologians argue that theology is the motivation to side with the poor.

2 b   'Marx, not theology, is the only way to bring justice to the oppressed.' Discuss.

3 Assess the view that the basic problem with liberation theology is that it has failed to use Marx sufficiently.

4 'The hermeneutical mediation is unnecessary.' Discuss.

Revision checklist

Can you give brief definitions of:

- *iglesia popular*
- preferential option for the poor
- pre-theological stage
- dialectical poverty.

Can you explain:

- why some consider liberation theologians too reductionist
- what is meant by infrastructural oppression
- what is meant by top-down and bottom-up theology.

Can you give arguments for and against:

- the use of violent revolution in liberation
- capitalism as idolatry
- the use of Marx by theologians.

Chapter checklist

This chapter considers how the Bible is interpreted by liberation theologians and its role in educating the poor to become socially and spiritually independent human beings. The key biblical themes are analysed including: Exodus, justice, the new Jerusalem and Jesus the liberator.

1 Hermeneutical circle

Key thought

Read page 82 on the hermeneutical circle. The general meaning of the hermeneutical circle is to read a text in its widest possible context, whereas the liberation theologians tend to focus on the relationship of the text to the situation of the poor.

Although liberation theology has grown out of a specific set of historical circumstances and developed as church leaders (priests, nuns, pastoral workers) have worked with the poor, the role of the theologian has been to reflect at a deeper scholarly level and to produce books to assist reflection. This kind of theoretical liberation theology is not intended to be read by the poor but rather to guide and inform church leaders in their local communities, especially when helping the poor and oppressed read the Bible – the core component of the second mediation.

Liberation theology has developed its own distinctive **hermeneutical circle** as a dialogue between the Bible as the Word of God and people living in a particular moment of history. The hermeneutic circle is the means by which:

- **theologians** reflect on the Bible from 'the underside of history' using the experience of the poor
- the **poor** learn to interpret the Bible themselves
- the **Church** community becomes more democratic and revolutionary.

a) Hermeneutics of suspicion

Cross-reference

Read pages 88–89 on Paul Ricoeur.

For many liberation theologians **Paul Ricoeur**'s idea of the hermeneutic of suspicion has provided a very important reminder that when reading a text such as the Bible, the poor as much as the professional theologian need to be aware that any interpretation is bound to be biased towards a certain official view. Ricoeur drew attention to the 'masters of suspicion' as he called them: Marx, Nietzsche and Freud. Marx questioned the political motivation by asking what economic advantage a person or institution gains by maintaining a particular belief; Nietzsche questioned the place of ideologies which diminish human authentic existence; Freud looked for unconscious repressed motives. By applying any of these suspicions when reading the Bible, the hope is that new fresh interpretations will emerge.

Liberation theologians also use suspicion to ensure that theology isn't merely repeating the official teaching of the Church and equally as a critical means of self-reflection to ensure that liberation theology itself avoids becoming dogmatic and alienating the very people it is intended to address.

i) Suspicion of what is not said

Freudian-type suspicion can be used to question what is *not* said in the text. For example, in Latin American Mary is a very popular figure, yet the biblical references to her are very few.

> *The written text must always make the reader wonder and ask about what was not written, what was lost, and what was left on purpose. A written text is always selective. The scriptural texts that speak of Mary are very few, but from these texts and different popular traditions, each historical epoch constructs an image of Mary and her past and present historical activity.*
>
> (Ivone Gebara and María Clara Bingemer, 'Mary', in Sobrino and Ellacuría, *Systematic Theology*, 167)

By asking what has been left out of the biblical text we are equally asking how and why the figure of Mary has developed as it has. By using the hermeneutic of suspicion, the figure Mary acts as a reminder that liberation applies specifically to women from the very beginning of Christian history to the present. Gebara and Bingemer call this a 'subversive memory' – even a 'dangerous memory' – because when she is removed from her usual chocolate-box depiction, Mary is a single working mother, an active member of the poor, whose message, like that of Jesus, looked for a radical reversal of social structures. Finally, Gebara and Bingemer use suspicion to question the Church's emphasis on Mary's virginity as a moralising point about ideal sexual purity. In the first century a virgin was a sign not of virtue but of failure, when society depended on having children – because 'survival is in children'. Mary's virgin body is a powerful sign of human failure and of being open to God's grace to transform and to deliver hope out of failure.

Cross-reference

See pages 130–131 on Mary's Song.

Cross-reference

Read pages 113–114 on Miranda and Marx.

Cross-reference

José Miranda, *Marx and the Bible*, page xi.

Cross-reference

Read Acts 4:32–35 and page 140 on the first Christian communities.

ii) Suspicion of anti-communism

José Miranda uses Marxist suspicion to re-read scripture independently from existing 'infrastructures' (church, class, European academic traditions, secularism, etc.) so that a 'theological reality' can emerge. Marx provides other insights, notably that in a capitalist system it is not only the poor who are alienated but also the oppressors. The hermeneutic of suspicion doesn't just put blame onto oppressors because 'injustice is more a work of the social machinery, of the system of civilization and culture, than it is of people's intentions'. Miranda goes further: his suspicion is aimed at those Christians who claim to be anti-communist, which he says 'without doubt constitutes the greatest scandal of our century'. He shows how much the Church is able to absorb current Marxist critique of society, because, in fact, the Bible already contains these ideas but in a more radical form – he considers how the early Christians practised a form of communism well before Marx developed the idea. Therefore, to reject the use of Marx as Ratzinger did in the *Instruction*, is in effect, to deny the essence of Christianity.

b) The poor as subjects

Whereas for Schleiermacher the hermeneutical circle was almost purely an academic exercise, for the liberation theologians the circle doesn't just include knowing a Bible passage in its historical context but also in the context of the poor's experience of the world. More in line with Ricoeur, authorship of the text is less important than the way reader and text relate to each other. The circle can be literal: the poor meet with a theologian (priest, nun, pastoral worker) who perhaps selects a passage for consideration and guides discussion through open-ended questions and provides necessary background information. But it is the poor who offer their perspective as 'readers' and in conversation with the text come to find their own interpretation. The dialogue is itself liberative; the poor are not being told what to think but to discover what it means to be their own subjects by thinking and doing theology themselves.

The circle might be seen this way:

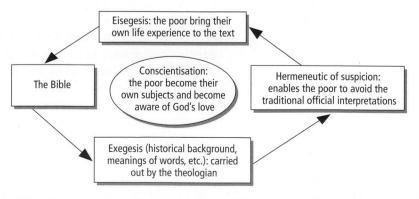

Cross-reference

Gustavo Gutiérrez, *Power of the Poor*, 45.

This is why, for Gutiérrez, becoming a human subject through the hermeneutical circle is ultimately *spiritual* as it requires an inward understanding of what it means to 'proclaim God as father in a world that is inhumane'. The circle moves from humans to God, from God to humans; from history to faith, from faith to history; from love of one's neighbours to the love of God the Father and from love of God the Father to love of neighbours; from human justice to God's holiness, and from God's holiness to human justice.

2 Conscientisation

Key word

Conscientisation is the process by which the oppressed come to see themselves as subjects not objects, human persons not slaves.

Key people

Paulo Freire (1921–97) was born in Brazil and lived through the Great Depression (1929). His experience led him to work against poverty. After reading philosophy at university, he worked on methods of teaching the illiterate poor. He was a member of the Christian Democratic Agrarian Reform Movement from 1964 and in 1968 produced his most influential book *Pedagogy of the Oppressed* which was banned in Brazil until 1974.

The process by which the poor become their own subject is called **conscientisation**. It is a process whereby a person learns to discard his false-consciousness, becomes fully in control of his own destiny and changes it. In Hegelian terms he or she realises that they are no longer defined as a 'slave' or object in the master–slave relationship, but are independent human subjects in their own right.

Education as conscientisation was developed by the Brazilian priest and educator **Paulo Freire**. Friere's methods have had wide acceptance. Working from a Marxist foundation Friere firmly held that the poor are not ignorant because they are poor but because they have been led to believe that only the priest or local official has authority because they are educated. Friere argued that education for the poor has to discard the northern European top-down view of school as imparting knowledge but to see education as a collaboration between learner and teacher. The process of learning is a dialogue; but the agenda is set by the learner and the teacher responds.

In his influential *Pedagogy of the Oppressed* Friere outlines four stages on how this process can be used in schools, but the method is true for any place where learning is active rather than passive:

- democratic dialogue in the classroom
- a curriculum situated in the learner's reality
- participatory teaching formats
- student-centred learning.

Conscientisation is a gradual process, not only for the learner but also for the teacher. As the learner gains in confidence and acquires critical consciousness, the teacher also has to constantly re-educate himself as circumstances change.

Friere's theory of education has a significant place in the biblical hermeneutic circle. As the poor learn to become their own interpreters, the theologian also has to relinquish his own position as expert and learn from the poor themselves.

3 Biblical liberative themes

As the poor and theologians read the Bible together, various themes and passages speak louder than others. As we have seen, the purpose of liberative hermeneutics is to allow these passages to inform and challenge the poor and theologians alike. Because the dialogue with the text is circular, no interpretation can ever be definitive, so the discussion of some of the key themes below is merely a summary of standard liberative responses to some popular texts.

a) Exodus paradigm

The 'exodus' theme is fundamental to many theologies of liberation because it describes the action of the poor (the Hebrew slaves) in solidarity against their oppressors (the Egyptians). The situation of exploitation has particular resonance with the poor of Latin America as the pharaoh represents the rich landowners of Latin America and the Hebrew slaves their own situation of economic exploitation.

i) God who hears

The God of Exodus is not the God of the philosophers such as Aquinas' Uncaused Causer, but a fully active God who 'intervenes in human history in the demand for justice' (Miranda). Nor is God the unknown impartial principle of the universe, but known and partial. God is partial because he sides with the poor against injustice; he is known because he is the personal God of Abraham, Isaac and Jacob. Finally, as the God who hears, God speaks through Moses as his prophet. It is Moses who enacts God's will and leads the people in revolution against their oppressors; this is one of the first slave revolts to be recorded in the ancient world.

ii) Land

The covenant promise to Abraham which is renewed with Moses is that the people will occupy their own land. Land is not an abstract spiritual notion but actual land where the Israelites will become their own masters and own the means of production. Ownership of land fulfils God's promise in Genesis 1:26 that humans will be his stewards of creation; the land not only provides physical sustenance but mental and spiritual satisfaction.

> And God blessed them, and God said to them, 'Be fruitful and multiply, and fill the earth and subdue it'.
>
> (Genesis 1:28)

iii) History

God's revelation is historical; it occurs at a particular time and place. Liberation theology is therefore always historical and particular, because transformative action is not abstract but deals with each

---

Key word

Paradigm is a conceptual model or framework of what something ought to be.

Cross-reference

Read page 26 on Aquinas.

Key quote

'Then the Lord said, "I have seen the affliction of my people who are in Egypt, and have heard their cry because of their taskmasters: I know their sufferings, and I have come down to deliver them out of the hand of the Egyptians, and to bring them up out of that land to a good and broad land, a land flowing with milk and honey".'

EXODUS 3:7–8

Key question

Can the Christian Church really justify private ownership of land?

Key quote

'Now the Lord said to Abram, "Go from your country and your kindred and your father's house to the land that I will show you. I will make you a great nation".'

GENESIS 12:1

Key quote

'Then the Lord said to Moses, "Go in to Pharaoh, and say to him, 'Thus says the Lord, the God of the Hebrews, "Let my people go, that they may serve me. For if you refuse to let them go and still hold them, behold the hand of the Lord will fall with a very severe plague upon your cattle"' … ".'

EXODUS 9:1–3

Key quote

'Woe to those who devise wickedness and work evil upon their beds! When morning dawns, they perform it, because it is in the power of their hand. They covet fields, and seize them; and houses, and take them away; they oppress a man and his house, a man and his inheritance.'

MICAH 2:2

Key quote

'Woe to you, scribes, Pharisees, hypocrites! For you tithe mint and dill and cumin, and have neglected the weightier matters of the law, justice and mercy and faith.'

JESUS IN *THE GOSPEL OF MATTHEW*, 23:23

situation as it arises. As Marx argues, historical change is dialectical, it often requires revolutionary action to overcome resistance – sometimes with force. In the Exodus story God calls Moses to revolutionary action against Pharaoh. In Latin American terms Pharaoh represents all those rich landowners, government officials even Church hierarchy who own the means of production. The church of the people is therefore called to be revolutionary, as Moses was.

b) Justice and judgement

In the eighth century BC, under political threat from Assyria, a new kind of prophet emerged. These prophets were individuals whose oracles were aimed at specific people (such as the king, rich landowners and priests). Unlike other prophets of the time they did not belong to an official group of court prophets, but their message nevertheless seemed to have reached the ears of the king. They were the conscience of Israel, speaking specifically about politics, land use, the market and religious practice and so on. In this oracle Amos mocks and condemns the rich who can't wait for the religious festivals to be over so they can continue to use their power to swindle the poor.

> *Hear this, you who trample upon the needy and bring the poor of the land to an end, saying 'When will the new moon be over, that we may sell grain? And the sabbath, that we may offer wheat for sale, that we may make the ephah small and the shekel great, and deal deceitfully with false balances, that we may buy the poor for silver and the needy for a pair of sandals, and sell the refuse of the wheat?'*

> (Amos 8:5–6)

Their message of judgement was not about God's final judgement but rather the political crisis which will occur if Israel does not reform her ways. The prophets regarded judgement to be as political as God's. These passages have deep resonance with the poor and their predicament in Latin America.

i) Justice

> *But let justice roll down like waters, and righteousness like an ever-flowing stream.*

> (Amos 5:25)

The heart of the message of the eighth-century prophets (Amos, Isaiah, Hosea and Micah) is justice. Justice for them is not only retribution (the punishment for wrongs) and distribution of goods to those who have a right to them, but a radically new idea that justice must also be a *relationship* based on love and mercy. Liberation theologians point out that there is a tendency for Christians to divide the Bible into the God of wrathful justice in the Old Testament and love in the New Testament. But this is wrong; there is no such dualism. The consistent picture in the Bible is that justice requires action as well as relationship. If this were not so, there would be no liberative praxis and no justice which seeks to reconcile oppressor and oppressed.

In summary, Jesus' teaching on righteousness continues the prophetic notion that true law is justice, compassion and goodness.

ii) Judgement of institutions

Just as Marx had warned against the dangers of institutions, so the prophets constantly spoke against the fossilisation of institutions which forget their primary function is to serve the people. Liberation theologians frequently regard these kinds of institutions as examples of contemporary **idolatry**. In Marx, idolatry is 'fetish', an unhealthy reliance on things. Idolatry is also a reversal and false-consciousness because it has turned an object into a subject with its own independent powers.

> *I hate, I despise your feasts, and I take no delight in your solemn assemblies. Even though you offer me your burnt offerings and cereal offerings, I will not accept them, and the peace offerings of your fatted beasts I will not look upon. Take away from me the noise of your songs; to the melody of your harps I will not listen.*

(Amos 5:21–23)

The root cause of modern idolatry is capitalism, but the Bible also makes a similar link. The prophets show how religion has been used as a way of covering up the exploitation of the poor. As Amos says, the rich appear to keep the religious festivals and offer sacrifices to God when their hearts are more set on stealing land from the poor and cheating them in the market place.

Jesus continues the prophetic judgement on religious fetishism. He cleanses the Temple accusing the priests, who ought to be its guardians, of turning it into a 'den of thieves'. He singles out the Pharisees for their obsession with rituals such as hand washing and food laws. In the same manner as the eighth-century prophets he says they are hypocrites because, in their obsession with rituals, they have forgotten the weightier matters of law: mercy, justice and love.

d) Eschatology and reversal

Eschatology is the discussion of the last things, the moment when God's kingdom will be complete and the righteous will be rewarded. It is often associated with heaven and the state after death. Whilst liberation theologians don't necessarily reject this idea, they are suspicious of those theologians who use heaven as a reason for

Key word

Idolatry in theological terms is the worship of material things treating them to be greater than God. In general terms it can also mean an unhealthy reliance on material things.

Cross-reference

Read Mark 7:1–23 on Jesus' criticisms of rituals.

Key quote

'Go learn what this means, "I desire mercy, and not sacrifice". For I came not to call the righteous, but sinners.'

JESUS IN *THE GOSPEL OF MATTHEW*, 9:13

encouraging the poor to bear their sufferings in this world as a 'vale of tears' to be rewarded in the next. This view is wrong for two reasons:

- First, it yet again sets up dualisms between this world and the next, the material world and the spiritual world.
- Second, when Jesus talks of God's kingdom he means it in the concrete sense of God's rule in the material world now. If this were not so, then his message of social and spiritual reversal, reform and justice would have little meaning.

In short, those who use a future **eschatology** to maintain the status quo have deliberately created a false consciousness, a false hope, which needs to be 'unveiled' and revealed as false.

Cross-reference

Read page 18 on eschatology.

i) Jesus' eschatological manifesto

'The Spirit of the Lord is upon me … to set at liberty those who are oppressed, to proclaim the acceptable year of the Lord.' He closed the book, and gave it back to the attendant, and sat down; and the eyes of all in the synagogue were fixed on him. And he began to say to them, 'Today this scripture has been fulfilled in your hearing'.

(Luke 4:18–21)

Jesus' first sermon at Nazareth (Luke 4:16–30) has often been called by liberation theologians 'Jesus' manifesto for the poor'. In reading from Isaiah 61:1–2, Jesus reaffirms the continuity of God's consistent revelation from Old to New Testaments. His gospel or good news is the same as the eighth-century BC prophets, which is 'to preach good news to the poor', 'proclaim release to the captives' and 'set at liberty those who are oppressed'. In other words, this is the 'preferential option for the poor' who occupy the 'underside of history'. As Jesus' ministry frequently illustrates, the poor are those termed 'sinners' under Jewish law, such as prostitutes, lepers, tax collectors.

Cross-reference

Read Leviticus 25 on the law of Jubilee.

One final element of Isaiah's prophecy which Jesus confirms is that he, too, will preach the 'acceptable year of the Lord'. The acceptable year in the Old Testament is the **law of Jubilee**, when every 50 years all interest on loans were forbidden, land returned to rightful owners and slaves set free. The jubilee was a time when Israel made a commitment to live fully according to the covenant.

Cross-reference

Read page 108 on the motivations.

What makes Jesus' sermon radical is his claim, 'Today this scripture has been fulfilled in your hearing'. In other words, Christians are to treat every year as a jubilee. The idea is repeated in the Lord's Prayer which calls on people 'to forgive our debtors' (Matthew 7:12) both in a literal and spiritual sense. Carrying out Jesus' manifesto is what the Boffs mean by 'the Christological motivation'.

Key word

The Sermon on the Mount (Matthew 5–7) is a collection of Jesus' teaching on the relationship of the Jewish written law (the Torah) and his own interpretation. He calls on his followers to 'be perfect as your heavenly Father is perfect' (5:48).

ii) Being poor in spirit

Jesus' **Sermon on the Mount** begins by setting out the qualities required of the Christian disciple. These beatitudes include the quality of being hungry and thirsty for righteousness. The saying which has grabbed the attention of the liberation theologians is the first:

> *Blessed are the poor in spirit, for theirs is the kingdom of heaven.*

(Matthew 5:3)

Key quote

'They are preferred by God and by Christ not because they are good, but because they are poor and wronged. God does not will the poverty they suffer.'

LEONARDO AND CLODOVIS BOFF,
INTRODUCING LIBERATION THEOLOGY, 48

There is a variant reading in Luke's gospel (Luke 6:20), where he omits 'in spirit'. It appears that Matthew has made Jesus' words less exclusive and made poverty an attitude not just a literal physical state. But liberation theologians consider that both versions mean the same thing – Matthew's version emphasises what is implied in Luke. In both cases the phrase is intended to shock. In the Judaism of Jesus' time, to be rich was a sign that one had been blessed by God. Jesus, therefore, deliberately *reverses* this common view. But why does it necessarily follow that being poor means one is blessed? The Boffs suggest two reasons:

- Those who are **socio-economically poor** and oppressed (for example due to their sexuality, ethnicity, race) have to learn that God sides with them in a special way as exemplified in the life and death of Christ.
- Those who are **evangelically poor** are those poor in spirit who put others first in the service of God and the establishment of the Kingdom of God on earth. Those who are not socio-economically poor but make themselves evangelically poor do so in solidarity with the poor. As Gutiérrez says, it is because the poor exist that those who are not oppressed learn to become spiritually poor.

It might seem that the preferred state is socio-economic poverty. But poverty caused by an unjust society is very different from voluntary poverty which is done in order to resist the capitalist materialism of northern Europe. The aim of the gospel is for all Christians, including the socio-economic poor, to become evangelically poor.

iii) Mary's Song of reversal

Key word

The Magnificat or Mary's Song (Luke 1:46–55) is a popular song in many Christian traditions.

In Catholic Latin America the figure of Mary the Mother of Christ is a popular and inspirational figure. Mary is especially important for poor women because she gives hope to those who, like her, are poor single parents and yet who are chosen by God. Her song, **The Magnificat**, recorded in Luke's Gospel, powerfully expresses how by choosing Mary to bear Jesus, God has sided with those of 'low degree' (Luke 1:52). The central theme of the Magnificat is reversal. God's mercy is on those who are open to him, but he will 'put down the mighty from their thrones' (Luke 1:52). In dramatic terms, especially in the Latin American context, the greatest social reversal will be when he sends away the rich empty handed and the hungry have an abundance of food. The Magnificat is:

a war song, a song of God's combat in human history, God's struggle to bring about a world of equal relationships, respect for every person, in whom the divinity dwells.

(Ivone Gebara and María Clara Bingemer, 'Mary', in Sobrino and Ellacuría, *Systematic Theology*, 169)

iv) Matthew 25

For I was hungry and you gave me food, I was thirsty and you gave me drink, I was a stranger and you welcomed me, I was naked and you clothed me, I was sick and you visited me, I was in prison and you came to me.

(Jesus in *Gospel of Matthew* 25:35–37)

The Parable of the Sheep and Goats (Matthew 25:31–46) is, along with Exodus, one of the most popular liberative biblical texts. Here are some of the points liberation theologians have made:

- It is significant that those who regard themselves as being religiously good (the 'righteous') but who are without praxis are those singled out for condemnation.
- Judgement occurs whenever anyone fails to act justly – Last Judgement does not occur only at the end of time.
- Justice is not a special kind of Christian justice but it restores those things which are owed to all humans.
- Praxis is based on a universal sense of human goodness. This idea is repeated four times so reinforces the basic idea that providing food, shelter, water, medicine and support for those in prison are common goods for all societies.
- The passage is not about charity (the obvious way of responding to the poor) but dealing with structural sin. When those accused say 'when did we see you hungry …' their blindness is due to the fact they are so much part of the system that they 'see and see without perceiving' (Isaiah 6:9).

v) The new Jerusalem

In Revelation 21 John's vision is of a world transformed and the new Jerusalem coming down from heaven to earth. In this **utopia** God will wipe away all tears, there will be no death, suffering, crying or mourning. The feature of this passage is that it is not an otherworldly state, a promise of reversal of fortune after death, but *this* world transformed. So, the question is how can such an obvious utopia not be a cause of false consciousness, just as Marx accused religion of doing when it used heaven as a means of allowing injustice to continue? Gutiérrez's reply is that genuine utopias are not sources of alienation because unlike ideologies which are by definition not of this world, utopia is a vision of what is possible but has yet to happen. Quoting Friere, Gutiérrez argues that Christian utopia has two forces, denunciation and annunciation:

Key quote

'The repudiation of a dehumanizing situation is an unavoidable aspect of utopia … This is why utopia is revolutionary and not reformist.'

GUSTAVO GUTIÉRREZ, *A THEOLOGY OF LIBERATION*, 218

Key word

Utopia can mean 'no place' (an imaginary perfect world) or a 'good place'. Because of its ambiguity Boff prefers the term 'topia' to refer to this world transformed.

Key question

Is the belief in the Kingdom of God as a utopia a cause of false consciousness?

Cross-references

Read pages 100–101 on Marx and religion.

Gustavo Gutiérrez, *A Theology of Liberation*, 218.

Key quote

'And I saw the holy city, new Jerusalem, coming down out of heaven from God.'

REVELATION 21:2

- **Denunciation**. Utopias cause people to denounce the present unjust order.
- **Annunciation**. Utopias announce what is not yet but will be; it is a 'creative imagination which proposes the alternative values to those rejected' (Gutiérrez).

Revelation 21 as a utopia is a call for solidarity by announcing what is possible and denouncing injustice, and by doing so establishes a political praxis in solidarity with the oppressed. What sets this apart as a Christian 'historical project' is the Christian eschatological motivation of love.

4 Jesus the liberator

Key quote

'For the Son of man also came not to be served but to serve, and to give his life as a ransom for many.'

JESUS IN *MARK'S GOSPEL* 10:34

Cross-reference

See Chapter 4 on the Jesus of history and the Christ of faith distinction.

Key thought

Read pages 9–10 on Augustine on sin and human nature and compare to liberation theology's notion of sin.

Although liberation theology begins with the poor in history, it is the person of Jesus who most clearly expresses the fact that God sides with the poor in history by fully entering into the state of human poverty. But because liberation theologians understand the human situation in socio-economic terms, Jesus' life and death is presented not in some abstract sense as paying off human sin, but liberation from the very structures of society which have created injustice, poverty, oppression and exploitation. Liberation theology is therefore wary of making a sharp differentiation between the **Jesus of history** and **the Christ of faith**, although the distinction helpfully highlights the relationship between political and spiritual liberation.

a) Types of sin

The term 'sin' is not used a great deal in northern European theology today because when people think of it they tend to express it internally in Augustine's sense of personal struggle against a wayward will. Although the term 'evil' is sometimes used, it is not considered to be the result of sin but extreme psychological disorder. The prevailing mood of liberal humanism does not talk of human corruption but lack of reason.

But in Latin America sin is visible, social and extreme. It is seen in countless numbers of murders, disappearances, extreme poverty and political corruption. Although liberation theologians accept that sin is personal, they also consider that sin describes the unjust structures of society which even 'good' people are part of.

i) Structural sin

The idea of 'structural sin' is one of the great contributions of liberation theology to contemporary theology. Structural sin can be defined simply as follows:

When humans sin, they create structures of sin, which in their turn, make human beings sin.

(José Ignacio González Faus, 'Sin', in Sobrino and Ellacuría,
Systematic Theology, 198)

Structural sin means that humans are alienated from each other because at a deep level there is no recognition of each other as humans. In non-theological terms Marx says that alienation is not just failing to own the means of production but being dehumanised by the lack of control one has of one's life. This applies equally to owner as well as worker. Structural sin is manifested in **infrastructural** and **superstructural oppression** – especially infrastructural.

Cross-reference

See page 110 on infrastructural and superstructural oppression.

Liberation theologians argue that this *collective* sense of alienation is already contained in the Christian doctrine of original sin. Sin cannot exist in isolation; sin exists because humans are fallen and corrupt and this state is continually perpetuated through false-consciousness. Faus gives the following example of structural sin:

The two ruling systems of our world are based upon a lie that is never stated but transmitted through injustice of their socio-economic relations. The false truth of capitalism is that a human being is not worth anything. The false truth of the communism existing at the moment is that a human being is always an enemy.

(José Ignacio González Faus, 'Sin', in Sobrino and Ellacuría,
Systematic Theology, 199–201)

From these two false ideas stem many atrocities. Faus gives the example of capitalist owners who, during a great earthquake in Mexico City, saved their machinery before their workers.

ii) Sin and creation

With the insights of structural sin, liberation theologians return to the biblical view of sin as expressed by Paul in Romans 8. Paul argues that sin has not only corrupted society but the structures of creation itself. This is a crucial point for Christianity. If sin remains structural then the solution is purely political and social. If sin is seen only in personal terms then redemption does not need Christ's death. But by seeing sin as a corruption of creation, then redemption can only be through God's reconciliation of the whole world (physically and spiritually) in Christ. Therefore when Jesus is called 'the liberator' of sin, both dimensions of the world are addressed: the political and the spiritual.

Key quotes

'We know that the whole creation has been groaning in travail together until now; and not only creation, but we ourselves.'

ST PAUL, *LETTER TO THE ROMANS*, 8:22

'In Christ God was reconciling the world to himself.'

ST PAUL, *SECOND LETTER TO THE CORINTHIANS*, 5:19

Diego Rivera (1886–1957) *The Revolutionary as a Christ-like figure*

b) Jesus the liberator

All liberation theologians reject the dualism of Jesus of history/ Christ of faith distinction. They do so because by detaching the Christ of faith from history, Christianity becomes merely an idea and the characters of the gospels not real people but stereotypes of people, as Gutiérrez says, 'reciting a script'. By starting with the Jesus of history, then it follows that Jesus was part of the political world and his life engaged with real political issues. Again it is important to stress, as Gutiérrez does, that it is not just Jesus' teaching which matters, but his life of action. For without actual physical engagement with those around him, Jesus' words could so easily become detached and spiritualised. By calling Jesus the liberator, his historical life continues to play a part in the historical conditions of every historical age. As Leonardo Boff says:

> *A Christology that proclaims Jesus Christ as the Liberator seeks to be committed to the economic, social and political liberation of those groups that are oppressed and dominated. It purports to see the theological relevance of the historic liberation of the vast majority of people in our continent.*

> (Leonardo Boff, *Jesus Christ Liberator*, 266)

i) Jesus as Zealot but not a Zealot

The gospels present Jesus as one who engaged with the political authorities of his day. In siding with the poor, the oppressed and marginalised it was inevitable that religious leaders would wonder by what authority Jesus was challenging their interpretation of the Law. The sign on the cross 'King of the Jews' (Mark 15:26) is an indication that from a Roman perspective he was executed as a political rebel. Yet, Jesus wasn't merely attacking the establishment; his teaching on the Kingdom of God was looking for more than this; what he wanted was a transformation of society itself.

This is why Gutiérrez argues that in one sense Jesus was a **Zealot** but he was also more than a Zealot. He was a Zealot because some of his close disciples (such as Judas, James and John) were either directly or indirectly associated with the Zealots. Some of Jesus' actions appeared to support the idea that he expected God to establish with them a new kingdom (Matthew 11:12) – at the Feeding of 5,000, the people even wanted to make him a king (John 6:15).

On the other hand, it would be quite wrong to depict Jesus only as a Zealot. Those quest theologians who have tried to fit Jesus into a particular role have had to conclude that in some sense Jesus failed in his efforts. This is why, as Gutiérrez argues, Jesus is not a Zealot. Jesus was suspicious of 'messianism' which the gospels frequently recall as the so-called **messianic secret** because, as Gutiérrez says:

Key question

Have liberation theologians put too much emphasis on the Jesus of history?

Key word

The **Zealots** were made up of a number of first-century Jewish movements who were looking for God to act to renew Israel by ridding her of her enemies and establishing God's kingdom on earth.

Cross-reference

Read page 61 on the messianic secret.

The liberation which Jesus offers is universal and integral; it transcends national boundaries, attacks the foundation of injustice and exploitation and eliminates politico-religious confusions, without therefore being limited to a purely 'spiritual' plane.

(Gustavo Gutiérrez, *A Theology of Liberation*, 213)

ii) Jesus as revolutionary prophet

Key quotes

'If Jesus were alive today, He would be a guerrillero.'

CAMILLO TORRES

'Is it not written, "My house shall be called a house of prayer for all nations?" But you have made it a den of robbers.'

JESUS IN MARK'S GOSPEL, 11:17

Jesus' Cleansing of the Temple (Mark 11:15–19) and attack on Temple institutions place him firmly in the prophetic tradition of one who was deeply suspicious of the religious authorities of his time. Like the great prophets of the eighth century BC before him, the core of his teaching was that revolution is only properly possible when God is *not* treated as an abstract object of faith but as Father. Then it becomes possible that humans as subjects and God also as subject, can act in solidarity with one another in revolutionary praxis. Jesus as human subject represents God's radical involvement with humans.

Put in Marxist terms, Jesus' words and actions as revolutionary prophet demonstrate that religion has actually alienated people and made them depend on human religious institutions. Some liberations theologians go so far as to suggest that Jesus' attack on the Temple was not merely to reform it but actually to abolish it altogether.

To summarise, Jesus is the liberator in four interconnected ways:

- **Social/political**. Jesus acts in solidarity with the socially marginalised and oppressed such as lepers, tax collectors, prostitutes. His role is similar to those of the Zealots.
- **Moral**. Jesus attacks hypocrisy of the law, 'the sabbath was made for man, not man for the sabbath' (Mark 2:28).
- **Religious**. Jesus' Cleansing of the Temple and his criticisms of the Pharisees' obsession with the rituals or the 'traditions of men' (Mark 7:1–8) liberate from religious fetishism.
- **Spiritual**. Jesus' vicarious death for the sins of the world is also a renewal of personal spirituality. His death graphically illustrates the reversal the cross performs, because in coming 'not to be served but to serve' (Mark 10:45) Christians know that martyrdom may be inevitable.

Summary diagram

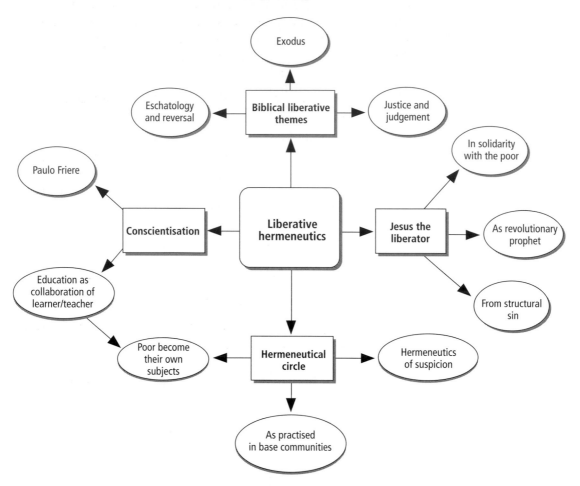

Study guide

By the end of this chapter you should be able to explain how a liberative interpretation of the Bible forms a central role in the second mediation in the process of conscientisaton and the means of establishing God's Kingdom as a state of justice on earth.

Essay questions

1a Explain liberation theology's teaching on eschatology and sin.

The essay might begin by explaining that for liberation theologians sin is not just personal but social. Sin is therefore structural because it has infected the very structures of society, much as the eighth-century prophets described Israel at the time. In Marx's terms the base or infrastructure has alienated people from each other so that those who are removed from owning the processes of production are dehumanised and powerless. In eschatological terms, the Kingdom demands radical reversal – as the Magnificat outlines. Matthew 25 describes how it is those who administer to the poor, alienated and oppressed who are members of the Kingdom, not those who are religiously good. The Kingdom is not just a final state as the Kingdom is in the 'midst of us' (Luke 17:21).

1b 'The causes of sin are always social not personal.' Discuss.

The argument might agree that, according to the doctrine of original sin, sin is always collective as it is the condition of being human. Societies and political systems are always far less able to act in a virtuous way than individuals. Deeper social structures are far less easy to change than individuals.

On the other hand, as Augustine graphically described, the individual will is far too rebellious for us to contain and sin is always dealt with through personal repentance and reflection. The Lord's Prayer asks for forgiveness of personal sin not social or structural sin.

Further essay questions

2 a   Explain how the Bible is used in the process of conscientisation.

2 b   'The Bible is more revolutionary than Marx.' Discuss.

3 'The Christ of faith is unimportant for liberation theologians.' Discuss.

4 Assess the view that of all the biblical themes, the Exodus is the most important.

Revision checklist

Can you give brief definitions of:

■ hermeneutical circle
■ hermeneutic of suspicion
■ conscientisation
■ structural sin.

Can you explain:

■ the significance of the Exodus paradigm
■ Jesus' eschatological manifesto
■ biblical teaching on justice and judgement.

Can you give arguments for and against:

■ Jesus as a Zealot
■ utopia as a cause of false consciousness
■ capitalism as a source of idolatry and fetish.

BASE COMMUNITIES

Chapter checklist

This chapter considers what is meant by 'church' and how through historical circumstances small grassroots 'base communities' within the Church evolved to tackle pastoral, social and political issues. The theological justification and future of base communities form the second part of the chapter.

1 New communities

In the early 1960s 'Church base communities', or *comunidades eclesiales de base* (CEB) emerged out of a dire need to provide practical as well as spiritual solidarity for the poor. There is no one definition of what a CEB is, but Berryman offers the following:

> *small lay-led communities, motivated by Christian faith, that see themselves as part of the church and that are committed to working together to improve their communities and to establish a more just society.*
>
> (Phillip Berryman, *Liberation Theology*, 64)

The definition may not sound controversial, but CEBs have posed a number of practical and theological challenges to the Church. Most fundamentally they question what is meant by the very idea of church.

a) What is church?

What is church and why does it matter? There are various models as to what church might be:

- **Functional**. Church is any community of Christians meeting in fellowship, or *koinonia*, to learn and function as a group with common values and aims. As Jesus says, 'where two or three are gathered in my name, there am I in the midst of them.'
- **Teleological**. The one true Church is a future perfect state of which any human institution can only be an imperfect version.

Key quote

'For where two or three are gathered in my name, there am I in the midst of them.'

JESUS IN *THE GOSPEL OF MATTHEW* 18:20

Key quote

'And I tell you, you are Peter, and on this rock I will build my church.'

JESUS IN *THE GOSPEL OF MATTHEW* 16:18

Key question

What are the characteristics of an ideal community?

Key people

Christiania was created as a separate 'state' in Copenhagen in 1971. Its aims, according to its founder Jacob Ludvigsen, are: 'a self-governing society whereby each and every individual holds themselves responsible over the wellbeing of the entire community'.

Key quote

'The Church is in history, but at the same time she transcends it. It is only with the "eyes of faith" that one can see her in her visible reality and at the same time in her spiritual reality as the bearer of the divine life.'

CATECHISM OF THE CATHOLIC CHURCH,
PARAGRAPH 770

- **Ontological**. The one true Church was founded by Christ when he made Peter its guardian. The Holy Spirit sustains and continues to make it a spiritual reality on earth.

b) Experiments in living

The idea of Church matters because this is how Christians organise themselves and justify their purpose. This doesn't just apply to Christians. 'Experiments in living', as they have been termed, are created when a group of people self-consciously opt for a different lifestyle because they feel that the present social arrangements fall short of what they consider to be the best way to live. For example, the kibbutz movement arose from Jews who had moved to Israel from Europe wanting to create radically egalitarian communities where land, labour and friendship would be shared without hierarchy. Some were inspired by Marx, whilst religious Jews felt that this was the authentic way their ancestors had first occupied the land. More recently in Copenhagen the state of **Christiania** was created as a self-sufficient hippy commune. But in time, all experiments in living lose momentum and become more conservative. It is then that they have to decide whether to reform or accept that the original purpose has changed. In its origins the Christian Church was another experiment in living; the development of CEBs question whether it is now time to reform the Church.

Traditionally the Roman Catholic Church has an ontological and teleological view of Church. This means its hierarchy of pope, bishops and priests is there as a result of the continuing activity of the Holy Spirit – not because the people have elected them. The Church's primary role is therefore as an intermediary of God's grace in the sacraments – particularly the celebration of the mass or Eucharist by the priest.

Protestant churches, on the other hand, tend to have a more functional view of Church and to regard its priests or ministers as those best educated to lead the people, but they are not ontologically different.

c) Two challenges

Now the company of those who believed were of one heart and soul, and no one said that any of the things which he possessed was his own, but they had everything in common. And with great power the apostles gave their testimony to the resurrection of the Lord Jesus, and great grace was upon them all. There was not a needy person among them, for as many as were possessors of lands or houses sold them, and brought the proceeds of what was sold and laid it at the apostles' feet; and distribution was made to each as any had need.

(Acts 4:32–35)

The social and pastoral crisis in Latin America has forced the Catholic Church to consider two basic ideas about what it means to be Church:

- **Pastoral/political basis**. Jesus' teaching on the poor suggests that the pastoral role of the Church is its role in the transformation of society. In making a preferential option for the poor, the Church can no longer remain politically neutral in society; the celebration of the sacraments does not address the fundamental concerns of the gospel.
- **Egalitarian basis**. According to Acts 4 the earliest Christians formed a radically egalitarian form of church based on Jesus' pastoral teaching. It appears to have been a 'grassroots organisation' where the poor and church leaders met together sharing food, property and money equally.

The legitimacy of base communities as 'experiments in living' since the early 1960s poses a set of particularly difficult problems for the Catholic Church. The new communities question whether the Church is functional or ontological or teleological; whether priests are equal with the people and serve their needs or are primarily there to administer the sacraments; whether the role of the Church is to be politically neutral and support the government or become politically active.

However, unlike the kibbutzim of Israel, base communities were not founded consciously but rather emerged in response to several pastoral crises. The theological and sociological justifications have followed later.

2 Origins and development

CEBs were not created consciously but resulted over a period of time in response to three factors:

- **Lack of priests**. The Roman Catholic Church in the late 1950s suffered from an acute shortage of priests. In many shanty towns there was only one priest for 20,000 baptised Catholics; the situation was slightly better in Brazil with one priest to six thousand parishioners. Without priests there could be no celebration of mass, or instruction or guidance. Consequently, religious practice was very low – around five per cent of baptised Catholics attended church (even lower amongst men).
- **Threat from Protestant churches**. The Church was losing ground to the effective young Protestant and evangelical churches and especially from 'fundamentalist' Christian groups who offered the people 'religious' solutions to their poverty. These churches

did not need trained celibate clergy and could therefore respond quickly to the needs of the people.

Cross-reference

See pages 109–111 on the 'see–judge–act' process which was developed into the three mediations.

- **European church experiments**. Catholic 'worker-priests' in Europe were experimenting with new ways of dealing with social problems by bringing the church into the workplace. The new pastoral methods, such as the **see–judge–act** process, were being developed to deal with social and pastoral problems. Some of these worker-priests were bringing their methods to Latin America.

a) Creation of the first CEBs

The response to these challenges was gradual and piecemeal. Some bishops tackled the lack of priests by training local leaders to deliver the teaching of the church as 'lay deacons' or 'catechists'. Their job was to read the materials produced by the Church and to conduct the 'priestless mass' for the people. Very quickly the 'huts' built for these meetings also became the village focal points for *all* village meetings, both religious and secular. The creation of the Barra do Pirai in Brazil in 1958 is often seen as the origin of the CEB movement.

By the mid-1960s a more conscious sociology was being applied, encouraged by the ecclesial reforms of Vatican II. The encyclical *Lumen Gentium*, for instance, spoke of the 'pilgrim church' promoting equality and co-responsibility of people within the church community. Sociological theory helped to develop the significance of working with small 'primary groups' as cells within existing parishes or existing communities.

The political situation (dictatorship, mass deaths and tortures), especially in Peru in the early 1960s, helped to turn the CEBs into political units working at the grassroots. The catechist's role was transformed from a passive priest-substitute to active 'animators' shaping and expressing the ideas and needs of the community.

In 1975 the first meeting of all the CEBs (some 4,000) in Brazil was held. This was a significant meeting, for it indicated that the base community was itself part of a web of other communities, all with their own particular style yet bound by a common vision. The meeting was also attended by a number of professional theologians and sociologists and their presence illustrates another important feature of the CEBs which is the dialectic between idea (theology and sociology) and practice.

b) Impact

However, by the mid-1980s the CEBs themselves had lost some of their early momentum. A conservative Pope (John Paul II) and the reinstitution of democracy in Latin America had affected many middle-class supporters of the base community movement. The

Church argued that the lay-deacon had originally only ever been considered a stop-gap until the priest shortage had been resolved. But deeper than this was the fear that the model of the Church as the means of educating and administering the sacraments was being diluted for a more 'communistic' people's church.

CEBs only ever had a minor impact on parish life. It is estimated that about ten per cent of parishes in the continent had a CEB and even then only around one per cent of the parish population were active in them.

However, the use of numbers is only one way to measure success. The questioning method of reading the Bible using Friere's democratic **pedagogy** has radiated out from the few to the many at the grassroots level. It has made church workers more self-aware of their own top-down methods and more sensitive to consensual democratic methods of community life. Liberative biblical hermeneutics have enabled the poor and oppressed to become more aware of their religious commitments: the symbols and utopian vision of what society could be like has often brought families together and helped resolve differences.

c) Popular Catholicism

CEBs have also had to make the Church confront the role and place of popular Catholic practice in the continent. For most of the poor the official Church is a distant and often largely irrelevant presence. Religion for the masses is the celebration of saints' days, processions and superstitious views of the power of the sacraments. Whereas the Church since Vatican II has focused on the problems of secularisation, the problem in Latin America is not European secularism but centuries' old village and shanty town peasant religion.

One response is for the Church to condemn all pagan type practice – to ban processions and to remove images of the saints. However, the CEB movement has suggested a more subtle alternative.

The psychological insights of **Carl Jung** has helped theologians to understand that humans naturally use symbols to express their deepest spiritual needs. As every society does this in its own way, these symbols should not be demolished but understood as the means by which the poor have found hope and solidarity. By discussing what their practices mean in the CEBs, the poor have come to understand their own spirituality in relationship to the official teaching of the Church. The dialectic is enriching for both popular and official church.

Cross-reference
Read page 125 on Friere's pedagogy.

Key thought
An example of popular Catholicism is 'Our Lady of Guadalupe' in Mexico which is the most visited Catholic pilgrimage destination in the world.

Key people
Carl Jung (1875–1961) was a Swiss psychologist. He argued that the mind naturally puts ideas into symbols, which is why religions, folk stories and art appeal because they express deeper levels of human consciousness.

3 Theology of base communities

a) The meaning of 'base'

Although the term 'base' grew out of the need to literally offer a local base or communal meeting point, base has been understood theologically and sociologically in several different ways.

i) Base as reversal

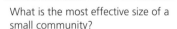

Key question

What is the most effective size of a small community?

As reversal, base challenges the hierarchy of a Church with a top-down theology. The 'base' refers to the poor, the oppressed whose experience of God often alienates from the formal church but who, nevertheless in their popular form of Catholicism, experience community in a more immediate and human way. Beginning at the base of society is a reminder that, as St Paul says, Christian communities do not discriminate on grounds of sex, race and class, for 'all are one in Christ Jesus'. In Latin America base communities aim to subvert prejudice. That means, for example, including men who often play little part in the formal Church and indigenous Indians who have been excluded from the official structures of society.

Cross-reference

St Paul *Letter to the Galatians* 3:28.

ii) Basic units

Some have preferred to talk of 'basic' communities. Basic suggests that the CEBs are not independent from the Church parish structure but comprise small units of people meeting, talking and worshipping together. This makes good sociological as well as theological sense. Sociologically, people work best in small groups. Most sociologists agree that no friendship group extends to much more than 30 or so friends with whom a person can maintain regular contact. A base community of 30 people or less, therefore, becomes a true community of friends.

Theologically, Jesus told his disciples that they should not think of him in master–servant terms but as friends. In the idealised picture of the first communities, Luke portrays the basic communities sharing their assets in ways reminiscent of Engels' phrase, 'from each according to his ability, to each according to his need'.

Key quote

'No longer do I call you servants, for the servant does not know what his master is doing; but I have called you friends, for all that I have heard from my Father I have made known to you.'

JESUS IN *THE GOSPEL OF JOHN* 15:15

iii) Base as mind–body unity

Using the term base locates community in the world of history and is a living example of why mind–body dualism should be rejected. This has important sociological implications. It suggests that, as there is no separate spiritual and secular history, the Church has no exclusive control over salvation.

Furthermore, as humans are psychosomatic unities, then their political, social and spiritual lives are equally important. 'Church', therefore, is to be found just as much in attending to a dispute over refuse collection as it is in receiving Holy Communion.

Key question

Does the new Jerusalem symbol create the wrong idea of Church?

Cross-reference

Read pages 131–132 on the new Jerusalem.

Key quote

'And he said to me, "It is done! I am the Alpha and Omega, the beginning and the end. To the thirsty I will give water without price from the fountain of the water of life".'

REVELATION 21:6

Cross-reference

Leonardo Boff, *Church: Charism and Power*, 33.

b) The new Jerusalem

We have already considered the image of the new Jerusalem in its eschatological role as the establishment of the Kingdom on earth. Traditionally, Jerusalem as the bride is associated with the Church, but for liberation theologians the bride is not an abstract idea any more than the Kingdom is merely an idea, but a living community in this world transformed. The **new Jerusalem** is a symbol of the Church as a community in a restored Eden; God and people live in harmony without hierarchy.

However, it is not necessarily obvious that the new Jerusalem image does avoid an otherworldly view of the Church. Leonardo Boff argues that rather than describe the new Jerusalem as an utopia, or 'no-place', it should really be considered a 'topia' – an actual place. Revelation 21 is therefore a powerful vision of hope. Others are less sure; it doesn't seem that Revelation 21 really supports a view of Church which is revolutionary but a traditional teleological otherworldly type which, as Marx put it, has created 'illusionary happiness' and an 'illusionary sun' round which to revolve as a form of escapism.

c) Prophetic and functional

Leonardo Boff's theological critique of the Church echoes that of the Reformers such as Calvin and Luther. Just as they had been inspired by the prophets of the Old Testament to question the functioning of the Church, Boff also calls on the Church to exercise its prophetic voice and see that by trying to be politically neutral it has been exploited by the ruling classes to promote and sanction their own interests. The Church is not neutral but by default has become part of the ruling class society.

The CEBs, on the other hand, remind the Church what its role should be; they offer a proper democratic process, where priests, nuns and lay workers work in cooperation with the people. Boff doesn't reject the place of priests and nuns but, he says, 'the hierarchy is functional and is not an ontological establishment of classes of Christians'. In other words, the role of clergy is organisational (functional) not God-given (ontological).

But despite Boff's call for church reform, in practice, as Berryman notes, priests and theologians remain conservatively respectful of the Church and its institutions. If the Church were really to act prophetically, as Boff suggests, then it should really question whether priests remain celibate and male; it should question whether the Eucharist be administered only by an ordained priest; it should consider the people to be as much Church as ordained ministers. In other words, if the theological logic which justifies base communities is right, then the reform of the Church needs to be of the magnitude of the Reformation in the sixteenth century.

4 Theology at work

A base community meeting of Sao Joano Mereti, Rio De Janeiro

There is no set way in which a CEB operates. A great deal depends on how many people comprise a particular base community, why it was formed, what its purpose is and what particular methods it has developed.

a) The three mediations in action

In Andrew Dawson's description of a typical CEB the see–judge–act method is used. We see how the three 'mediations' function in practice.

- **Attendance.** CEBs may comprise 10–60 people who meet once or twice a week coordinated by a lay worker or facilitated by a local priest or nun. A CEB could be one of several CEBs in the same parish. A meeting might begin with a song or prayer.
- **Seeing.** Members of the group contribute their own experiences of the week in what some refer to as the *revisio de vida* (life review).

Cross-reference

Quotations and references are from Andrew Dawson, 'The origins and character of the base ecclesial community: a Brazilian perspective', in Rowland, *Cambridge Companion to Liberation Theology*, 117–118.

> *Such concerns and events might include, for example, news of illness through lack of adequate sanitation facilities, proper housing or malnutrition, the sharing of hardships caused by redundancy or low pay, and information upon someone injured on account of dangerous working conditions.*

- **Judging.** The 'animator' or coordinator may choose a biblical passage to read and discuss together putting into practice the hermeneutic circle. Then,

> *the biblical text is interrogated and made relevant to the life setting of the group. In such a way, the scriptural passage speaks in retrospect concerning recent events, whilst at the same time giving encouragement to those gathered concerning the week to come.*

● **Acting**. Finding solidarity in the group, the people are 'spurred on' to deal with the practical problems found in the bairro. This might be done through the setting up or support for

local community centres, women's groups, cooperative ventures, political parties and unions, youth clubs, and ad hoc campaigns in the pursuit of a local health clinic, sanitation facilities, school and public transport provisions.

b) The future

There are now far fewer CEBs in Latin America than in the heyday of the 1970s. Some argue that their decline is symptomatic of the failure of liberation as a whole, but before one can make that kind of assessment, we need to know what the possible factors are for decline and whether these will have long-term effects on the movement.

i) Decline

Decline has been put down to some of the following factors:

● The optimism of the CEBs in the 1960s and 1970s has not brought about the democratic changes hoped for. Even though the military dictatorships have declined, the poor are not better off. Disappointment has affected CEBs as well as other political movements in Latin America.
● The Church authorities have become more conservative and many bishops have closed down, or at least discouraged, CEBs.
● CEBs lack leadership. Leaders or animators have either left and become members of local political parties or were killed or 'disappeared' (presumably killed by government forces). With the loss of a whole generation of church leaders, the CEBs have lacked direction and motivation.
● The poor have become more religiously conservative; people prefer attending church mass rather than being involved in the political scene.

ii) Alienation

CEBs embody almost all of liberation theology's ideas of the 'people's church' (*iglesia popular*). But is it really inclusive? CEBs have never become part of middle-class Catholic life because their education and involvement in political life is already catered for. The worry is that, far from reforming the Church, the CEBs alienate those who are not poor but nevertheless wish to be part of the Church.

iii) Cautious optimism

Despite the problems and criticism outlined so far, others remain optimistic. Where a bishop has encouraged CEBs – especially in a rural area – CEBs have continued to flourish. Whilst urban CEBs

Key question

Will CEBs make the Church more democratic in the future?

have fared less well, often because men have had to travel long distances to work and concentrated on their family life, urban CEBs have focussed instead on programmes to help drug users, prostitutes and the homeless. CEBs continue to monitor and expose corrupt government officials.

CEBs have not brought about a second reformation, but their impact on the Catholic Church and on non-Catholic churches has been significant in making them all more democratic and perhaps closer to the Christian communities of the very early Church.

Summary diagram

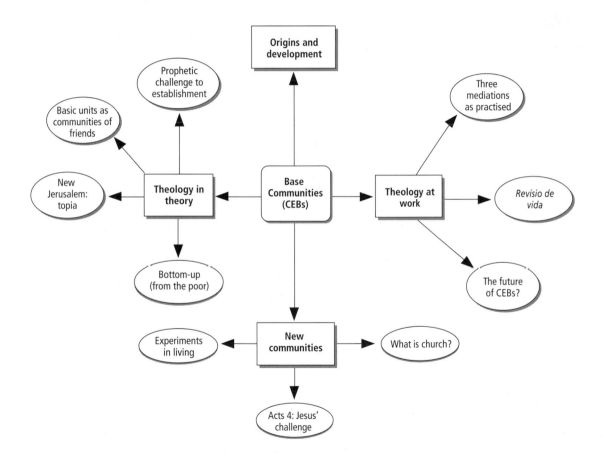

Study guide

By the end of this chapter you should be able to explain how CEBs were created in response to a shortage of priests and the failure of the Catholic Church to provide pastoral aid to the poor. You should also be able to discuss the theological reasons why many are critical of CEBs.

Essay questions

1a Explain the theological justification for base communities.

Essays might begin by referring to the Roman Catholic Church's *Lumen Gentium* which encouraged the Church to be a pilgrim church on earth for all people. The term 'base' can have various theological justifications from the poor who are 'one in Christ', to a community of friends (John 15:15), to an organisation overcoming the false body–soul distinction and not distant from the people which it should be serving as the *iglesia popular*. Finally, using Revelation 21, the Church is described as a bride wedded to the people in a restored world.

1b 'Base communities alienate the people from the Church.' Discuss.

The argument might at first disagree with the statement. The CEBs give more involvement with the Church through enacting the three mediations and taking on more responsibility for social, pastoral and educational services to the local community. The symbols of the community have their own spiritual power (Jung). By being 'basic' communities they seek to carry out the basic conditions of the Church. Priests, nuns and other members of the Church hierarchy still, however, have their roles.

On the other hand, it might be considered that CEBs have a very functional view of Church. Church is not functional but ontological; its institution is established through the giving of the Holy Spirit via apostolic succession from St Peter onwards. By reducing the Church to its functions the sense of holiness and the purpose of the sacraments are greatly diminished. The people have created their own secular communities which are alienated from the Church.

Further essay questions

2 a Explain the reasons why CEBs have declined in numbers.

2 b 'CEBs continue to offer a powerful means of hope.' Discuss.

3 'There is greater theological justification for base communities than for the official Church.' Discuss.

4 To what extent are CEBs just utopian experiments?

Revision checklist

Can you give brief definitions of:

■ democratic pedagogy
■ *revisio de vida*
■ pilgrim church
■ New Jerusalem.

Can you explain:

■ the difference between the functional and ontological idea of church
■ the various meanings of 'base'
■ two reasons why CEBs came into being
■ how the mediations function in the CEB.

Can you give arguments for and against:

■ CEBs as a threat to the Church
■ the success of CEBs.

Chapter checklist

The chapter begins by looking at the responses of the Catholic and Protestant churches to liberation theology and then reviews three non-Latin American theologies of liberation (black African, dalit and gay). The final part of the chapter considers whether liberation theology has failed or has a future especially after the demise of communism.

1 Responses of Catholic and Protestant churches

Key question

To what extent has liberation theology fulfilled its aims set out in the 1970s?

At the start of Chapter 6 we considered Berryman's claim that liberation theology has the potential to have the same profound effect on society and the Church as the Protestant Reformation of the sixteenth century. As he said:

It is conceivable that liberation theology represents the initial phase of a comparable shift in the history of Christianity and that its impact will go far beyond the churches.

(Phillip Berryman, *Liberation Theology*, 6)

Berryman wrote this in 1987. So the question is: has liberation theology achieved any of this?

a) Catholic Church

Cross-reference

Read pages 116–17 on the *Instruction*.

The reaction of the Catholic Church consists largely of Cardinal Ratzinger's *Instruction*. The negative reaction of the *Instruction* was partly against the base community movement which was thought to be giving too much power to the people and therefore moving the centre of influence away from the Vatican, and partly the way some liberation theologians had made 'uncritical' use of Marxism. Ratzinger's *Instruction* reinforced the view that only the Church is the true mediator of Christ, through the sacraments, ordained priesthood and Magisterium (the official authority) of the Church. His major criticism was that liberation theology was too reductionist, too materialistic and too this-worldly.

However, despite these criticisms, many of the ideas of liberation theology have filtered their way into the official teaching of the Church. Social justice, empowering of the poor, conscientisation and preferential option for the poor are frequently used terms. For example, the Vatican's *Libertatis Conscientia* (1986), or 'On Christian Freedom and Liberation', frequently uses the terms 'liberation' and 'preference' in a similar way to liberation theology.

> *those who are oppressed by poverty are the object of a love of preference on the part of the Church.*

(*Libertatis Conscientia*, paragraph 68)

Likewise CAFOD (Catholic Overseas Development Agency) deals specifically with international development, has embraced many of the ideas of liberation theology such as praxis, solidarity, the poor as the underside of society and justice.

b) Protestant Churches

Liberation theology may have developed at first among Catholic theologians because Latin America is primarily Catholic, but it has influenced many Protestant theologians who have had a freer reign to develop their theology without the control of a centralised church hierarchy.

- **Marcella Althaus-Reid** is a good example of a radical feminist liberation theologian who was brought up a Catholic in Latin America but as a young adult left the Church and became a Protestant Christian. Her attack on Catholicism is that it has a repressed sexuality which has undermined the radical nature of Christian spirituality.
- Outside Latin America the Protestant churches have developed a wide range of liberative theologies arising from racial, ethnic, sexual and class oppression.
- **James Cone** is an example of a Methodist theologian from North America who was instrumental in the creation of black liberation theology.

2 Other theologies of liberation

Liberation theology has inspired many other contextual liberative theologies where a group has been marginalised, exploited and dehumanised by another group. The reason for alienation might be: class, colour, race, sexuality, or even poverty. Since Latin Americans used the term **irruption** to describe how the poor suddenly emerged from the underside of history, it has now become common to use the phrase to describe how other

Key quote

'We walk alongside poor and disadvantaged communities, making their cause our cause, uniting in action and prayer.'

WWW.CAFOD.ORG.UK

Key people

Marcella Althaus-Reid (1952–2009) was born and brought up in the bairro of Rosario, Argentina. She taught and published on contextual theology at Edinburgh University specialising in feminist and queer theology but also ran her own base communities for women in Dundee and Perth.

Cross-reference

Read pages 63–7 on Cone and black theology.

Key word

Irruption is the moment when an oppressed group suddenly emerges from the underside of history into consciousness.

oppressed groups have appeared, seeking to affirm their own identity and to be liberated from the dominant ideology and its system. The 1981 New Dehli meeting of **EATWOT** was entitled 'Irruption of the Third World'.

> *It is an irruption of all those who struggle for full humanity and for their rightful place in history.*

(EATWOT, New Delhi, 1981)

EATWOT's outlook is critical of the North American and European view that theology is universal which not only fails to take into account the particular experiences of Christians in their own cultural situation, but has been in part responsible for reinforcing economic and ideological oppression.

There are now many theologies of liberation. The rest of this section considers three: dalit theology from India; black theology from South Africa; and gay theology from northern Europe and North America. Each of these has an affinity with classical liberation theology (i.e. from Latin America) but there are some important differences which will be referred to briefly.

a) Dalit liberation theology

i) History

What makes **dalit** theology distinctive is that it has emerged from a religiously plural environment where Christianity is the minority religion in a predominantly Hindu society. The history of dalit oppression is ancient and woven into the fabric of Indian culture and history for thousands of years.

However, recent Indian history has altered the place of dalits, or untouchables. During British colonial rule they were known as 'depressed classes' and, even when India gained independence

Key word

EATWOT, or Ecumenical Association of Third World Theologians, was created in Dar-es-Salaam, Tanzania, in 1976. Through conferences and papers third-world theologians develop their theologies of liberation.

Key word

Dalit is an ancient word and can mean: downtrodden, broken, crushed. It has come to refer to those in Indian society who are outcaste and untouchable.

in 1947, they fared little better and were specifically named in the Indian Constitution as the 'Scheduled Caste'.

Various attempts have been made to remedy the situation. Gandhi called them 'harijan', or children of God, and in the 1970s the 'Dalit Panther Movement' of Maharashtra promoted the use of dalit as a term of pride and dignity.

However, even though the Indian Constitution of 1950 officially outlawed untouchability, the caste system still operates at a structural level. Dalits comprise 20 per cent of the population and 70 per cent of practising Christians. Even though Christianity has no official caste system, the churches (both the Roman Catholic and Protestant) have systematically denied dalits positions of responsibility and very few have been ordained priests/pastors or risen to positions of responsibility in the Church.

Dalit theology emerged in the 1990s, inspired by black liberation theology in the USA and people's liberation in Korea.

ii) Alienation and exploitation

In the traditional Indian caste system those who belong to the four castes, or **varnas**, have enjoyed certain privileges according to their place within their caste. The outcaste has been given various names such as 'avarrias' casteless, and 'chandalas' – worst of the earth. All these terms indicate how dalits are viewed and why as outcastes their lives are characterised by poverty, carrying out the most menial tasks which are forbidden to caste-born Indians. These tasks, such as removal of dead bodies and cleaning, make them the 'untouchables' as Hindu purity laws forbid touching such people for fear of becoming religiously unclean. In villages dalits are denied land, they are not allowed to enter temples for worship, and they are forbidden to use public water. Even within the Indian church dalits have been buried in separate places in the churchyard and they are not expected to marry anyone who belongs to a caste.

Dalit Christians are alienated three times over: by the state (in the Indian Constitution); in Hindu culture; and by the Church.

iii) Conscientisation and experience

In common with all liberation theologies, dalit theology begins with the God who sides with the poor and Jesus the dalit who, as liberator, restores human dignity to its fullness. Likewise, dalit theology also finds inspiration in the Exodus paradigm, especially the period when the Israelites wandered for 40 years in the wilderness, as this resonates with their own lack of land and permanent home as they wander from village to village.

Conscientisation tends to focus not just on the promise of a land flowing with milk and honey (i.e. rights and liberties) but an internal restoration of the self as one made in the image of

Key thought

The Christian population in India is about 25 million, of whom 20 million are of dalit origin.

Key word

Varnas, or castes, comprise: brahmin (priest/teacher), ksatriyas (ruler/soldier), vaishyas (merchants) and shudras (labourers).

God. Dalit theology finds inspiration in God who, in becoming a servant, endures the pain of rejection and death on the cross as an inevitable consequence of a religiously stratified culture. As the word dalit (in Hebrew as well as in Sanskrit) also contains the idea of 'poverty of spirit', Jesus' beatitude 'blessed are the poor in spirit' has special meaning for those who are downtrodden economically, psychologically and spiritually.

God's preferential treatment of the poor is an entirely free act not under the power of eternal dharma which controls class (as it is taught in traditional Hinduism). Likewise, dalits are encouraged to understand that their condition is not the result of past **karma**. Just as Jesus defied the priests and upper castes of his day in the Cleansing of the Temple and rejection of Pharisaic rituals, dalits are liberated from their sense of being religiously and socially subhuman.

Key word

Karma in Hindu thought is the law of cause and effect where all actions in our past and present lives determine what kind of person one is.

iv) Praxis and analysis

The death of Jesus on the cross is especially significant for dalit liberative praxis as his death establishes through his resurrection new communities in which there is neither 'free nor servant' (Galatians 3:28). Dalit theologians have a vision of society where all are transformed, not just the untouchables so that oppressors (those people of caste) are transformed in their confrontation with dalitness.

Dalit praxis has also challenged the way converts to Christianity from Hinduism have been taught to understand Christianity from classical Hindu texts. These inevitably have promoted Brahminism and with it the varnas (castes); Christian theology in India is now being forced to rethink the caste question.

v) Liberation theology and dalit theology

The two theologies share a great deal in common. Both focus on the historical plight of the marginalised and both seek reversal of those who, for centuries, have been the unnoticed underside of history and to bring them into the public sphere in the Church and society. But Dalit theology, more so than classical liberation theology, illustrates quite how deep structural sin can penetrate as it is reinforced by organised ideology. A Marxist analysis is therefore considered to be useful but too narrow in its analysis.

Biblical hermeneutics form a central means of conscientisation. Some dalit theologians have worried that an exclusive dependency on the Bible has marginalised dalit culture and history. Just as Latin American theologians have incorporated popular religious culture, so more recent dalit theologians have made more use of dalit Hindu culture and sought a less confrontational dialogue with Hinduism.

b) Black African liberation theology
i) History

The colonialism of South Africa began when Dutch traders set up a permanent base there in 1652. In 1795, when the British arrived, society was split between the Dutch Afrikaans speakers and English speakers.

Both British and Afrikaans felt that they had a God-given right to the land. When Boers or Dutch farmers trekked north to escape the British colonists, they felt this was divinely commanded. Equally, Cecil Rhodes argued that the British were establishing a new Israel and had a right to expel heathens from the land or convert them.

The discovery of diamonds was a major cause of the Boer wars (1880–81 and 1899–1902). In 1910 the South African Act gave power to whites and the Native Land Act deprived natives of many rights to land. The nationalists came to power in 1948 and created the idea of **apartheid**, a theological and political notion that as God had ordained separate nations, then the only way to achieve peace was through a policy of separating whites from non-whites. Apartheid was given official backing by the Dutch Reformed Church who justified it in biblical terms as God protecting his elect (the Afrikaans) against the British 'pharaohs' in order to establish a holy and pure white church.

However, there were many, both black and white, who considered apartheid to be morally and religiously wrong. Black resistance grew and in 1960, the **ANC** organised a crowd of over 7,000 black Africans to gather at the police station in Sharpeville to protest against the hated pass book. The police opened fire and killed 69. This marked the first of many protests and the black consciousness movement was inspired by people such as Steve Biko and Desmond Tutu. Finally in 1994, Nelson Mandela was freed from prison and elected the first black president of South Africa.

ii) Alienation and exploitation

Black African theologians argue that the major cause of alienation is the white psyche dating back to the time of the Emperor Constantine in the fourth century when he transformed Christianity by making it the official religion of his empire. The white, northern European, Christian church has, from this time, adopted a 'triumphalist' view of the world and its theology has been used to reinforce political expansion of Christian monarchs. Jesus as lord of the universe has been the banner which white nations have used to dominate the world. Massive exploitation was in part the result of the British Empire and her 'domesticated British God', as **Simon Maimela** puts it, but also the Afrikaner Calvinist teaching on the political purity of the 'volk' (the people), predestination, election and separation of races.

Key quote

'This theology of glory has encouraged South African whites to develop an attitude of priding themselves as worthier persons than the people of color by virtue of belonging to Western civilization and by being the elect of God to promote Christianity.'

SIMON S. MAIMELA, *BLACK THEOLOGY OF LIBERATION*, 187

Key word

Apartheid is an Afrikaans word meaning 'separation'.

Key word

ANC, or African National Congress Party, was founded in 1912 and has been the ruling party in post-apartheid South Africa since 1994.

Key people

Simon Maimela (1944–) was the first lecturer in black theology at the University of South Africa from 1980–96. During this time he was international coordinator of EATWOT. His many books include *Proclaim Freedom to My People* (1987).

Key quote

'For my part, its [apartheid] most vicious, indeed, its most blasphemous aspect, is not the great suffering it causes its victims, but that it can make a child of God doubt that he is a child of God.'

ARCHBISHOP DESMOND TUTU, QUOTED IN MAIMELA *BLACK THEOLOGY OF LIBERATION*, 189

Cross-reference

See pages 65–67 on Cone's teaching on blackness.

Key people

Allan Boesak (1945–) is a minister of the Dutch Reformed Church, politician and campaigner against apartheid. He was one of the early writers on black African liberation theology.

Key people

Desmond Tutu (1931–) was the first Anglican Archbishop of Cape Town. He campaigned against apartheid and won the Nobel Peace Prize in 1984.

For black Africans the most profound sense of alienation was in the constant use of the official term 'non-white' to describe them; their beliefs and culture were regarded as worthless because they were in effect non-persons. Structural sin was maintained by the myths of white supremacy, triumphalism and election and ultimately reinforced by the biological argument that black society is in every way inferior to the successes achieved by white civilisation. The outward superstructural aspects of exploitation could be seen everywhere in South Africa from separate schools, churches, housing and in those who held positions of power.

iii) Conscientisation and experience

The first stage of conscientisation is to recover African culture and history as rich and diverse, pre-dating European settlement and now omitted by many of the official history books. With this comes a realisation that there is a distinctive African spirituality which values the individual in relationship to his community and ancestors.

Whereas for Cone blackness had been a call to protest, in South Africa blackness looks for change by discovering an authentic culture which has been suppressed for two hundred years. The process of reconstructing an authentic culture is controversial but has been significant in the critique of white culture and society. **Allan Boesak** is critical of Cone's overemphasis on blackness as a condition of God's revelation. For him, blackness in African black theology is about becoming a person fully created in the image of God. Blackness is also about applying a hermeneutics of suspicion to existing colonial theology which appears to be neutral and 'colour blind'.

iv) Praxis and analysis

Desmond Tutu has, for decades, stood firmly by his notion of the 'rainbow nation' and, like Martin Luther King in the USA, his campaigns for reconciliation have been instrumental in changing politics and the Church. However, not everyone considers that Tutu has been radical enough. Some consider that he is too establishment and as an Anglican still too much part of South Africa's colonial past. These are some of the reasons why the African Independent Churches (AIC) were formed to break away from mainstream churches and they developed their own indigenous Christian worship.

In general, black African theology has not been as radical as its North American parallel; African Christian worshippers are by nature more conservative than black Americans. Quite often critics comment that there has been less effective church praxis often because black theologians have not developed their theology in the church communities but in the academic, detached environment of

Key word

The **Kairos Document** was issued in 1985 and signed by 150 signatories. Kairos in Greek means 'time' and the document called for Christians to act now against injustice.

Key word

Enculturation is the adaptation of one set of cultural values to another culture.

Key question

Is there a need for gay liberation theology?

Cross-reference

Read Michael Wilcockson, *Social Ethics*, Chapter 3 on sexuality.

Key thought

For many, gay liberation would also include lesbian, gay, bisexual and transsexual people (LGBT).

universities. Nevertheless, the production of the **Kairos Document** in 1985 by a group of South African theologians criticising the apartheid state caused immediate debate throughout the world. One of its targets was what it called 'state theology', theology which has been used by churches and government to justify racism, capitalism and totalitarianism.

v) Liberation theology and black theology

Black African theology shares many of classical liberation theology's ideas, especially the notion that theology is to be grounded in historical experience. In adapted form all of the following are central to black African theology: the Exodus paradigm where God sides with the oppressed; the repossession of land as covenantal promise; and Jesus as servant whose death and resurrection transform despair into hope.

On the other hand, black African theology has not developed a Marxist-type socio-analytic mediation, although it shares the same suspicion of those church people who try and spiritualise Christianity by removing it from the political arena.

It is the process of **enculturation** of European culture to African culture in worship and spirituality where black African theology is most significantly different from Latin American theology. Nevertheless, some argue that greater use of Gutiérrez's critique of development would help in the maturing process by giving black African theology its own distinct cultural identity.

c) Gay liberation theology

i) History

Gay liberation has not been the product of a specific geographical location as is the case for Latin American liberation theology. Nevertheless, as a contextual theology it has developed in northern Europe and North America as a result of general shifting attitudes to sex and sexuality. In secular society the liberalising homosexual laws since 1967 in the United Kingdom, for example, have forced the Church to reconsider its traditional attitudes to homosexuality, lesbianism and bisexuality. Christian churches have had to face criticisms from groups such as Stonewall who regard traditional Christian teaching on homosexuality as oppressive and bigoted. Stonewall have 'outed' Christian clerics who have privately admitted to being gay as an indication that within its walls the Church practises double standards. The Church of England's publication *Issues in Human Sexuality* (1991) accepted that homosexuality is not a condition which a person chooses, and yet argues that in order for gay clergy to remain faithful to the Scripture, they have to be single and celibate.

Key quote

'The vocation of marriage is written in the very nature of man and woman as they came from the hand of the Creator.'

CATECHISM OF THE CATHOLIC CHURCH,
PARAGRAPH 1603

Key quote

'It is the conviction of the members of the Lesbian & Gay Christian Movement that human sexuality in all its richness is a gift of God gladly to be accepted, enjoyed and honoured as a way of both expressing and growing in love, in accordance with the life and teaching of Jesus Christ.'

STATEMENT OF CONVICTION, LESBIAN &
GAY CHRISTIAN MOVEMENT
(WWW.LGCM.ORG.UK)

Key people

Michel Foucault (1926–84) was a French philosopher, historian and sociologist. Through his multidisciplinary analysis of prison, madness and medicine he developed his distinctive view of power and knowledge. This approach was developed in his influential three volumes *The History of Sexuality* (1976–84).

ii) Alienation and exploitation

Traditional views of Christian marriage and sex which are strictly monogamous and heterosexual are considered to be the model of society in microcosm. As gays have not been part of this, they have naturally been excluded from one of the central aspects of Christian life in the formation of families. Theological language can be dehumanising: take for example Catholic Church's use of 'intrinsically disordered' to describe homosexual orientation, meaning that gay sexual relationships can never achieve their reproductive purpose according to the order of nature.

iii) Conscientisation and experience

Conscientisation through the reading of scripture requires scripture to be understood in its proper historical context. Scenes such as Sodom and Gomorrah (Genesis 19:1–8), for example, where homosexuality is judged by God with brimstone and fire (Genesis 19:24) is not a condemnation of gay *relationships* but homosexual rape. In the New Testament St Paul appears to single out homosexuality as an example of depravity (1 Corinthians 6:9–11 and Romans 1:18–32). But on closer reading this turns out to be an example chosen from the many Jewish purity laws (Leviticus 18) which prohibited the mixing of opposites and in particular homosexual prostitution.

Finally, Jesus' ministry and teaching frequently focused on the 'sinners', the oppressed underside of Jewish society, and shockingly he used them as examples of those who would enter the Kingdom of God before the righteous. Reversal has particular resonance with gay liberation, as homosexuality has variously been termed perverted or inverted.

Many Christian theologians have deliberately developed a 'reverse' or 'queer discourse', not only to empower themselves but also to deliberately subvert the power structures of the Church.

iv) Praxis and analysis

Whereas for classical liberation theology Marx provided a useful sociological tool in the first mediation, many gay liberation theologians have preferred **Michel Foucault**'s philosophy as a means of analysing the oppressive power structures which have marginalised lesbians and gays. Queer theorists (those who have developed Foucault's ideas on sexuality and reverse discourse) are not satisfied with a church which merely tolerates non-heterosexuality but challenges it to a more thorough-going shift in consciousness which will open up a wide variety of human relationships. Queer theologians, such as Elizabeth Stuart, wonder whether the Church can ever meet the challenge. At a less extreme end, gay Christian groups, such as the Lesbian & Gay Christian

Key quote

'Pseudo-radicals have no interest in non-monogamous, flamboyant, lesbian, gay and bisexual people.'

ELIZABETH STUART, 'SEX IN HEAVEN', IN *SEX THESE DAYS*, 187

Key word

Hegemony means a monopoly or domination of one idea or institution over all others.

Cross-reference

Read pages 97–98 on north European dualisms.

Movement, arrange events for solidarity and support and also to ensure that the gay voice is heard in the Church and represented in society as a whole.

v) Liberation theology and gay theology

Although there are economic issues to be considered and Marxist-type analysis is certainly appropriate, gay theology focus is less on ownership of the economic means of production and more about reconsidering the whole of theological sexual discourse. This has also been the preoccupation of many feminist theologians, but the particular insight offered by queer liberation theology is the challenge to the duality of the male–female sexual **hegemony** of western Christianity. Like Latin American liberation theologians, gay liberation theology also uses a hermeneutic of suspicion to 'query', or 'indecently undress' as Althaus-Reid argues, north European heterosexual male–female sexual **duality**.

3 Is there a future for liberation theology?

Cross-reference

Read pages 117–19 for Kee's argument.

Despite Ratzinger's efforts to silence Leonardo Boff and Gustavo Gutiérrez, liberation theology continued. It may have become more circumspect in its use of Marx but the question is whether political circumstances have changed so much that liberation theology no longer has a role to play.

a) General criticisms and responses

i) Poverty is too limited a view of Christian theology

Critics of liberation theology are doubtful whether a whole theology can be constructed on such a limited view of the world.

Cross-reference

See page 96 on Gutiérrez and the nature of poverty.

- Gutiérrez assumes that the poor somehow have a spiritually superior position over those who are privileged in material terms. He argued that siding with the poor is to enable us 'to become rich' spiritually. But why should this be so? Being poor could equally mean that a person is dangerous, deceitful and untrustworthy, in short, no different from anyone else – just human.
- Although it is reasonable in numerical terms to argue that the vast proportion of the world live in poverty, there are millions who do not and for them a theology which is 'preferential' can rapidly equate being poor with being good and being rich or well-off with being bad.
- It can strain the metaphor too far to attach 'poverty' to any group which is oppressed in some way – women, homosexuals, blacks and so on. If wealth and privilege can be regarded as a kind of oppression, then this might also be construed as a form of poverty.

Liberation theologians are fully aware of these criticisms. Liberation theologians don't claim that liberation is the only way to do theology, but they ask their critics what theology means if it is to be more than an intellectual exercise. It is true that being poor in the economic sense doesn't make a person good, but a person who sides with the poor recognises that the structures of society cannot be right.

ii) Over-optimistic

Another frequent criticism is that liberation theology suffers like so many utopian visions from an over-optimistic expectation of what can be achieved. Critics argue that not only has the liberation utopia failed to achieve any significant results, economically, socially or spiritually but it is also a major source of false consciousness.

Those who defend liberation theology argue that Western theologians and critics simply don't realise how much the Bible has helped the poor to develop a spirituality which has inspired them to interpret life from fresh perspectives. The hermeneutical circle has been exported throughout the world and altered the collective spirituality of communities in ways which cannot be quantified. The tendency in northern Europe is to measure success in empirical terms such as the numbers attending church; liberation theologians argue that spirituality is more subtle than this and cannot be judged merely in numerical terms.

b) Liberation and capitalism

Key question

Does the Christian hope for a utopia cause false consciousness?

The fall of the Berlin Wall on 9 November, 1989

The single greatest challenge to liberation theology has been the collapse of the Berlin Wall in 1989. The removal of the wall between West and East Berlin marked the end of communism, the failure of socialism to work on a grand scale and the triumph of capitalism. In addition, as many Latin American countries have embraced democracy and capitalism, liberation theology's socialist vision is no longer attractive or plausible.

The reaction of liberation theologians has been to withdraw from the bairros and offer a revised version of liberation theology which is not interested in specific political praxis but general ideas of liberation and concern for the poor. Consider this statement from Sobrino responding to his critics in 1995 that liberation theology has had its day and is no longer relevant:

As for the notion that liberation theology is no longer relevant due to the fall of socialism, let us observe that socialism was never at the root of this theology, although obviously – as with some of the encyclicals of Pope John Paul II it may have contributed to the critique of capitalism and the positing of certain utopian horizons. The origin, thrust, and direction of the theology of liberation is not in socialism, but in the experience of God in the poor, an experience of grace and exigency. Therefore so long as this experience exists and is conceptualized, there can be a theology of liberation. And so long as oppression exists, there must be a theology of liberation.

(Jon Sobrino, in *Systematic Theology*, ix)

Key people

Ivan Petrella (1969–) is Argentinian and teaches social theory and liberation theology at the University of Miami, USA. His books include *The Future of Liberation Theology* (2004).

Key word

Endism is the belief that history has 'ended' with capitalism and liberal democracy as there is no better system which can follow it.

Cross-reference

Ivan Petrella, *The Future of Liberation Theology*, vii.

What is odd about Sobrino's justification (and this is shared by many other theologians) is that he claims 'that socialism was never at the root of this theology'. But if this is true, then what was early liberation theology doing if it wasn't offering a critique of development and dependency caused by capitalism? In his analysis, **Ivan Petrella**'s thesis is that liberation theologians have abandoned their central defining plank, the 'historical project'. The historical project establishes theology in the actual conditions of history, challenging political and economic organisations so as to ensure that it doesn't become an ideology or generalised theology. But this is exactly what it has become. When Sobrino said that experience of oppression has to be 'conceptualised', he is making theology no different from the standard European theologies which liberation theologians originally criticised.

Liberation theologians appear to have succumbed to what is called **endism**, the view that history has 'ended' in the sense that capitalism and its ideology, liberal democracy, cannot be bettered. 'Small wonder', Petrella comments, 'that liberation theology seems stagnant; small wonder that many think liberation theology is dead.' So the question is whether liberation theology can adapt itself and recover some of its originality and purpose in the twenty-first century world.

As Alistair Kee suggests, liberation theologians may have helped the poor to understand their intrinsic value, but this is, using Marx's dictum, just interpreting the world, the point is still to *change* it.

i) Plurality of capitalism

The major failing of early liberation theology is that it treated capitalism as if there was only one kind and this is the reason why theologians seemed so readily to accept endism. In **Roberto Unger**'s analysis, the liberation theologians have fallen into what he calls the 'naturalistic premise', the belief that there are only very limited ways in which society can be organised. They have done the very thing they criticise others for doing and that is idolising capitalism and then being seduced by it as a **fetish**. But there is a possible way out of this. As Petrella argues, if only they could see that capitalism has many forms, then liberation theologians could be at the forefront of those who are offering a hermeneutic of suspicion of endism and then seek alternatives. Capitalism doesn't need to exploit and if Kee is right even Marxists realise that capitalism is a necessary condition for socialism. Liberation theologians could play a vital part challenging some versions of capitalism and adapting others within the Christian idea of the Kingdom of God.

ii) Renewed use of the social sciences

It has been a mistake of liberation theologians to regard the social sciences merely as instruments of analysing economic society as part of the socio-analytic mediation. It is a mistake because it creates a dualism between the material world (analysed by the social sciences) and God (analysed by theology), when the originality of early liberation theology was to challenge this way of thinking: God sides with the oppressed *in history* and is not separate from it. Petrella's challenge is for liberation theologians to fully integrate the social sciences (including Marx if necessary) into theological discourse, just as the early work of Gutiérrez did when he challenged developmentalism.

In conclusion, socialism may have not seemed to have worked, but neither has capitalism wiped out poverty. Theology in itself cannot offer economic solutions but it can reflect on the place of humans in creation and influence budgets to favour the poor. By working with economists and politicians to tackle injustice, the Church is more than just a conscience but can point to those who have been forgotten and who occupy the underside of history. Liberation theology must reinvent itself. Petrella presents three challenges. Liberation theology:

- must free itself from Church and university control which 'domesticate' it and hinder it from becoming fully involved in the world

---

Key question

Can liberation theology reinvent itself in the twenty-first century?

Key people

Roberto Unger (1947–) was born in Rio de Janiero and is presently professor of law at Harvard Law School. His major works includes *Politics: A Work in Constructive Theory* (1987).

Cross-references

Read page 128 on Marx's view of fetish.

For Kee's argument read pages 117–18.

Key question

Should theology be involved with politics?

Key quote

'Theology must be political if it is to be evangelical.'

CHRISTOPHER ROWLAND, *THE CAMBRIDGE COMPANION TO LIBERATION THEOLOGY*, 241

Cross-reference

Ivan Petrella, *The Future of Liberation Theology*, 149.

- 'must recover politics on a grand scale'
- 'must cease thinking of capitalism as a monolithic whole' and see all economic systems as incomplete.

Summary diagram

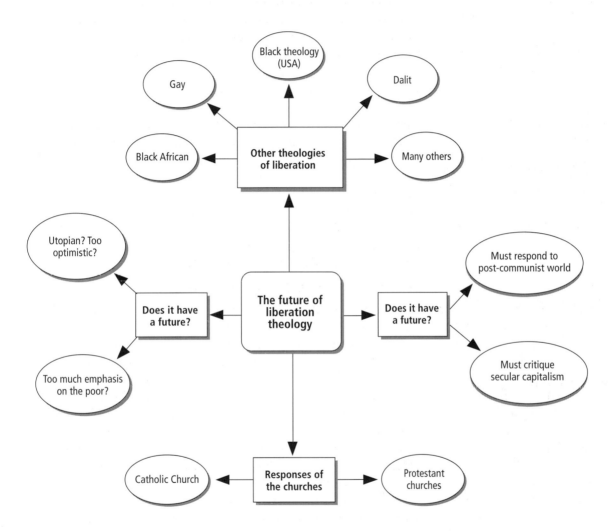

Study guide

By the end of this chapter you should be able to describe and explain different types of liberation theology and discuss whether liberation theology as a whole can meet the challenges of the twenty-first century after the collapse of communism.

Essay questions

1a Explain how liberation theology has developed in South Africa.

Essays might begin with a very brief outline of the history of South Africa and the relationship between the Dutch Boers, British and indigenous peoples which led to apartheid and oppression of black Africans. Through the formation of the ANC, the Sharpeville riots and eventual establishment of Nelson Mandela as president in 1994, South Africa might have gained her freedom theologically and religiously, but there is still much to be done. The Church is regarded as triumphalist as the preserve of the volk. Black theologians consider structural sin is maintained by myths of whiteness. The Exodus paradigm is less significant than the 'kairos', the 'now' of the Kingdom and desire for the recovery of black African culture and spiritual identity.

1b 'Liberation theology has no future now that communism has failed.' Discuss.

The argument might begin by agreeing that along with the analysis of many scholars since 1989, capitalism has appeared to triumph over communism, and liberation theologians have given up their original vision of a transformed society and instead opted to speak in general terms about the poor and injustice. Furthermore, with the demise of the CEBs, liberation theology has literally and symbolically removed itself from the bairros and favelas as many South American countries have embraced democracy and enjoy the material success of capitalism.

On the other hand, Petrella and others argue that liberation theology has a new opportunity to act on the world stage and challenge the culture of secular endism and tackle the forms of capitalism which continue to create an underclass. It needs to have the boldness to consider that a spiritual challenge to secularism is still a much needed 'historical project'.

Further essay questions

2 a Explain how the Protestant churches have responded to liberation theology.

2 b 'Protestant liberation theology is more successful than Catholic liberation theology.' Discuss.

3 'Politics corrupts theology; theology diminishes politics.' Discuss.

4 Assess the view that liberation theology has been the most important development in Christianity in the past 50 years.

Revision checklist

Can you give brief definitions of:

- irruption
- EATWOT
- Kairos Document
- dalit
- endism.

Can you explain:

- how the Exodus paradigm has been used in dalit theology
- the historical and theological reasons for apartheid
- how gay liberation theologians use a hermeneutic of suspicion and reversal.

Can you give arguments for and against:

- whether there is a need for gay liberation theology
- whether liberation theology is too optimistic
- liberation theology's chief failure is its very limited view of capitalism.

GLOSSARY

accommodation as used by Calvin, means that God limits and adapts his revelation so as to be best suited to human finite minds.

actus purus is Latin meaning 'pure act' and describes God's constant creative activity.

Aitia is the Greek used by Aristotle meaning cause, law or characteristic.

ANC or African National Congress Party, was founded in 1912 and has been the ruling party in post-apartheid South Africa since 1994.

akrasia is the paradox that when a person S chooses voluntarily to do action B, they do so even though they appear to think that alternative A is better.

allegory is where a character or event in a text symbolically represents another deeper, spiritual, philosophical or political idea.

apartheid is an Afrikaans word meaning 'separation'.

apophatic way is derived from the Greek meaning 'to show no'. Apophatic theology therefore talks in terms of what God is not, i.e. God is unknowable, God is not evil, God does not occupy time and space.

atheological is Plantinga's term referring to those who reject theological claims as false.

atonement means literally at-one-ment and in Christian terms is the process by which God reconciles the world to himself by removing the barrier of sin.

bad faith or *mauvaise foi* is the inauthentic life which is not lived freely but according to a stereotype or preconceived image or idea.

bairro is Portuguese for 'neighbourhood' and often refers to the shanty town or favela areas occupied by the poor.

Biblical inerrancy means that the Bible is without error or fault.

Big Bang is the cataclysmic event scientists estimate to have taken place 14 billion years ago which brought the universe and time into being.

bourgeoisie and **proletariat**. Bourgeoisie are all those who own the means of production and proletariat are the workers who have no ownership or direct control over production according to Marx.

capitalism is the belief that human societies flourish best when operating in a free competitive market motivated by profit.

capriciousness means to act in sudden and unexpected ways for no apparent reason.

category mistake occurs when factual statements are confused with value judgements, or historical knowledge is confused with faith knowledge.

CELAM stands for *Consejo Episcopal Latinoamericano* or Latin American Episcopal Conference.

concupiscence is sexual lust but can also refer to uncontrolled desires of all kinds.

conscientisation is the process by which the oppressed come to see themselves as subjects not objects, human persons not slaves.

contextual theology considers that the role of theology is to reflect and articulate Christian ideas in response to a particular historical situation or experience.

continence means self-restraint especially to abstain from sexual pleasures. Augustine describes continence using the metaphor of a beautiful woman.

correlation as used by Calvin, means that whatever humans say about themselves implies something about the nature of God and whatever we say about God implies something about the nature of humans.

creationism is the belief that the Bible and not evolutionary science offers the correct view of how the world was created.

creed means belief and is a concise, formal and authorised summary of Christian belief and teaching. There are various creeds notably the Apostles' Creed (c. 90) and Nicene Creed (c. 374).

cupiditas and *caritas* are two Latin key words used by Augustine meaning love. *Cupiditas* is selfish love. *Caritas* is generous love.

the Cynics were an ancient Greek philosophical movement who taught that the good or virtuous life should be lived in accordance with nature and not by social convention.

dalit is an ancient word and can mean: downtrodden, broken, crushed. It has come to refer to those in Indian society who are outcaste and untouchable.

deism is the belief that God is an ultimate cause or principle but that he plays no active part in the universe.

demythologising is the process by which ancient myths or metaphors used to express deep religious and philosophical experiences of the world are stripped of their imagery (which has falsely been treated in objective factual terms) to recover their original existential experience.

dependency theory describes how an external dominant political power causes a weaker political power to become dependent on it as in a master–slave relationship.

design argument or the argument for design infers that as the world everywhere shows signs of order and purpose then it must have a designer. That designer is God.

development describes the process of improving the quality of human lives by raising living standards through an increase in incomes and levels of food production, along with growth in medical services and education.

developmentalism is a negative form of development which has led to dependency. The term is used by Latin American liberation theologians.

dialectic describes the creative tension between conflicting ideas or states which resolves into a synthesis. The synthesis might then find itself in conflict with a new state of affairs.

dipolar relationship in process theology describes the way God persuades rather than orders creation to fulfil its potentials.

divine simplicity is the principle that God exists as one single entity. He cannot be divided (into matter and form), he has no parts and has no dimensions.

doceticism is the view that Jesus as a divine being only appeared to be human. Docetism is rejected by mainstream Christianity because it suggests that if Jesus was not fully human, then his death for the sins of the world is false.

doctrine means teaching and has come to mean the official teaching of the Church on key areas of Christian theology such as the Incarnation, the Trinity, Grace, God and so on. Doctrines are frequently discussed and refined by theologians.

EATWOT or Ecumenical Association of Third World Theologians, was created in Dar-es-Salaam, Tanzania, in 1976. Through conferences and papers third-world theologians seek to develop their theologies of liberation.

eisegesis means 'reading into the text'. Meaning is not fixed by the text but is a relationship between the reader's own agenda and experiences and the text itself.

election is the Christian doctrine that salvation is possible because God chooses to redeem humans first.

enculturation is the adaptation of one set of cultural values to another culture.

endism is the belief that history has 'ended' with capitalism and liberal democracy as there is no better system which can follow it.

ens and esse are two Latin terms Aquinas used to explain existence. *Ens* is a thing's being and *esse* is the way it exists.

eschatology means literally 'discussion of the last things' and is the time when the present age comes to completion and creation achieves perfection. Some consider that it refers not to the future of the world but to our own journey towards moral and spiritual completion.

exegesis means 'reading out of the text'. Meaning is located in the text and is there simply waiting to be read.

exodus is the liberation of the Hebrew slaves from Egypt led by Moses.

the Fall is the moment described in Genesis 3 when Adam and Eve rebelled against God and were punished by being expelled from Eden (paradise).

false consciousness describes how a person or people may hold a view of the world which they consider to be true when in fact it is fundamentally false.

fideism is the requirement that revelation is absolutely required for the human mind to know anything about God's existence or nature with certainty.

Gnostic Christians considered the world to be evil and corrupt and created by a lower being. Salvation lay in acquiring special knowledge or gnosis which would enable them to escape the world and to be united with God.

grace is God's generous, undeserved and free act of love for the world, expressed supremely in the giving of his son Jesus Christ in order that humans might overcome their sinful natures.

hegemony means a monopoly or domination of one idea or institution over all others.

hermeneutic of suspicion questions the underlying political and psychological motives which often form interpretations.

hermeneutical circle is the process of interpretation which reads a text in its widest possible context.

hermeneutics is the art of interpreting a text.

historical materialism is Marx's central idea that the material forces of nature and human societies have a dialectical relationship. Matter and human minds are in constant tension.

idolatry in theological terms is the worship of material things treating them to be greater than God. In general terms it can also mean an unhealthy reliance on material things.

image of God (or in Latin *imago Dei*) as used in Genesis 1:27 has been the subject of considerable interpretation: a) the human rational self; b) the power for humans to act as God's stewards on earth; c) human free will; d) human ability to be in relationship with God as mirror of the divine.

imago Dei is the Latin phrase meaning image of God.

immanence describes God's omnipresence and involvement in the particular processes and events of the universe.

incarnation refers to God as Word (the second person of the Trinity) becoming fully human in the person of Jesus Christ.

indeterminate is a mathematical term to mean that there are any number of solutions to a problem.

infrastructural oppression arises from the basic organisational beliefs of society which are biased against certain types of people because of their race, class, age or sexuality.

integral means essential, vital and fundamental.

irruption is the moment when an oppressed group suddenly emerges from the underside of history into consciousness.

Jesus Seminar was founded by Robert Funk and John Crossan in 1985. Scholars debate and then vote on which sayings of Jesus from the Gospels and the *Gospel of Thomas* (not found in the New Testament) they think are authentic and then publish the results.

Kairos Document was issued in 1985 and signed by 150 signatories. Kairos in Greek means 'time' and the document called for Christians to act now against injustice.

karma in Hindu thought is the law of cause and effect where all actions in our past and present lives determine what kind of person one is.

kerygma in Greek means 'preaching' and is used by scholars to refer to the earliest message of Christianity.

Kingdom of God is the Age to Come and in Jesus' teaching referred to a future transformation of this world.

Lessing's Ditch is the principle of the 'proof of power' that unless a Christian claim can be rationally justified then it should be discarded. In Lessing's words, 'That, then, is the ugly great ditch which I cannot cross, however often and however earnestly I have tried to make that leap'.

The Magnificat or Mary's Song (Luke 1:46–55) is a popular song in many Christian traditions.

Manichees believed that suffering and evil in the world are not caused by God but by a lower power. Humans have two souls: one which desires God and the other desires evil.

mediation is a distinctive phase of theological praxis.

messianic secret describes the number of occasions in Mark's Gospel where Jesus says he is not the messiah. These were added after Jesus' death by the Gospel writer to explain why Jesus was not considered to be the messiah in his lifetime.

monarchian means the unity of God. It is also used negatively to refer to those who have reduced the place of the Son in the Trinity by making Jesus an inspired prophet of God, not God himself.

myth is a story which conveys deep human experiences of the meaning of the world and our place in it.

natural theology considers that God can be known through reason and observation of the natural world.

neo-Platonism is the term scholars use to refer to the followers of Plato in the third century AD, notably Plotinus (c. 205–270). They were dualists believing there are sharp differences between thought and reality, matter and the One (or God), body and soul. The One can only be achieved once the soul has separated itself from all thought and material influences.

neo-Thomism refers to the modern revival and adaptation of Aquinas' teaching.

ontological refers to being or the nature of existence.

original sin is the Christian notion that despite being created in the image of God, all humans fail to fulfil this potential. This is the human condition. Original sin is different from actual sins which are committed by individuals.

orthodoxy means right teaching.

orthopraxis means right action.

paradigm is a conceptual model or framework of what something ought to be.

Parousia in Greek means 'arrival' and usually refers to the return of Christ at the coming of the Kingdom and final judgement. This is sometimes referred to as the Second Coming.

plenitude means fullness and describes the state of the greatest possible perfection.

point of contact is God's revelation in the world which provides humans with the first step to knowing him. The idea was put forward by Brunner and rejected by Barth.

post-Lapsarian means the world after the Fall of Adam and Eve, or simply the fallen world.

praxis is a critical or reflective process which moves from theory to action.

predestination is God's eternal plan or decree that humans will be saved because of God's grace in Jesus Christ. Some theologians argue that salvation is only for the few chosen elect.

preferential option for the poor is the Christian duty of the privileged to side with the poor in solidarity and act against exploitation.

pre-theological in liberation theology is the stage prior to any theological reflection when acting in solidarity with the poor is more important than official Christian teaching.

Protestant was a termed coined in 1529 when six princes and 14 German cities protested against the restrictions placed on those who wished to belong to the Reform movements. It has come to refer to the churches and people who support the theology and practices developed during and after the Reformation.

providence is God's action in the world generally (as creator) and specifically (in human history and miracles).

Puebla state is situated in Mexico and was the location of the third meeting of the CELAM in 1979. The meeting there is usually referred to simply as 'Puebla'.

quantum physics suggests that the behaviour of sub-atomic particles are predictions based on probabilities and not certainties as in Newtonian physics.

redemption is when humans are freed from sin, suffering and death. In Christian thought redemption of the world is through Jesus Christ.

reductionism means to explain something in more basic, usually physical, terms. Reductionist arguments are often in the form 'X is nothing but …'.

reformed epistemology describes the view held by some modern theologians and philosophers in the Calvinist tradition (eg. Alvin Plantinga, Nicholas Wolterstorff and Michael Rea) who believe that belief in God is a 'properly basic belief'. Epistemology is the philosophical study of knowledge and how we know things.

regeneration in Christian terms is the process of renewal, restoration and recreation associated with baptism and other sacraments of the Church.

revealed theology considers that God can only be known when he lets himself be known. This might be through a prophet, scripture, prayer, etc.

scepticism is the position which tends to doubt what others hold to be true.

secular is concerned only with non-religious matters.

sensus divinitatis is the Latin phrase used by Calvin meaning a 'sense of God' or 'sense of the divine'.

the Sermon on the Mount (Matthew 5–7) is a collection of Jesus' teaching on the relationship of the Jewish written law (the Torah) and his own interpretation. He calls on those who follow it to 'be perfect as your heavenly Father is perfect' (5:48).

si integer stetisset Adam is the Latin phrase used by Calvin meaning 'if Adam had remained upright'.

substantial and **accidental change**. A substantial change is one where matter undergoes a change which cannot be reversed; an accidental change is where matter remains the same but other factors (such as place and quantity) can be reversed.

superstructural oppression occurs in the organisation of institutions arising from the basic (or infrastructural) beliefs of society.

synchronic and **diachronic exegesis** Synchronic interprets the biblical text in its final form. Diachronic investigates the text as it has developed historically over time.

tautology is when the same thing is said twice using different words making it redundant or unnecessary.

theism is the belief that God is more than a principle but can be experienced personally.

the Trinitarian view of God is central Christian teaching that God is one but reveals himself as three 'persons'; Father, Son and Holy Spirit.

utopia can mean 'no place' (an imaginary perfect world) or a 'good place'. Because of its ambiguity Boff prefers the term 'topia' to refer to this world transformed.

varnas or castes, comprise: brahmin (priest/teacher), ksatriyas (ruler/soldier), vaishyas (merchants) and shudras (labourers).

the will in Augustine's thought is the aspect of the image of God which distinguishes humans from all other animals.

the Zealots were made up of a number of first-century Jewish movements who were looking for God to act to renew Israel by ridding her of her enemies and establishing God's kingdom on earth.

An excellent interactive multimedia website in which scholars present many of the ideas and people discussed in this book, may be found on the St John's Nottingham 'timelines' website: http://stjt.org.uk

Althaus-Reid, Marcella *Indecent Theology*. Routledge, 2000.

Augustine *Confessions* (Translator: R.S. Pine-Coffin). Penguin, 1961.

Augustine *City of God* (Editor: David Knowles. Translation: Henry Bettenson). Penguin, 1972.

Baker, Deane-Peter 'Plantinga's Reformed Epistemology: What's the Question?' *International Journal for Philosophy of Religion*, volume 57, number 2. Springer, 2005.

Barbour, Ian *Nature, Human Nature and God*. SPCK, 2002.

Barbour, Ian G. *Issues in Science and Religion*. SCM Press, 1966.

Barth, Karl *The Knowledge of God and the Service of God* (Gifford Lectures 1937–1938) (Translators: J.L.M Hare and Ian Henderson). Hodder and Stoughton, 1938.

Barton, John (editor) *The Cambridge Companion to Biblical Interpretation*. Cambridge University Press, 1998.

Berryman, Phillip *Liberation Theology*. I.B. Taurus, 1987.

Bockmuehl, Markus (editor) *The Cambridge Companion to Jesus*. Cambridge University Press, 2001.

Boff, Leonardo *Jesus Christ Liberator*. SPCK, 1980.

Boff, Leondardo and Boff, Clodovis *Introducing Liberation Theology*. Burns and Oates, 1987.

Brown, Peter *The Body and Society*. Columbia University Press, 1988.

Bultmann, Rudolf *The History of the Synoptic Tradition*. Basil Blackwell, 1968.

Bultmann, Rudolf *Primitive Christianity*. Fontana Library, 1960.

Calvin, John *Institutes of the Christian Religion* (1559) (Edited: John T. McNeill. Translator: Ford Lewis Battles). Westminster John Knox Press, 2006.

Carmichael, Liz *Friendship*. T & T Clark, 2004.

Catholic Church *Catechism of the Catholic Church*. Geoffrey Chapman, 1994.

Cone, James H. *Black Theology and Black Power*. Orbis Books, 1989.

Cone, James H. *God of the Oppressed*. Orbis Books, 1997.

Davies, Brian *The Thought of Thomas Aquinas*. Oxford University Press, 1992.

Dawkins, Richard *The God Delusion*. Bantam Press, 2006.

Dowey, Edward A. *The Knowledge of God in Calvin's Theology*. William B. Eerdmans Publishing Company, 1994.

Evans, G.R. (editor) *The Medieval Theologians*. Blackwell Publishing, 2001.

Gunton, Colin E. *The Christian Faith*. Blackwell Publishing, 2002.

Gutiérrez, Gustavo *A Theology of Liberation*. SCM Press, 2001.

Harrison, Carol *Augustine*. Oxford University Press, 2000.

Hart, Trevor A. (general editor) *The Dictionary of Historical Theology*. William B. Eerdmans Publishing Company, 2000.

Hawking, Stephen W. *A Brief History of Time*. Bantam Press, 1988.

Hedley, Douglas *Living Forms of the Imagination*. Continuum, 2008.

Holgate, David and Starr, Rachel *Biblical Hermeneutics*. SCM Press, 2006.

Hume, David *Dialogues Concerning Natural Religion* (1779) (Editor: Martin Bell). Penguin, 1990.

Kee, Alistair *Marx and the Failure of Liberation Theology*. SCM Press, 1990.

King, Martin Luther *The Knock at Midnight: The Great Sermons of Martin Luther King, Jr* (Editor: Clayborne Carson and Peter Holloran). Abacus, 2000.

Macquarrie, John *In Search of Deity* (Gifford Lectures 1988–1984). SCM Press, 1984.

McGrath, Alister E. *Christian Theology*. Blackwell Publishing, 2007 (4th edition).

McLellan, David (editor) *Karl Marx: Selected Writings* (2nd edition). Oxford University Press, 2000.

Migliore, Daniel L. *Faith Seeking Understanding* (2nd edition). William B. Eerdmans Publishing Company, 2004.

Miranda, José *Marx and the Bible*. Orbis Books, 1974.

Morgan, Robert with Barton, John *Biblical Interpretation*. Oxford University Press, 1988.

Niebuhr, Reinhold *Moral Man and Immoral Society*. Charles Scribner's Sons, 1960.

Pattison, George *A Short Course in Christian Doctrine*. SCM Press, 2005.

Petrella, Ivan *The Future of Liberation Theology*. Ashgate, 2004.

Ricoeur, Paul *The Conflict of Interpretations*. Continuum, 2004.

Rowland, Christopher (editor) *The Cambridge Companion to Liberation Theology*. Cambridge University Press, 1999.

Sanders, E.P. *Jesus and Judaism*. SCM Press, 1985.

Sartre, Jean-Paul *Existentialism and Humanism*. Methuen, 1973.

Schleiermacher, Friedrich *Hermeneutics and Criticism* (Editor: Andrew Bowie). Cambridge University Press, 1998.

Schweitzer, Albert *The Quest of the Historical Jesus* (3rd edition 1954). SCM Press, 1981.

Sobrino, Jon and Ignacio Ellacuría (editors) *Systematic Theology. Perspectives from Liberation Theology*. SCM Press, 1996.

Te Velde, Rudi *Aquinas on God*. Ashgate, 2006.

Thompson, Mark D (editor) *Engaging with Calvin*. Apollos, 2009.

Ward, Keith *God, Chance and Necessity*. Oneworld, 1996.

Wilkinson, Michael B. and Campbell, Hugh N. *Philosophy of Religion for AS Level; Philosophy of Religion for A2 Level*. Continuum, 2009.

Wright, N.T. *Jesus and the Victory of God*. SPCK, 1996.

INDEX

60400

YALE COLLEGE
LEARNING RESOURCE CENTRE